ADAPTIVE PARSING
Self-Extending Natural Language Interfaces

THE KLUWER INTERNATIONAL SERIES IN ENGINEERING AND COMPUTER SCIENCE

NATURAL LANGUAGE PROCESSING AND MACHINE TRANSLATION

Consulting Editor

Jaime Carbonell

Other books in the series:

EFFICIENT PARSING FOR NATURAL LANGUAGE: A FAST ALGORITHM FOR PRACTICAL SYSTEMS, M. Tomita
ISBN 0-89838-202-5

A NATURAL LANGUAGE INTERFACE FOR COMPUTER AIDED DESIGN, T. Samad
ISBN 0-89838-222-X

INTEGRATED NATURAL LANGUAGE DIALOGUE: A COMPUTATIONAL MODEL, R.E. Frederking
ISBN 0-89838-255-6

NAIVE SEMANTICS FOR NATURAL LANGUAGE UNDERSTANDING, K. Dahlgren
ISBN 0-89838-287-4

UNDERSTANDING EDITORIAL TEXT: A Computer Model of Argument Comprehension, S.J. Alvarado
ISBN: 0-7923-9123-3

NATURAL LANGUAGE GENERATION IN ARTIFICIAL INTELLIGENCE AND COMPUTATIONAL LINGUISTICS, Paris/Swartout/Mann
ISBN: 0-7923-9098-9

CURRENT ISSUES IN PARSING TECHNOLOGY, M. Tomita
ISBN: 0-7923-9131-4

CONCEPTUAL INFORMATION RETRIEVAL: A Case Study in Adaptive Partial Parsing, M. L. Mauldin
ISBN: 0-7923-9214-0

GENERALIZED L. R. PARSING, M. Tomita
ISBN: 0-7923-9201-9

ADAPTIVE PARSING
Self-Extending Natural Language Interfaces

by

Jill Fain Lehman
Carnegie Mellon University

SPRINGER SCIENCE+BUSINESS MEDIA, LLC

Library of Congress Cataloging-in-Publication Data

Lehman, Jill Fain.
Adaptive parsing : self-extending natural language interfaces / by Jill Fain Lehman.
p. cm. -- (Kluwer international series in engineering and computer science. Natural language processing and machine translation)
Includes bibliographical references and index.
ISBN 978-1-4613-6610-2 ISBN 978-1-4615-3622-2 (eBook)
DOI 10.1007978-1-4615-3622-2
1. Natural language processing (Computer Science) 2. Human-computer interaction. I. Title. II. Series. III. Series: Kluwer international series in engineering and computer science.
QA76.9.N38L44 1992
006.3'5--dc20 91-35582
CIP

Originally published by Kluwer Academic Publishers in 1992
Softcover reprint of the hardcover 1st edition 1992

Printed on acid-free paper.

To Mom and Dad and Ken—
for always making me *get the dictionary*

"I don't know what you mean by 'glory,' " Alice said.

Humpty Dumpty smiled contemptuously. "Of course you don't—till I tell you. I meant 'there's a nice knock-down argument for you!' "

"But 'glory' doesn't mean 'a nice knock-down argument,' " Alice objected.

"When I *use a word," Humpty Dumpty said, in rather a scornful tone, "it means just what I choose it to mean—neither more nor less."*

"The question is," said Alice, "whether you can *make words mean so many different things."*

"The question is," said Humpty Dumpty, "which is to be master—that's all."

— *Lewis Carroll*
Alice's Adventures in Wonderland

Table of Contents

Foreword

As the computer gradually automates human-oriented tasks in multiple environments, the interface between computers and the ever-wider population of human users assumes progressively increasing importance. In the office environment, for instance, clerical tasks such as document filing and retrieval, and higher-level tasks such as scheduling meetings, planning trip itineraries, and producing documents for publication, are being partially or totally automated. The range of users for office-oriented software includes clerks, secretaries, and businesspersons, none of whom are predominantly computer literate. The same phenomenon is echoed in the factory production line, in the securities trading floor, in government agencies, in educational institutions, and even in the home. The arcane command languages of yesteryear have proven too high a barrier for smooth acceptance of computerized functions into the workplace, no matter how useful these functions may be. Computer-naive users simply do not take the time to learn intimidating and complex computer interfaces.

In order to place the functionality of modern computers at the disposition of diverse user populations, a number of different approaches have been tried, many meeting with a significant measure of success, to wit: special courses to train users in the simpler command languages (such as MS-DOS), designing point-and-click menu/graphics interfaces that require much less user familiarization (illustrated most clearly in the Apple Macintosh), and interacting with the user in his or her language of choice. The latter category includes spreadsheet programs for interacting with accountants, markup languages for interacting with editors and writers, and natural languages for interacting with just about everyone else in a wide variety of tasks ranging from data base query to expert system command interfaces. By "natural language," of course, we mean English, French, German, Spanish, Japanese, etc. or, rather, the subset of the selected language needed for the range of tasks at hand. The central philosophy is to build the interface so as to exploit existing human means of communication—to adapt the computer to human abilities, rather than vice-versa.

Natural language interfaces are not yet in widespread use for a variety of reasons, ranging from the sheer complexity of the natural language comprehension task to ergonomic limitations such as poor typing skills in some user populations and lack of robust error-recovery methods. The technology, however, moves inexorably forward: newer and faster language comprehension methods are under development. The accuracy and speed of speech-recognition systems is approaching acceptable levels, hence permitting the substitution of a microphone for the keyboard. And the computing power available on the desktop is approaching the levels required for real-time language comprehension. Is it then only a matter of time before natural language becomes a ubiquitous interface technology? A few scientific challenges remain, such as semi-automated customization of the linguistic knowledge to the task-domain and to the idiosyncracies of the individual user.

Jill Fain Lehman addresses the second of these challenges in this monograph: how to build a self-adapting natural language interface that learns the modes of expression of each particular user, thereby improving interpretation accuracy over time. Heretofore, natural language interfaces suffered from inherent fragility because their coverage (grammar and vocabulary) were necessarily limited, and any user utterance outside this self-imposed boundary would cause an interpretation error. The better systems provide some diagnosis of the error permitting the user to rephrase and hopefully complete the intended communication. Would it not be much better if the interface learned the new word or grammatical construct, so next time it would understand it correctly without necessitating a clarification subdialog? Such is the motivation for the work described in this book: habitability means never having to say you're sorry, twice. In other words a major component in making a natural language interface habitable, beyond those enumerated by Harry Tennant [69] is the ability to accommodate necessarily unpredictable idiosyncratic usage of language, and to do so systematically and reliably.

If natural language interfaces require extensive coverage, why not build an all-encompassing grammar and dictionary to cover all possible normal, ideolectic, and idiosyncratic usage of language in all domains? Setting aside the sheer enormity of such a task, there are inherent problems in that similar or even identical expressions used in different domains by different users can have different meanings. In other words, as the number of possible interpretations of natural language utterances grows so does the language comprehension time and the ambiguity of the resultant interpretations. The problem of occasionally not understanding an idiosyncratic expression would be replaced by the problem of repeatedly having multiple spurious interpretations of the same utterances. Such a tradeoff is not necessarily beneficial. Instead, Lehman chooses to start with a kernel grammar and dictionary and augment it incrementally on an *if-needed* basis when interpretation impasses are reached and resolved. Moreover, she chooses to do so separately for each frequent user of the interface. Lehman's philosophy is adapting the computer interface to the needs of human users carried to its ultimate extreme: adaptation to each and every frequent user.

In order for automated adaptation of a natural language interface to be effective, certain assumptions must be verified, such as cross-user linguistic variability and within-user linguistic constancy. In other words, if there is no idiosyncratic linguistic usage, adaptation is not required, and if each user changes her language daily adaptation is not possible. Lehman verifies both assumptions with longitudinal hidden-operator experiments, and goes on to design, build, and evaluate a natural language interface that adapts to the linguistic preferences of each individual user, demonstrating significant improvements in comprehension accuracy. To determine how this adaptation technology is developed and applied, of course, requires reading the book. The ability to adapt to individual frequent users is one more key component towards the development of habitable natural language interfaces with widespread user acceptance.

—Jaime Carbonell

Acknowledgements

Many people have contributed to this book. What follows is undoubtedly an incomplete list, both in those it mentions, and in the ways in which I counted on their support. Thanks, first, to Jaime Carbonell, Allen Newell, Tom Mitchell, and Wendy Lehnert who formed the thesis committee for the research on which this book is based. Completion of the experimental work required help from a variety of sources: David Nichols, Kelly F. Hickel, Michael and Julie Shamos, Marion Kee, and the willing participation of the ten users. The generous enviroment at Carnegie Mellon University and its School of Computer Science, and especially the help of Sharon Burks, were also instrumental in finishing this work. Special thanks to Angela Kennedy Hickman for her painstaking review of various stages of this manuscript. Finally, thanks to Philip Lehman; the degree to which he contributed to this work is immeasurable, as are his contributions to my life.

This research was partially supported by the Defense Advanced Research Projects Agency (DOD), ARPA Order No. 4976, and monitored by the Air Force Avionics Laboratory under Contract F33615-87-C-1499. The author was partially supported by a Boeing Company fellowship. The views and conclusions contained in this document are those of the author and should not be interpreted as representing the official policies, either expressed or implied, of the Defense Advanced Research Projects Agency, the Boeing Company, or the U. S. Government.

ADAPTIVE PARSING
Self-Extending Natural Language Interfaces

Chapter 1
Introduction

1.1. Natural language interfaces

A long-term goal of natural language processing is to provide users with an environment in which interaction with computers is as easy as interaction with human beings. Most programs with which users interact can be thought of as having two parts. The *front-end*, or communication interface, allows the user to specify the next thing to do, while the *back-end*, or application software, executes the specified action. In essence, the philosophy behind the design of natural language interfaces is to permit the user the full power and ease of her usual forms of expression to specify the task she wants to accomplish.

Although ease of use is always a desirable design characteristic, it is especially important for the unsophisticated user. Indeed, supporting the increasing number of naive users is a main justification of research in designing natural language interfaces. The interests of naive users lie solely in the functionality of the application domain. They may have only the vaguest model of how software systems are organized, and it may not be cost-effective to try to improve that model (see, for example, [43]). For these users, the artificial command languages provided for communication often seem arbitrary and non-intuitive. In particular, the difficulty with a system-supplied command language is that it requires the user to learn both the system's task model and its communication model simultaneously. The burden is on the user to express her intent completely and unambiguously within the forms provided by the interface designer. Thus, depending upon the user's level of experience and the complexity of the interface, the software originally intended to increase her productivity often becomes the new bottleneck. By allowing the user to interact via an English language front-end, however, the need for a separate communication model disappears, and the burden of clarifying intent is moved to the natural language interpreter.

The examples below demonstrate how a natural language interface facilitates interaction. They are taken from the LADDER system [34] which is made up of a natural language front-end (based on LIFER [33]) and a database about naval vessels (formatted using DATALANGUAGE). LADDER assists the user in an information retrieval task by translating English questions into appropriate DATALANGUAGE queries which are used to search the database.

LADDER: Print the length of the Kennedy.
DATALANGUAGE: ((NAM EQ JOHN#F.KENNEDY) (?LENGTH))

LADDER: Give me the name and location of the fastest american oilers.
DATALANGUAGE: ((* MAX SPEED) (NATION EQ US)
((TYPE EQ AO) OR (TYPE EQ AOR))
(?NAME (?LOC)))

It is clear from the examples above that the ability to request information in English greatly simplifies the user's task. It frees her from the need to remember particular field names and values in the database, as well as the particular syntax and database relations associated with the DATALANGUAGE formalism.

1.2. The dilemma

Although LADDER recognizes a number of equivalent ways of phrasing each meaningful database query, its coverage is by no means complete. Thus, a user's natural form of expression may be semantically well-formed but still uninterpretable by the system. For example, the starred sentences below are considered "ungrammatical" by LADDER, despite the fact that their unstarred counterparts will produce the appropriate response.

What is the nearest oiler?
What is the nearest oiler to the Constellation?
*What is the closest oiler near to the Constellation?
*Name the oiler closest to Constellation.

How far is it to Norfolk?
How far away is Norfolk?
How many nautical miles is it to Norfolk?
How many miles is it to Norfolk from here?
*What's the distance between here and Norfolk?
*From here to Norfolk is how many miles?

What are the length, width, and draft of the Kitty Hawk?
Display the length, width, and draft of the Kitty Hawk.
*Give Kitty Hawk length width draft.
*Length width draft Kitty Hawk?

These examples demonstrate an unfortunate fact. No existing interface permits the full range of potentially relevant vocabulary and syntax, non-standard turns of phrase, and ungrammatical utterances that are part of real language use [12]. This limitation stems from two sources: our inability to anticipate all possible inputs the user might generate and the computational cost of processing all of the inputs we can anticipate.

The computational cost of understanding an utterance depends, in general, on the amount of ambiguity in the grammar. Consider language understanding as a search problem in the space of partially instantiated meaning structures. Using this view, the relationship between ambiguity and computational cost can be expressed simply: the more ambiguity there is in the grammar, the larger the search space becomes. In short, the nature of language is such that a complete analysis, even if possible, is hardly useful. If we try to anticipate all the lexical meanings and linguistic forms the system might encounter, we will formalize enough of English to make the effects of ambiguity computationally intolerable [23].

As the number of permissible forms of reference grows, ambiguity tends to grow as well. As ambiguity grows, so does the amount of processing required to understand an utterance. Thus, there is an essential trade-off in interface design: efficiency (good response time) versus *habitability* (ease of use, as measured by a high acceptance of initial phrasings) [9, 69, 72]. We can favor one factor or the other by manipulating the size of the grammar. A system with a small grammar sacrifices habitability for efficiency. From the user's point of view, such a system is characterized by:

- fast response time
- usually producing a single interpretation of the utterance
- poor coverage, often requiring rephrasing by the user

In contrast, an interface with a large grammar sacrifices efficiency for habitability, presenting the user with:

- slow response time
- frequently producing multiple interpretations for an utterance
- good coverage, requiring few rephrasings by the user

Thus, in choosing a sublanguage, an interface designer is faced with a dilemma. A small grammar with minimal ambiguity has the advantages of fast processing and a single interpretation for most accepted utterances, but the disadvantages of poor coverage and brittleness. As the designer tries to extend the sublanguage, coverage is increased but processing time and the number of interpretations produced for each utterance tend to grow as well.

Historically, designing an interface has involved choosing a fixed grammar that attempts to balance the trade-off between efficiency and habitability. Thus, any design requires some degree of compromise along each dimension. Although a small number of users may find that the designer's choice of sublanguage corresponds well to their own natural languages, most users will not. In fact, any fixed grammar results in two kinds of mismatch between the language expected (the system's language) and the language encountered (the user's language). The first kind of mismatch is caused by utterances the system can understand but that the user will never employ. The second kind is caused by utterances that the user employs but that the system cannot understand. The individual pays a price for each of these mismatches: time is wasted both in allowing for utterances the system will never encounter and in trying to resolve utterances the system was not designed to interpret. Thus, the designer makes compromises without any guarantee that the extensions made to the grammar conform to the needs of the particular user who must endure the performance degradations.

In Section 1.1, we claimed that the philosophy behind the design of natural language interfaces is to permit the user the full power and ease of her usual forms of expression to accomplish a task. At odds with this philosophy is the computational barrier created by natural language's inherent ambiguity; as the size of the permissible grammar increases, system performance decreases. Thus, current natural language interfaces tend to fail in two ways. First, they fail philosophically because any fixed grammar limits the user to an arbitrary subset of her natural forms of expression. Second, they fail theoretically because any attempt to extend the available sublanguage to meet the expressive needs of all users results in intractability.

1.3. Towards a solution

At first glance, the efficiency/habitability trade-off seems to be unavoidable. It would appear that no matter how we improve coverage, response time must suffer, and vice versa. In reality, there is a hidden assumption underlying previous interface designs: the assumption that a single parser must be able to understand every user. If we discard this assumption, we can take advantage of the possibility that each individual does not always use all of language. In everyday tasks, such as going to the store or eating at a restaurant, we find repetitive behavior [61]. In this research, we demonstrate that this type of stereotypy need not apply only to action, but may also apply to language when the principal method for accomplishing a task is linguistic. We argue further that under appropriate circumstances people are both *idiosyncratic* and *self-bounded* in their language use. In other words, users do not prefer the same forms of expression, and each user naturally restricts her forms of expression to the subset of language that she used to accomplish the task in the past (see Section 3.5).

If people are self-bounded in their language use, then a system that can learn those bounds need not define all meaningful forms of expression *a priori*. Rather, it need only learn the particular forms preferred by a given user. We call the gradual augmentation of a kernel grammar to include the user's preferred forms of expression *adaptive parsing*. In essence, the purpose of adaptive parsing is to learn a user's idiosyncratic style.

The basic challenges in constructing an adaptive parser are similar to those involved in the design of any learning system. How do we decide when to learn? How do we decide what to learn? What learning method will bring the new knowledge to bear during search only when that knowledge is appropriate? The model of adaptation presented in Chapter 2 answers these questions in the context of language acquisition in a goal-oriented, interactive environment. The model demonstrates how an expectation-driven parser can learn by noticing violated expectations, explaining them as deviations with respect to a current grammar, and then deriving new grammatical components based on the explanations.

An adaptive parser need not suffer from the problems described in the previous section. The process of adapting a grammar to reflect the language of an individual user directly addresses the issue of extendability. When the goal was to understand every user with a single system, the limit on extendability was the union of all idiosyncratic grammars. The ambiguity inherent in such a language description placed the goal computationally out of reach. In adaptive parsing, however, we are concerned with only one idiosyncratic grammar at a time. The crucial observation is that the user's self-bounded behavior places a natural limit on the degree of extendability required of the system and, therefore, on the amount of ambiguity that must be tolerated during search.

Adaptation to a self-bounded grammar addresses the mismatch problem as well. As long as the user's preferred forms of expression are represented in an initial, minimally ambiguous grammar, or their representation is derivable from it through adaptation, mismatch is controlled. This is because the system reflects only those inefficiences actually embodied in the ambiguity of the user's particular linguistic style. Of course, tractability cannot be guaranteed absolutely—it is still a function of the amount of stable ambiguity in the individual's idiosyncratic grammar. Yet, in Chapters 4 through 9 we show that by relying on the self-bounded behavior of the user, we trade the current impossibility of understanding every individual effectively for the likelihood of understanding any individual well.

1.4. The frequent user

In the previous section, we claimed that under appropriate circumstances users will demonstrate idiosyncratic and self-bounded linguistic behavior. The most important of these circumstances is that the user has frequent interactions with the system. Effective adaptation relies on the user's stereotypy; without repetition, no stereotypical behavior will develop. With only sporadic interactions, the infrequent user's model of how to use the system remains relatively constant and uninformed. For her, a flexible natural language interface may be accommodating, but an adaptive interface provides no advantage. For the frequent user, however, adaptation is advantageous. Through regular interaction, the frequent user's methods become stylized, and her model of how to accomplish the task grows in ways that are particular to her experiences. This stylization is exactly what an adaptive parser comes to reflect, at the very least increasing the efficiency of the frequent user's interactions over those of the infrequent user.

Adaptation has another advantage for the naive frequent user. As she becomes increasingly expert in her interactions, she may want the convenience and speed of an abbreviated language such as a system-supplied command language [29, 48, 58]. By permitting lexical abbreviations and the introduction of terse structures, the same process of adaptation that allows non-standard turns of phrase and ungrammatical constructions also permits the user to develop a concise, idiosyncratic command language as part of its natural function. Although we cannot guarantee that each individual's command language will be as efficient as a system-supplied one, it is still likely to be more habitable as there is no guarantee that the user's experience has rendered the system designer's choice of sublanguage any more intuitive. In addition, a user who must interact frequently with a number of different application programs will rarely find any common philosophy in their interface designs. Even after reaching "expert" status, she will be forced to keep a multitude of conventions in mind (or manuals in her pocket) if she wants to take advantage of the conciseness and execution speed of simpler command parsers. In theory, a single adaptive interface to a variety of application programs solves this problem in a unified way with minimal cognitive load on the user.

For the naive frequent user, adaptation serves to develop the parser in the same directions the user is developing. Learning a particular interface user's style can be recast as learning an idiosyncratic command language. Under conditions of frequent use, the benefits of such a system include better performance and a smooth transition for the user from naive to expert status.

1.5. Conclusions

The main conclusion of this research is that adaptive parsing is a desirable and expedient method of natural language interface design when users act in a linguistically idiosyncratic and self-bounded manner. Adaptation reflects the idea that regularity of language use over time introduces a source of search constraint that can compensate for individual linguistic freedom. In other words, a grammar extended in response to a user's idiosyncratic language is naturally bounded in its growth by the user's reliance on forms that have been effective in the past. In this way, we can achieve both efficiency and habitability in a small to medium-sized interface by allowing the contents of individual grammars to be determined through interactions with individual users.

Support for this conclusion is established in three steps. First, we present a model of adaptive language acquisition capable of learning different idiosyncratic grammars with a single, general mechanism. Second, we demonstrate that with frequent interactions a user limits herself to a restricted subset of forms. Her subset is significantly smaller than the full subset of natural language conceivably appropriate to the task, and quite different from the idiosyncratic subsets of other users. Third, we examine in detail a computational realization of the model as a system able to perform effectively in the presence of spontaneous user input. The usefulness and robustness of adaptation is demonstrated by the system's ability to capture both the regularity and idiosyncracy in the natural grammars of eight users.

1.6. Reader's guide

This section gives a brief synopsis of each of the remaining chapters for the convenience of readers with particular interests. A basic understanding of adaptive parsing can be acquired from Chapters 1 through 3 and Chapters 9 through 11. The remaining material (Chapters 4 through 8) describes an implemented adaptive interface at a level of technical detail that is likely to be beyond the interests of the casual reader. A more cursory understanding of the implementation can be acquired, however, by reading the introductory sections of each of those chapters as well as Sections 4.1 and 8.7.

Chapter 2 describes the model of adaptive parsing and introduces such notions as deviation, recovery, and least-deviant-first search. The chapter also states clearly the assumptions underlying the model and poses a number of testable hypotheses to justify the assumptions. In the final sections of Chapter 2, we discuss alternative approaches to adaptation and prior research in language acquisition.

Chapter 3 discusses a set of hidden-operator experiments in which users interacted with a simulated adaptive interface based on the model described in Chapter 2. The results of the experiments support the behavioral assumptions of self-bounded, idiosyncratic language use under conditions of frequent interaction. In addition, the experiments provided a large set of spontaneously generated utterances, a small subset of which helped guide the subsequent design of a working interface. All data collected from the experiments was used in the evaluation of that interface, as described in Chapter 9.

Chapter 4 begins the discussion of CHAMP, an implementation of the model as a working adaptive interface. This chapter presents the overall design of the system and examines its knowledge representations in detail.

Chapter 5 introduces the bottom-up parser. The chapter is designed to familiarize the reader with the basic parsing mechanism before introducing the complexities associated with error detection, error recovery, and adaptation. The final section of the chapter presents an extremely detailed example of parsing a grammatical input.

Chapter 6 extends the basic parsing algorithms to include error detection and error recovery. The extensions turn the bottom-up parser described in the previous chapter into a least-deviant-first bottom-up parser.

Chapter 7 examines the portion of the interface responsible for resolving multiple interpretations of an utterance. In particular, we examine the role of the user and of the domain databases in providing additional constraint for the understanding process.

Chapter 8 describes CHAMP's method of adaptation and generalization. We demonstrate how the explanations produced by error recovery and verified by resolution are transformed into the new grammatical components that recognize formerly deviant input directly in future interactions. Adaptation turns the least-deviant-first bottom-up parser described in Chapters 6 and 7 into the full adaptive parser found in CHAMP.

Chapter 9 evaluates CHAMP in two ways. First, we examine how the performance of the implementation compares to the performance displayed by the experimental simulation of the model for the same data. Second, we validate our preliminary results in on-line experiments with two new users.

Chapter 10 discusses general issues in adaptive interface design, outlining some problems and tradeoffs that seem to be inherent in learning language from real user interactions.

Chapter 11 concludes with a review of the main results of the research and directions for future work.

Chapter 2

System Behavior in an Adaptive Environment

The goal of an adaptive parser is to acquire an idiosyncratic grammar with minimal ambiguity and maximal coverage through repeated experience with a user. To attain this goal a system must have both a method for expanding the search space in the presence of an unparsable input and a method for augmenting the grammar to recognize the unfamiliar structure directly in future interactions. Using such methods the system can extend an initial grammar to handle new forms, or variants of existing forms, whether they be truly ungrammatical constructions, or grammatically valid extensions to an initial grammar whose coverage was less than complete.

In the next section we introduce some of the notions fundamental to our model of adaptive parsing—deviation, recovery, and least-deviant-first search—in the context in which they first appeared. Section 2.2 then refines and generalizes these ideas and presents our model of adaptation. The assumptions that underlie the model are examined in Section 2.3, while the last two sections of the chapter compare the model to other adaptive approaches and natural language interface designs.

2.1. Foundations: Least-deviant-first parsing and MULTIPAR

Our approach to adaptive parsing is based in part on ideas first explored in the flexible parser MULTIPAR [17, 52]. MULTIPAR was designed to overcome certain specific types of extragrammatical behavior frequently displayed by interface users: simple spelling errors, some word-order or phrase-order inversions, missing case markers, missing determiners, and semantic inconsistencies.

Like most natural language parsers, MULTIPAR's performance can be described as search through the virtual space of possible parses for a given input. In most parsers, search is constrained by the violation of *expectations* inherent in the grammar; for example, the expectation that a preposition introduces a postnominal case, or the expectation that a particular lexeme acts as verb. When an expectation is unmet, the search path is abandoned. Since some ungrammatical constructions were tolerated by MULTIPAR, however, the system could not necessarily limit search by rejecting a partial parse when an expectation was violated. Instead, if the linguistic *deviation* belonged to one of the anticipated types of extragrammatical behavior, the system invoked an associated *recovery strategy* to compensate. Suppose, for example, that a user typed:

"Move the accounts directory the file Data3."

MULTIPAR compensated by inserting a case marker where one was missing, arriving at the correct interpretation:

"Move to the accounts directory the file Data3."

Thus, compensating for the deviation allowed the parse to continue, at the cost of some loss of confidence in the resulting meaning structure for the utterance. In order to produce the best meaning and to constrain search if too many expectations were violated, each type of violation was assigned a degree of deviance. Deviant partial parses were inserted into a queue and explored in a *least-deviant-first* manner. This means simply that grammatical parses were attempted first, parses containing minor deviations such as orthographic anomalies next, and paths with more serious grammatical deviations were examined only if no meaning could be constructed using less serious deviations.[1]

In MULTIPAR the loci at which expectations could go unmet were predetermined, fixed points in the grammar. These recovery points were empirically selected based on the most frequently encountered user deviations in a number of informal studies. Although strictly grammatical input was preferred, particular types of ungrammaticality could be tolerated. Thus, in some sense, when we built MULTIPAR we simply extended our notion of what we would be willing to consider part of the grammar to include those classes of extragrammatical constructions most often produced by interface users. With increased flexibility, MULTIPAR was an improvement over stricter interfaces, especially for the sporadic user. In designing an interface for the frequent user, however, we want to take advantage of the stylization that occurs with frequent interaction to provide a system capable of capturing an idiosyncratic grammar developing over time. Unfortunately, the static model of deviance and recovery embedded in MULTIPAR is inadequate to this task. By predetermining the recovery points, MULTIPAR can anticipate only a small subset of the possible deviations in an utterance, denying the user true idiosyncracy of expres-

---

[1]This description of MULTIPAR does not usefully distinguish the system from earlier work by Kwasny and Sondheimer [44], or Weischedel and Black [73] which explored the ideas of deviance and relaxation in Augmented Transition Network grammars (ATNs) [76]. Although MULTIPAR can be said to share the same abstract point of view, it differed significantly from these other systems both in the generality of its approach and the scope of extragrammatical phenomena it tolerated.

sion. In addition, because MULTIPAR cannot change its definition of what is grammatical, it also cannot improve its performance in response to regularity in the user's language; once a deviation, always a deviation.

Like its predecessors, MULTIPAR's limitations stem from the design goal of understanding everyone. Nevertheless, the system serves as an introduction to the fundamental point of view of parsing as deviation detection and recovery in a least-deviant-first search. In the next section we see how these ideas can be extended to accommodate the frequent user.

2.2. The model

Recall that the goal of an adaptive parser is to acquire an idiosyncratic grammar with minimal ambiguity and maximal coverage through repeated experience with a user. In essence, the system must remember the recovery actions performed in the presence of an unfamiliar utterance, and then augment the grammar with a representation that can parse the same structure directly. Thus, in order to take advantage of regularity in language use over time, we must generalize the key concepts of deviation and recovery to be independent of any particular grammar. We begin by introducing the following definitions:

- **Kernel grammar**: the lexicon and syntactic forms that are present in the system prior to interaction with any user (by "syntactic" we mean only *a related set of expectations*—the model may be applied to semantic grammars [7, 8] as well as traditional syntactic ones). The kernel grammar organizes information about typical forms of reference. For example, the pattern "<month> <day> , <year>" is a typical form of reference for a date.
- **Domain concepts**: the actions and objects that are meaningful referents in the task domain. A domain concept organizes the static information (such as semantic constraints and default values) that is associated with an action or object. Thus, the **day** concept might limit the value bound to <day> in "<month> <day> , <year>" to a number between one and thirty-one, while the **date** concept might enforce a tighter upper-bound depending upon the value of <month>.
- **System form/kernel form**: any form in the kernel grammar, lexical or syntactic.
- **Deviation**: the violation of an expectation as embodied in a syntactic form. Four types of deviation, other than misspelling, are possible:
    - the lack of expected text (deletion error)
    - the existence of unexpected text (insertion error)
    - the presence of text other than the text expected (substitution error)
    - the presence of expected text in an unexpected location (transposition error)

Note that misspellings correspond to exactly the same four categories but for letters in words rather than phrases in sentences [16].

- **Recovery action:** one of insertion, deletion, substitution, transposition, or spelling correction. Each action compensates for one type of deviation. The recovery action for a deletion error is insertion; for an insertion error, it is deletion; transposition and substitution are their own inverses.
- **Deviation-level:** a value that indicates the number of deviations permitted at a given point in the search for a meaning representation for the utterance. Search at Deviation-level 0, for example, succeeds only for utterances directly parsable by forms already in the grammar. Adopting the least-deviant-first method, the deviation-level is increased whenever all paths at the current level have failed. Thus, if search for a "grammatical" interpretation is unsuccessful, Deviation-level 1 is considered, parsing utterances that require only one recovery action. At Deviation-level 2, two recovery actions are permitted along a search path, and so forth.
- **User form/derived form:** a new lexical or generalized syntactic form created in response to the successful application of one or more recovery actions in the presence of deviant input. These forms are added to the specific user's "adapted kernel" (the kernel grammar remains unchanged).
- **Adapted kernel:** a grammar that includes both system and user forms. An adapted kernel is specific to a single user.
- **Current grammar:** the lexical and syntactic forms available at a given point in time. Deviation is always defined relative to the current grammar which may be either the kernel grammar or an adapted kernel.

The set of four deviations and their corresponding recovery actions were chosen for two reasons. First, for completeness: every utterance can be mapped into a grammatical form by zero or more applications of insertion, deletion, transposition, and substitution. The second reason for the choice is the set's lack of commitment to any underlying linguistic theory stronger than a basic ordering assumption. Instead, the set gives the system a kind of *linguistic weak method* for understanding that seems appropriate for an initial exploration of language acquisition through adaptation.

Sample sentences at various levels of deviation and the recovery actions that correct them are shown in Figure 2-1. The system form in the example is given in standard BNF notation: terminals appear as tokens, non-terminals are enclosed in angle brackets, optional constituents are enclosed in square brackets, alternatives are separated by a bar and an asterisk is read as the Kleene star: "zero or more instances of." Thus, the system form in Figure 2-1 would be paraphrased as, "The word *add* or *schedule* optionally followed by *a* or *an*, followed by one of *meeting*, or the extension of the non-terminal *meal*, followed by zero or more marked cases for add." Beneath each deviant sentence we introduce the notational conventions used for indicating the four kinds of error: deleted segments are reintroduced in square brackets, inserted segments are surrounded by "><," transposed segments are underlined, and substitutions are italicized.

System form: add | schedule [a | an] meeting | <meal> <marked-add-case>*

0 deviations: "Schedule lunch with Bob at 12"
1 deviation: "There is a dinner at AISys at 7:00 p.m."
notation: "*There is* a dinner at AISys at 7:00 p.m."
Recovery:
1. substitute "add" for "There is"
2 deviations: "Meeting with Philip on June 15 10 to 11 a.m."
notation: "[Add] Meeting with Philip on June 15 [from] 10 to 11 a.m."
Recovery:
1. insert "add" before "Meeting"
2. insert "from" before "10"
3 deviations: "I have to be at AISys for a meeting at 7:00 p.m."
notation: "*I have to be* at AISys >for< a meeting at 7:00 p.m."
Recovery:
1. substitute "add" for "I have to be"
2. transpose "at AISys" to postnominal position
3. delete "for"
4 deviations: "On June 11 there is an AISys appt 7 p.m."
notation: "On June 11 *there is* an AISys *appt* [at] 7 p.m."
Recovery:
1. transpose "On June 11" to postnominal position
2. substitute "add" for "There is"
3. substitute "meeting" for "appt"
4. insert "at" before "7 p.m."

Figure 2-1: Sample deviant sentences and recovery actions with errors indicated by notational convention.

Using the definitions introduced above we describe the essence of our model for adaptive parsing in the following manner. For each utterance, we perform a least-deviant-first parse. If the utterance can be understood using only the domain concepts and the current grammar then a meaning structure is produced at Deviation-level 0 and no adaptation is necessary. If the utterance is deviant with respect to the current grammar then one or more recovery actions are required and a derived form is constructed to capture the effects of recovery. In short, the adaptive understanding process is one in which we look for the simplest combination of deviations that help explain a particular input utterance and store some generalization of that explanation as a new user form.[2] Figure 2-2 displays the model schematically.

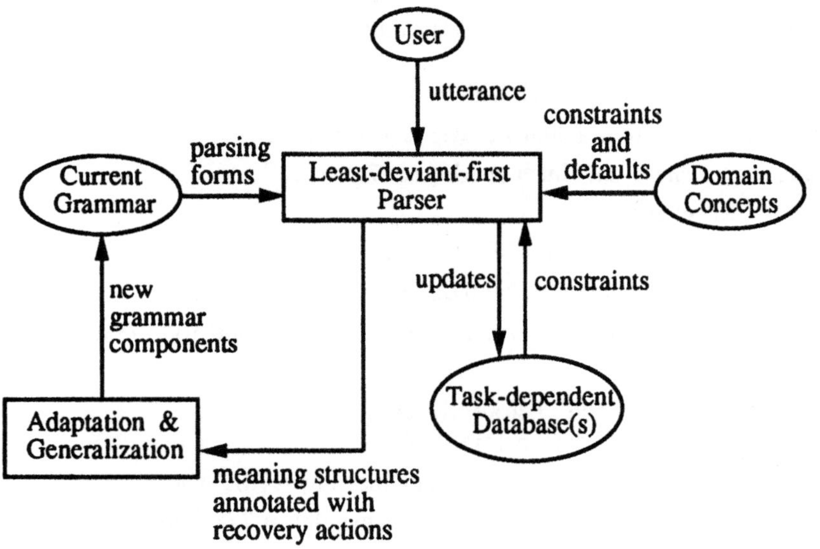

Figure 2-2: Schematic representation of the adaptive understanding model (ovals are knowledge sources, rectangles are processing components).

As an example of adaptive understanding let us consider the sentences in Figure 2-1 as sequential utterances from a single user. The first utterance is non-deviant with respect to the kernel grammar. As a result, a meaning can be assigned at Deviation-level 0 and the database updated to reflect the user's request. The next utterance requires one recovery action to explain the substitution of "There is" for "add". Thus, the second utterance produces two results: the database is updated and a new form is added to the grammar making "add" and "there is" synonymous. The new grammar component is generalized so that the two lexical entries act as synonyms regardless of the context in which the relation was learned (here, a <meal> followed by a marked location and a marked time). In this way, when the four deviation utterance in Figure 2-1 is encountered, only three recovery actions need be applied; the appearance of "There is" in the final sentence is now non-deviant with

---

[2]A word of caution is appropriate here for readers familiar with the machine learning literature. The term "explanation" is used throughout this work in an intuitive sense rather than in the technical sense associated with Explanation-Based Generalization [53]. In terms of our model, "explaining" an utterance means using the grammar and recovery actions to associate a meaning to the input. The process by which the meaning is constructed cannot be considered a "proof" in the EBG sense because the construction may require an inductive step during error recovery (and, hence, the "proof" may be wrong).

respect to the user's adapted kernel and the first substitution recovery in the list has become unnecessary.

What are the aspects of a user's idiosyncratic language that are amenable to adaptation? Note that although the model in Figure 2-2 makes no commitment for or against any particular kind of grammatical component, we are nonetheless limited to learning what is representable within the grammar and, more importantly, to what is explainable using our general but knowledge-poor notions of deviation and recovery. Thus, we are theoretically free to represent the kernel so as to learn morphology, syntax, semantics, or even discourse phenomena. The degree to which the inclusion of any of these categories is appropriate, however, depends upon an affirmative response to two questions:

1. Is there regularity in the user's behavior along this dimension? For example, is she consistent in her method of abbreviation, her choice of imperative or declarative form, her word choice, or her order of subtask performance?
2. Can those regularities be captured in useful, predictive ways? In other words, can we design a representation for the grammar that, in conjunction with our model of deviance and recovery, is adequate to capture the user's actual conditions on usage?

In the particular implementation of the model described in the following chapters, we show that an affirmative response to these questions can be given for a semantic grammar augmented with context-sensitive search constraints. The kind of grammatical components the system learns, therefore, are idiosyncratic vocabulary and syntactic structure.

How does our model achieve the goal of acquiring an idiosyncratic semantic grammar balancing minimal ambiguity and maximal coverage? In initial interactions with a user, we expect the number of deviant utterances to be fairly large, although the degree of initial disparity between the kernel grammar and the user's grammar clearly depends on both the choice of system forms and the user's idiosyncracies. Utterances that can be explained without too much uncertainty (for example, containing at most two deviations) give rise to generalized user forms and thereby create an adapted kernel. By extending the grammar in response to real instances of behavior, we increase the system's linguistic coverage in useful directions while incorporating only the ambiguity intrinsic to the user's idiolect. As the adapted grammar and the user's language converge, the likelihood that an existing form serves as an adequate explanation of an utterance increases. At the same time, the average amount of search required to understand the user should decrease as more utterances are judged grammatical rather than deviant. Thus, as long as the user continues to rely primarily on those forms she has employed successfully in the past, the system's recognition capability and response time asymptotically approach the optimal performance given any stable inherent ambiguity in the user's grammar.

When a novice user becomes more expert she may wish to move away from full sentences and toward the kind of terse utterances that resemble a command language. Should linguistic behavior begin to vary, there would follow a transition period of decreased system performance. The decrease occurs because the system must widen its search to explain the new, deviant utterances. As the new set of preferred forms stabilizes, however, the system's recognition capability and response time again asymptotically approach the optimal performance for the new adapted grammar.

2.3. Assumptions and hypotheses

The model of adaptation introduced in the previous section relies implicitly on a number of assumptions. The purpose of this section is to make those assumptions explicit. Since assumptions about human behavior cannot be taken for granted, we pose those assumptions as testable hypotheses (proving the hypotheses is the subject of Chapter 3). We begin by adopting:

A1. The Single-user Assumption: Any instance of the parser is confined to interaction with a single user over time.

By assuming A1, we presuppose that the system is intended to benefit frequent users. Thus we restrict the set of pertinent tasks to those requiring recurring interaction with an individual. A1 serves as a precondition for the following hypotheses:

H1. The Regularity Hypothesis: In a natural language interface used by the same individual over time, the user tends to rely on those forms of expression that she remembers as having worked in the past. In other words, we assume that frequent use leads the user to a *stylized* and *self-bounded* grammar.

H2. The Deviation Hypothesis: Self-bounded behavior is more appropriately described as asymptotic to a fixed set of structures. When a user deviates from her canonical utterances, she does so in small, idiosyncratic ways.

H1 tells us that adaptation is a useful technique if we can guarantee that the user's grammar will not grow indefinitely. It leads us to expect that the amount of search performed by the system will drop sharply after an initial learning phase as the set of utterances understood by the system and those employed by the user converge. H2 reminds us, however, that we cannot simply choose a point at which to stop adapting; small changes may continue to occur sporadically. In Chapter 3 we will see strong empirical support for these hypotheses.[3]

Current natural language interfaces work, at least in part, because they restrict the search space of meaningful utterances to those to which the application program can respond. By assuming all utterances must make sense in the context of a fixed set of actions, objects, and descriptive categories, the parsing process becomes one of resolving the references in an utterance to the concepts in the domain. In other words, the utterance "Schedule a meeting at 4 p.m." is meaningful only if the domain concepts for **add-to-calendar, meeting** and **time** are well-defined. In an adaptive parser, restriction to a fixed set of referents is extremely important. For if an utterance cannot be recognized and new domain concepts can be introduced, then we are faced with the following dilemma: it will not be possible to distinguish between the case where the unrecognized utterance is a new form referring to known concepts (and thus guaranteed to be meaningful), and the case where the unrecognized utterance refers to an unknown concept (possibly one to which the application program cannot respond). Thus, we adopt:

A2: The Fixed Domain Assumption: The task domain is fully specified in the sense that no object or action meaningful to the application is unrepresented in the underlying system. The only exceptions permitted are categories explicitly designated as extendable—the members of such a category may change but the classification of a category as extendable or non-extendable may not.

Extendable categories in our domain include locations and people's names. As Kaplan [37] points out, these are the kinds of categories whose membership must be permitted to grow in a cooperative interface. If we did not include extendable categories as an exception to the Fixed Domain Assumption, every unknown segment would have to be resolved as either a substitution or insertion. Allowing extendable classes does add a certain degree of indeterminacy—an unknown segment must be considered a possible instance of a known extendable class as well as a substitution or insertion—but the benefits far outweigh the cost. It is unreasonable to assume, for example, that new people are never met and new places never visited; an interface capable of understanding real user input cannot afford such an assumption.

---

[3]There may be times when true exploratory behavior is employed by the user, violating H1 and H2. In effect these times are similar to the state of the parser before its first interactions with the user and many predictions based on history will not pertain. At times of exploration, as in the initial stage of use, we expect poorer performance. H1 and H2 imply that instances of exploratory behavior are relatively rare; the evidence in Chapter 3 supports this as well.

In Chapter 5 we show how learning new instances of extendable classes can be accomplished naturally within the adaptive parsing framework. Here we note only that the exception to the Fixed Domain Assumption does not entail the dilemma we mentioned above. Since the number of meaningful types is fixed, the introduction of a new token cannot correspond to a concept with which the application is unfamiliar.

In addition to providing a powerful mechanism for constraining search, Assumption A2 serves as the precondition for a final hypothesis:

H3: The Fixed Kernel Hypothesis: The kernel grammar for an adaptive parser need contain only a small set of system forms—in general only one form of reference for each meaningful domain action and object. Any user can be understood by then extending the grammar as a direct result of experience with the individual, using the paradigm of deviation detection and recovery in a least-deviant-first search.

The point of an adaptive parser is not just to recognize a large set of natural language utterances, but to control search by recognizing that set of utterances most likely to be used by a particular individual. The Single-user Assumption (A1) says that we need a different instance of the interface for each user; the Fixed Kernel Hypothesis says that we need design only one initial interface for all individuals.

2.4. Adaptation vs. customizable and instructable interfaces

Past solutions to the frequent user's problems have been limited to customizable or instructable interfaces. The difference between the two approaches rests upon whether changes to the interface occur during system building (customizable) or system use (instructable).

Customizable interfaces permit special vocabulary and grammatical forms to be integrated into a base system. In the case of systems like INTELLECT[4] [29, 30] and LanguageCraft[5], the extensions are added once by the interface designer. This kind of customization may make the system friendlier to the sporadic user (by increasing the probability that a naturally-occurring utterance is meaningful), but it does not actually address the frequent user's problems because the system's notion of what is grammatical cannot change over time. Although an effort is made to account for the most likely forms of reference, the user remains limited to a fixed subset of English.

---

[4]INTELLECT is a trademark of Artificial Intelligence Corporation.

[5]LanguageCraft is a trademark of Carnegie Group, Incorporated.

Alternatively, customization may be an on-going process performed by an on-site expert, as with RAMIS-English [43], LDC [3], and TEAM [26]. The primary drawback to this kind of customization is that it suffers from the mismatch problems outlined in Chapter 1—every user pays the performance price for the customizations desired by others. In addition, dependence on an expert means a potentially lengthy wait for the user's idiosyncratic grammar to become part of the system. In contrast, adaptive parsing makes the interface itself the on-site expert—only the individual's customizations are added to her interface, and added at the moment they are needed.

Like an adaptive interface, an instructable system can change dynamically in response to a single user's demands. Unfortunately, instructable interfaces require a language of instruction (distinct from the task language) as well as an interface to talk about language—introducing yet another version of the problem we are trying to solve. In order to control the learning dialogue, some systems, such as LIFER [34], ASK [70], NANOKLAUS [31], and UC Teacher [74], limit the instruction language to a fixed set of instructive forms. These forms, in turn, limit changes to the underlying subset of English—generally to the introduction of new vocabulary (either as synonyms or with corresponding concept definitions) or to a highly specialized set of alternate syntactic forms. In order to allow for true idiosyncratic variations in syntax, such systems would have to be extended significantly. At the very least, they would have to be given full access to their own grammar representations and an additional set of instructive forms that operate on that representation.

Even an extended instructable interface would be a poor solution to the frequent user's problems, however. For whenever the instruction language consists of a fixed set of instructive forms, the designer must choose those forms based upon some prior analysis. If all potential loci of change within the grammar are not equally available through the instruction language, it is possible to exclude the kinds of linguistic idiosyncracies the user finds natural. Since all loci must be available, the number of instructive forms is likely to be quite large. Presented with this diversity, a user may find the task of choosing the appropriate instruction uncomfortably complex—perhaps more complex than memorizing a fixed command language to the domain application and bypassing instruction altogether. On the other hand, an adaptive parser treats the violation of expectations at all loci uniformly, permitting syntactic as well as lexical variation and moving the burden of choosing the correct explanation of the deviation onto the system.

An alternative method for designing an instructable interface allows the user to employ natural language for the instruction task as well (see, for example [55]). In theory, the user could teach any idiosyncratic grammatical variation she preferred. To adopt this approach one must assume that people are reflective about how they use language, that they know and can express the rules that govern their own linguistic behavior. One must also assume that the task of understanding a user's utterance about her own language is somehow less difficult than understanding a user's utterance about a restricted task domain. Neither assumption seems warranted.

2.5. Prior research in adaptation

Previous work in automatic language acquisition falls broadly into one of two categories: theories of child language learning that try to account for existing developmental data, or fundamentally non-cognitive models that argue for a particular learning mechanism. Both sets of research differ significantly from the model outlined in Section 2.2—either with respect to their underlying assumptions or with respect to their range of performance.

Since our model is not intended as a theory of human language acquisition, it is not surprising that it proceeds from a different set of assumptions than systems that are so intended. There are a number of psychological models that offer an explanation of aspects of the observed developmental progression in children, particularly phenomena such as the omission of function words, gradual increase in utterance length, and order in which function words are mastered. Early research in this vein includes Langley's AMBER [45], an adaptive production system, and Selfridge's CHILD [62, 63], which evolved out of the conceptual dependency approach to language understanding [60]. The particulars of the acquisition process differ in these systems and differ from later research by Anderson [2], Berwick [5], and Pinker [57]. Yet despite various justifications, they all share one powerful assumption: the system (child) has access to the meaning of the utterance prior to any learning-related processing.[6] Even if the reasons for separating language understanding from language acquisition are well-founded in models of children, an adaptive interface's task is such that it cannot share this assumption. For an adaptive natural language interface the process of searching for the correct meaning structure and the process of learning new grammatical components are inextricably related.

In general, the second category of relevant research has been less concerned with the explanation of particular psychological phenomena than with advancing specific

[6]Anderson's LAS [1], which preceded the work cited above, was not explicitly a model of child acquisition and did not account for developmental data. It did, however, share the assumption mentioned.

mechanisms or structures as integral to some aspect of language learning. While our model fits comfortably into this context, it differs from each of these systems along one or more dimensions—most notably with respect to the range of types of linguistic knowledge it can acquire.

In 1975, Miller [51] described a tic-tac-toe playing system with a natural language interface that could compensate for "inadvertent ungrammaticalities" and learn new words and expressions in its domain. Although expectation-driven, like the model we presented in Section 2.2, Miller's system lacked generality. New words were learned by one mechanism, new syntax by another, and only when an unknown verb was encountered. In addition, the system compensated for some types of ungrammaticality consistently but without learning—the constructions could not be viewed as systematic attempts by the user to employ unanticipated forms. In sum, the simplicity of the domain hid a number of computational difficulties that might have become apparent in a more realistic task.

Granger's FOUL-UP [25] was also expectation-driven. Relying on conceptual dependency-based knowledge structures, FOUL-UP used both script-based intersentential and intrasentential expectations to infer single word meaning. Because of the representational scheme, there were different learning procedures for different word classes. The ability of the learning procedures to recover from violated expectations varied enormously depending on the unknown word's syntactic role: FOUL-UP recovered well in the face of unknown nouns, had difficulty with unknown verbs, and fell apart when confronted with unknown prenominal adjectives. Carbonell generalized much of Granger's work as part of his POLITICS system [10, 11], although he was concerned with learning only concrete and proper nouns. Extensions included adding expectations from goal-driven inferences and allowing the system to make potentially incorrect or overgeneral hypotheses and later recover from its own mistakes.

In a different vein, Berwick [4] presented an approach to single-word learning based on analogical matching between causal network descriptions of events. Similarly, Salveter [59] used successive event descriptions to extract the meaning of verbs.

Common assumptions among the single-word acquisition systems described above are that the input is both syntactically and semantically correct, and that only one word at a time is unrecognized. In contrast, our model of adaptation contains a uniform learning procedure capable of more than single-word acquisition without those assumptions.

Davidson and Kaplan [15, 37] took a different view of single-word learning. They argued that it was unrealistic to assume a complete and unchanging lexicon for some types of databases. To aid interface users under these conditions, they used a semantic grammar to generate all legal interpretations of the unknown word, then explored category assignments in order of the estimated cost of verification. Similarly, in the presence of an unknown word or phrase, the only non-deviant interpretation our model permits is the resolution of the segment as an instance of a known extendable class (see Section 2.3). In Kaplan and Davidson's work, however, the *only* extensions to the lexicon that were permitted were new ground instances of specific known classes (for example, a new ship name or port city); the query language itself was fixed. In contrast, our model of adaptation permits idiosyncratic vocabulary to be added to all word classes.

Zernik's RINA [79, 80, 81, 82] went beyond the single word to phrase acquisition. Specifically, RINA learned the meaning of idioms from multiple examples. Since idioms are a special kind of idiosyncratic language use, Zernik's work is of particular interest. Indeed, Zernik's approach to hypothesis formation and error correction is, in many ways, compatible with our own. Underlying RINA's design, however, is the assumption that the syntax of the utterance is correct, although it may be inadequate to resolve the meaning. Thus, an unparsable sentence is always taken as an indication of a gap in the system's semantic knowledge. With the exception of extendable classes, our model proceeds from the opposite assumption: an unparsable sentence indicates a new form of reference, not a new referent. Zernik's assumption provides his system with a strong mechanism for limiting search, just as the Fixed Domain Assumption provides a different but equally powerful method for search reduction in our model. The empirical studies discussed in the next chapter demonstrate that a fixed domain, variable language assumption is the more realistic one for task-oriented natural language interfaces. From this point of view, RINA's approach to learning and our approach to adaptation take complementary paths, a fact we reexamine in Chapter 10.

Berwick, too, explored multi-word constructions. In recent work [6] he has concentrated on learning finite subsystems of English (for example, auxiliary verbs and noun phrase specifiers) by induction of finite automata. To accomplish this he must assume that what constitutes a grammatical utterance can be captured at a single point in time by some core set of examples that spans the target linguistic space. He then can try successively more complex classes of automata until he arrives at the level that generates the core set without generating examples he knows to be outside that set. Thus, his techniques, though powerful, do not accord well with the conditions of language use under which an adaptive interface must perform—the minimally ambiguous set of utterances that must be accounted for does change over time (and vary across users). In addition, we could not bound the search for a class of automata using Berwick's method since we do not know *a priori* what the target linguistic space is, nor do we have examples known to be outside the set.

Expanding our view to include learning sentential forms, we find the early work of Siklossy [67] whose system (ZBIE) induced vocabulary and syntactic structure. For ZBIE to learn it had to be given both a natural language input and a functional language input. The latter was a tree structure intended to describe the same scene referred to by the natural language input (for example, "This is a hat" would be paired with "(be hat)" and "The hat is on the table" would be paired with "(be (on table hat))"). The system used its current grammar to translate the functional language description into a hypothetical natural language utterance, replacing functional tokens with language tokens when possible, or with a token representing an unknown when no language token was available. ZBIE's primary learning strategy was to match, left-to-right, the natural language hypothesis against the natural language input, trying to resolve unknowns in the hypothesis with unmatched tokens in input. Using the primary learning strategy, ZBIE could acquire new vocabulary and more economical versions of its grammatical patterns for very simple sentences. When the primary learning strategy failed, the system had a rudimentary method for building a new grammar pattern. Although noteworthy for its scope, Siklossy's approach is incompatible in two ways with the constraints imposed on a natural language learning interface. Whereas a learning interface cannot assume grammaticality, ZBIE functioned under the assumption that the utterance was syntactically correct. More importantly, ZBIE was given both a language utterance and a meaning structure as input whereas a learning interface's search for the meaning of an utterance is its fundamental task.

Also at the sentential level is work by Harris [28]. Although not advanced as a psychological model of child language acquisition, Harris's intent was to teach his robot natural language under the same conditions children learn it. By breaking acquisition down into distinct phases, he built a system able to learn both word meanings and sentential forms. In Phase I, the system received utterance-action description pairs and learned the meaning of individual words by building a correlation table. In Phase II, a kind of context-free-grammar was induced from a fixed set of sentences composed from the vocabulary learned in Phase I. Finally, in Phase III, the correlation table and grammar were used together to parse new utterances and respond appropriately. In order to expand the vocabulary, the system had to be returned to Phase I; similarly, to extend the grammar, it had to be returned to Phase II. This approach seems to lie somewhere between adaptation and instruction (the successor to this work, INTELLECT, was discussed in Section 2.4).

At the discourse level we find the recent work of Fink and Biermann, VLNCE [19], which notices and remembers regularities in interface behavior in order to help predict future actions. In contrast to our work, VLNCE tracks dialogue expectations in order to predict lexical items to correct for speech recognition failures. The system builds a *behavior graph* in which the nodes correspond to the meaning structures of utterances it has encountered—no record of the structure of the utterances themselves is kept. The *expectation parser* uses the behavior graph and an ATN-like network [76] to process the input. When lexical expectations are violated, the parser uses the expectations in the behavior graph to control the size of the search space during error recovery. Recovery corresponds to traversing portions of the network that correspond loosely to insertion and deletion errors; the error recovery procedures are hand-coded into the network in terms of the grammatical structure of each type of constituent (similar to MULTIPAR). The model of adaptation we have presented differs from this approach in three ways: first, it offers a uniform mechanism for error recovery that is defined independently of the grammar. Second, the model views errors as potentially reliable indicators of previously unknown regularities. In VLNCE an error is considered a transient result of the inadequacy of the speech recognizer. Finally, although this book examines only adaptation in a semantic grammar, we believe the same model could be used to learn discourse level phenomena as well (see the discussion in Section 2.2). In contrast, there is no readily apparent way to extend VLNCE to use grammar level predictions.

Young, Hauptmann, and Ward's MINDS system has a focus similar to VLNCE's [32, 77, 78]. Their approach also uses predictions derived from high-level knowledge sources (the dialogue level, problem solving knowledge, pragmatics, and user goal representation) to limit the search space during speech processing. VLNCE uses its high-level knowledge to correct errors the system generates. In contrast, MINDS uses knowledge to prevent the generation of interpretations that violate the predictions. It does this by restricting the set of possible word choices to those that index concepts that have been predicted to be active. As with VLNCE, MINDS learns changes only to its high-level knowledge sources; the syntactic and semantic information embedded in the grammar cannot change. In addition, the changes that are learned are expected to hold only in the short-term because they reflect the fluidity of the user's goals over the course of a dialogue. Our adaptive approach takes the opposite point of view; changes to the system occur at the syntactic level of a semantic grammar and reflect long-term regularities in the user's linguistic behavior. Although it is possible to see how short-term, high-level learning might be added to an adaptive interface (Section 2.2), it is less apparent how MINDS could be extended to learn long-term changes at the lexical and syntactic levels.

It is clear from our review of previous work that the model of adaptation described in Section 2.2 proceeds from a different, more realistic set of assumptions for natural language interfaces than those found in other language acquisition systems. The assumptions underlying our model enable the system to meet the frequent user's need for a dynamic grammar. The model itself provides a uniform mechanism for constructing new grammatical components—from sentential forms down to dictionary entries—in direct reaction to the user's changing linguistic demands. The mechanism is robust enough to understand and learn in the face of multiple errors in an utterance, and to permit unknown but meaningful segments to be resolved as either synonyms or new instances of known extendable classes. The system achieves its goal in large part by taking advantage of the natural, self-bounding behavior of frequent users. In the next chapter we examine our expectations about user behavior in detail.

Chapter 3
User Behavior in an Adaptive Environment

In formulating the adaptation model in the previous chapter we made some strong assumptions about users' linguistic behavior. Before investing the resources required to implement an adaptive interface, it seemed appropriate to ascertain the validity of those assumptions. To accomplish this, we used a technique that is fairly common in evaluating natural language interface designs—the hidden-operator experiment. A hidden-operator experiment is one in which the user believes she is interacting with a computer system, when, in reality, the feedback is produced by an experimenter simulating the system's behavior. To accomplish the simulation the user's typed input is viewed remotely by the experimenter who constructs a response according to the algorithm being simulated (see Figure 3-2). The experimenter's response is then sent to the user's terminal as the "system's" output.[7]

In addition to allowing us to test our assumptions about user behavior in an adaptive environment, the hidden-operator experiments described below had two other uses. First, they demonstrated that the model is capable of learning different idiosyncratic grammars with a single, general mechanism. Second, the interactions between the user and the simulated system provided a set of spontaneously generated utterances that could be used as part of an evaluation of the implementation (see Chapter 9).

In the next section we state the behavioral hypotheses to be tested. Sections 3.2 through 3.4 describe the experimental conditions. In the last section of the chapter we review the results of the experiment and demonstrate the validation of our hypotheses.

---

[7]For examples of other studies conducted under the hidden-operator paradigm, see [24, 39, 49, 68, 69]. The experiments and results described in this chapter were first reported in [47].

3.1. The behavioral hypotheses

There are three conditions under which our model of adaptative parsing is an appropriate method of interface design. We have already alluded to the first condition: self-bounded language use. Without asymptotic movement toward a fixed set of structures, no idiosyncratic style will develop. In addition, if the grammar grows without bound in relation to a finite task domain, the accompanying rise in ambiguity is likely to render the system's response time intolerable.

The second necessary condition is significant across-user variance. This requirement is implicit in the idea of idiosyncratic style. If all users employ the same restrictions on form and reference then a methodology such as that of Kelley [39, 40, 41] or Good *et al.* [24] is preferable; through a generate-and-test cycle one builds a single, monolithic system incorporating the complete common subset. Without natural idiosyncracy of expression, the monolithic grammar would not suffer from the mismatch inefficiencies discussed in Chapter 1.[8]

The final condition requires limited adaptability in the user. A non-adaptive approach to interface design assumes that the cognitive burden of learning the interface's sublanguage is a minor one. If the user is able to adapt quickly and with little effort to a fixed system, adaptation on the part of the system is no longer a clear advantage. Although Watt [72] has argued convincingly against the efficacy of relying on user adaptation, it is nevertheless of interest to test the claim of limited user adaptability empirically.

These three conditions correspond to an assumption that certain behaviors are characteristic of frequent users . If we require the conditions, we must show that the commensurate behaviors exist. We can satisfy the first two conditions by demonstrating that the Regularity and Deviation Hypotheses are true. These hypotheses, introduced in Section 2.3, state that with frequent interaction a user will develop, and come to rely on, idiosyncratic language patterns:

H1. The Regularity Hypothesis: In a natural language interface used by the same individual over time, the user tends to rely on those forms of expression that she remembers as having worked in the past. In other words, we assume that frequent use leads the user to a *stylized* and *self-bounded* grammar.

---

[8] Some empirical evidence supporting significant across-user variance can be found in [21, 22, 50]. Those studies, however, examined individual variation only at the word level. The experiments described in this chapter explore the degree of variation across all types of grammatical constituents.

H2. The Deviation Hypothesis: Self-bounded behavior is more appropriately described as asymptotic to a fixed set of structures. When a user deviates from her canonical utterances, she does so in small, idiosyncratic ways.

To satisfy the third condition we form:

H4. The Adaptability Hypothesis: a system that permits the natural expression of idiosyncratic language patterns through adaptation results in better task performance than a system that forces the user to adapt to it.

The series of hidden-operator experiments discussed in the remainder of this chapter validate our three behavioral hypotheses and give ample evidence that with frequent use the required conditions are met.

3.2. The experimental condition

A calendar scheduling task was chosen for the experiment because of its fairly well-defined semantics and its normal requirement of frequent interactions over time. In a hidden-operator design, users were told that they would be typing the input to a *natural language learning interface* that would increase its knowledge of English while helping them keep an on-line calendar for a busy professor/entrepreneur.

In each of nine sessions, the user was given ten to twelve pictorial representations of changes to be made to the calendar. The stimuli was pictorial in order to minimize its influence on the user's forms of expression. In general, users had little trouble interpreting the *subtasks*, two examples of which are shown in Figure 3-1. The picture on the left indicates that the ending time of John's June 26 speech research meeting should be changed to 11:30. The picture on the right indicates that Flight #616 on June 28 should be cancelled, and another flight scheduled, closer to six o'clock (performing the second subtask requires at least two utterances: one to look for a replacement flight in the airline database and one to make the change to the calendar). The user was asked to effect the change in each picture by typing her commands as if she were "speaking or writing to another person." Although no time limit was enforced, the instructions told users to proceed to the next subtask after three unsuccessful tries.

In responding to a user's utterances, the hidden operator had the user's current grammar and lexicon available. With that information, an utterance was judged either *parsable* (no deviations), *learnable* (at most two deviations), or *uninterpretable* (more than two deviations). The algorithm for making the deter-

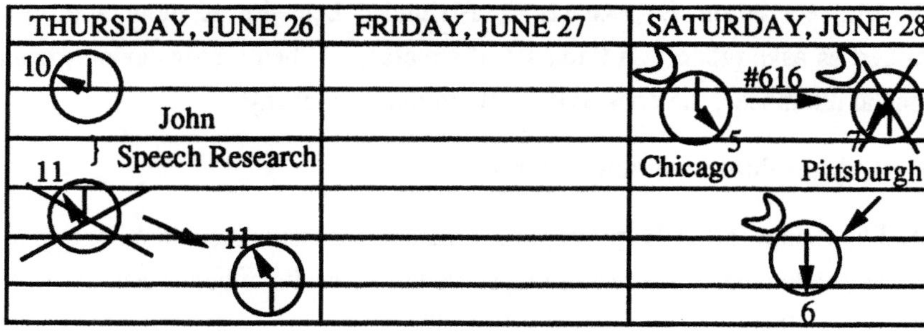

Figure 3-1: Sample pictorial stimuli for the hidden-operator experiments.

Reprinted with permission of Springer-Verlag

mination and the actions taken by the hidden operator in response are presented in Figure 3-2.

There are a number of observations to be made about the rules in the figure. First, note that Rule 2 adds new instances to extendable classes without considering the resolution as a deviation. The rationale is straightforward: as the grammar approaches its bound, the probability that an unknown segment corresponds to a new instance must increase. In the limit, all unknowns can be resolved in this way. Since new instances of known classes are exactly the sort of change that continues to occur even after the grammar has stabilized, we want to make learning them relatively inexpensive and routine. In the algorithm above, learning new class instances is accomplished at Deviation-level 0.

Another point of interest is the limit of two deviations in a learnable utterance in Rule 3. The model presented in Chapter 2 has no inherent limit; search continues in a least-deviant-first manner until a verified interpretation is found. In practice, however, some limit is necessary to control the amount and quality of interaction with the user. In general, a sentence with more than two deviations produces a large number of poor explanations.[9]

The algorithm's definition of *learnable* (Rules 3 and 4) points to a difficulty in the experimental method. If the hidden operator's response time was to be reasonable, not all adaptations to the grammar could be done "on-line." Certainly simple dele-

[9]The number of explanations produced increases as a function of both the deviation-level and the relative ambiguity of the constituents hypothesized to be present. Explanations at higher deviation-levels tend to be poorer because the recovery actions are largely knowledge-free. If they encoded more knowledge, more deviation could be tolerated successfully. Unfortunately, knowledge is not only power—every piece of knowledge built into a system is also an assumption the system may be unable to relax. Chapter 11 discusses this issue further.

1. IF the utterance can be understood using the current grammar and lexicon,
   THEN consider it *parsable* and tell the user that the action has been carried out.

2. IF there are unknown segments in the utterance,
   THEN try to resolve them as instances of extendable classes through interaction.

   2a. IF they are resolvable in this way,
   THEN add the new instances to the appropriate classes and goto 1.

3. IF the utterance can be understood by positing at most two deviations with respect to the current grammar,
   THEN consider it *learnable* and ask the user to verify the interpretation.

   3a. IF the user verifies the interpretation and the deviations are simple,
   THEN change the grammar and tell the user the action has been done.

   3b. IF the user verifies but the deviations are not simple,
   THEN tell the user the action has been done and change the grammar after the session is over.

   3c. IF the user does not verify but there is another interpretation
   THEN goto 3a.

   3d. IF the user does not verify and no other *learnable* interpretation exists,
   THEN consider the utterance *uninterpretable*, indicate to the user which portions were understood, and ask her to "Please try again."

4. IF the utterance is composed of constituents from which a legitimate database action can be inferred and within which no more than two deviations occur,
   THEN consider it *learnable* by "constructive inference," and verify as above.

5. IF most of the user's sentences were *parsable* during the session,
   THEN give her supplementary instructions at the beginning of the next session that encourage her to perform the task as quickly as possible.

Figure 3-2: Rules followed by the hidden operator in simulating the adaptive interface.

tions and substitutions could be accomplished quickly, but complex changes had to be delayed until the session was over. A change was considered complex if there were a number of ways it could be integrated into the grammar; between sessions, one new form was chosen. Sentences that were learnable by constructive inference (Rule 4) were almost always complex in this sense because the model does not specify a method of generalization. Although we discuss this (and other) problems of underspecification in Chapter 9, we note here that the delayed adaptations for complex forms did not seem to effect materially those aspects of performance we were examining.

Finally, Rule 5 mentions "supplementary instructions" asking the user to perform the task as quickly as possible. While it has been observed that given a natural course of events users will come to employ terser, more economical language [29, 40, 48, 58], it was unclear whether nine sessions would be adequate time for the tendency to be manifested. The point of providing the additional instructions was to subject the model to more extreme linguistic behavior within the time available. Note, however, that the supplementary instructions were not given until the user's grammar had stabilized substantially (see, for example, Figure 3-3). By perturbing the stable situation, we were also able to examine the model's performance when behavior begins to vary (as discussed in Section 2.2).

3.3. Control conditions

The experimental condition described in the previous section (the "Adapt" condition) was designed to test our hypotheses about the development of self-bounded, idiosyncratic grammars. To evaluate the counterargument to adaptation that maintains that the user will naturally adapt to the system's limitations faster than the system can usefully adapt to the user's idiosyncrasies, we designed two variations on the previous experimental condition.

In the "No-Adapt" condition, the experiment was conducted as outlined above with the following exceptions:

- Users were told the system was a natural language interface (not a learning interface).
- The kernel grammar was never changed.
- No supplementary instructions were given.

Although the system remained more permissive of extragrammaticality than the average natural language interface (by allowing up to two deviations with respect to the kernel grammar), the boundaries of the grammar *were* rigidly fixed. Any improvement in performance would therefore be attributable to the user's adaptability.[10]

[10] Because it was important to keep the criteria for parsability the same under all conditions, the kernel grammar for this condition was extended in one respect: use of articles was made optional. This is the most common ungrammatical construction displayed by interface users. If the grammar had not been extended in this way, most sentences would have involved more than two deviations and, without learning, the results from this condition would have been comparable almost exclusively to session one of the Adapt condition.

The "Adapt/Echo" condition was included in response to arguments by Slator *et al.* [68] that users want to learn, and will learn, a mnemonic command syntax and domain-specific vocabulary. When given the graphics command language equivalent to their natural language input, Slator's users were able to gradually integrate the terser forms into their utterances. It was unclear whether individuals would show the same propensity in interactions with an adaptive system. Users in the Adapt/Echo condition were given the same instructions as those in the Adapt condition except that they were told the system would display a paraphrase of their utterance in an "internal form" that they were free to incorporate into their commands or to ignore, as they saw fit.

3.4. User profiles

All of the users were female adults between twenty and sixty-five years of age. None had prior experience with natural language interfaces. Each was employed as a secretary or executive assistant in either a business or university environment. Although not every user maintained a calendar for her employer, each had kept a personal calendar for at least one year.

Sessions were run at approximately 24 hour intervals (except User 1 whose sessions were run twice a day with a five hour break). The number of sessions varied in the two control conditions in accordance with the availability of the users. Table 3-1 summarizes the relevant user information.

U	Other	Own	Job	EC	Ss
1	2.25	1	univ-psy	A	9
2	0	1.33	company	A	9
3	1.5	2	company	A	9
4	2	4	company	A	9
5	0	4	univ-cs	A/E	3
6	0	10	univ-cs	No-A	3
7	0	"always"	company	A/E	5
8	4.5	40	univ-eng	No-A	5

Table 3-1: Summary of user information.
(Key: U = user, Other = years keeping calendar for another,
Own = years keeping own calendar, Job = employer, EC = experimental condition
(A = Adapt, A/E = Adapt/Echo, No-A = No-Adapt), Ss = number of sessions)

3.5. Results and discussion

The results for users in the two adaptive conditions indicate a high degree of self-limiting behavior, converging towards a user-specific recurrent subset of English. There was virtually no overlap of derived forms at the sentential level across users; non-sentential similarities were limited primarily to missing articles and some common phrase marker substitutions. This profile of within-user consistency and across-user variability confirms the expectations in the Regularity and Deviation Hypotheses and satisfies the first two conditions necessary for an adaptive approach to interface design.

Figure 3-3 shows the approximate number of changes to the grammar over time for each of the four users in the Adapt condition. Figure 3-4 shows the same information for the Adapt/Echo condition. Both figures indicate, by user and session, the number of new constructions per *interpretable* sentence which is calculated as the total number of changes to the grammar divided by the total number of *parsable* and *learnable* sentences. The number of *uninterpretable* sentences in a session is given in parentheses next to the fraction. The computation of the total number of changes to the grammar did *not* include learning new instances of extendable classes because the tokens in the stimuli corresponding to unknown names were the same for all users. Shaded areas of Figure 3-3 indicate sessions following the introduction of the supplementary instructions to work quickly.

Figures 3-3 and 3-4 show both the effect of the choice of kernel forms and the difference in the rates at which language stabilization occurs. Observe that User 1's grammar requires the least learning and stabilizes quickly. She began with terse utterances and a vocabulary that was quite close to the kernel chosen for the experiment. User 2's grammar showed less initial resemblance but she employed it consistently and thus stabilized quickly as well. User 3 had a tendency to be both polite and verbose, so her utterances were more likely to contain new forms and stabilization occurred more slowly. User 4 showed the most rapid stabilization because, although the new forms she introduced in sessions one and two were not terse, they were quite "natural:" they were used consistently and without modification in subsequent sessions.

User 5's behavior is of limited interest as she became ill after the third session and her participation was discontinued. User 7's graph shows much the same trend as that found in the Adapt condition. Neither User 5 nor User 7 showed integration of the command language paraphrase, results at odds with Slator's general claims. Our

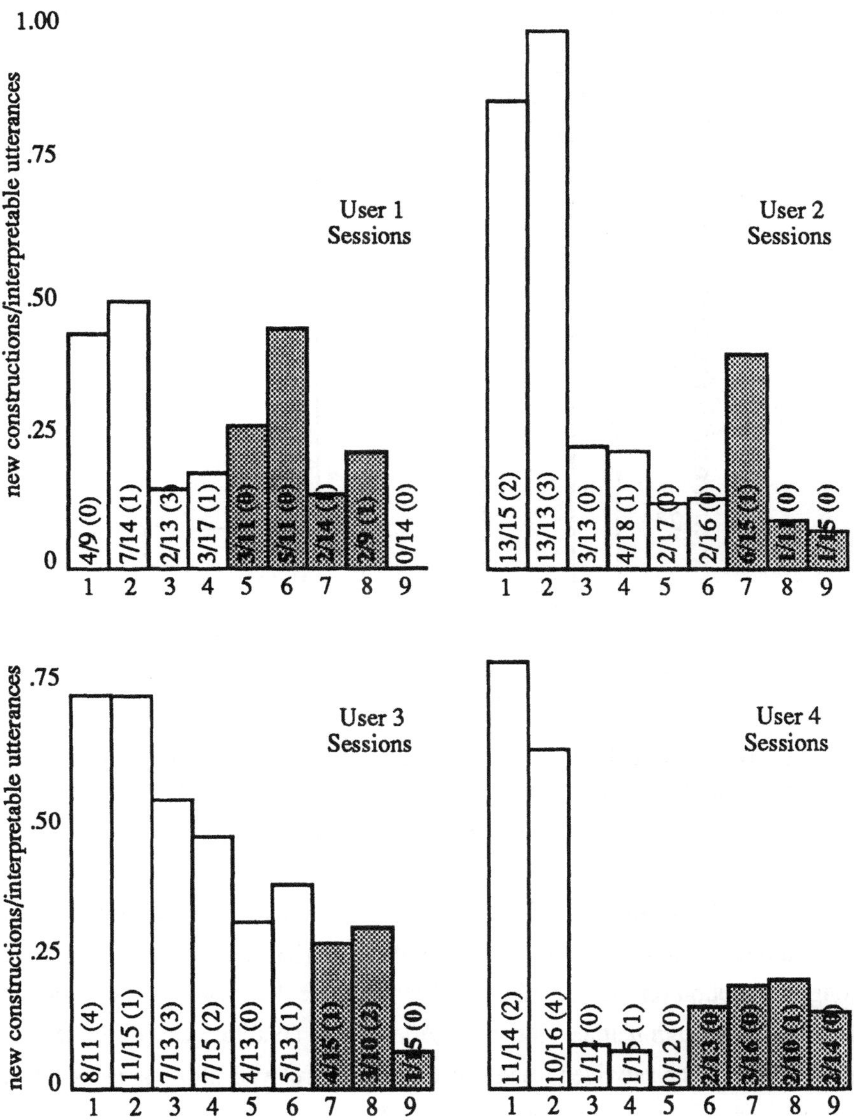

Figure 3-3: Self-limiting behavior in the Adapt condition as measured by the number of new constructions/the number of interpretable sentences (shaded sessions followed supplementary instructions to work quickly, # of unparsable utterances for each session is given in parentheses).

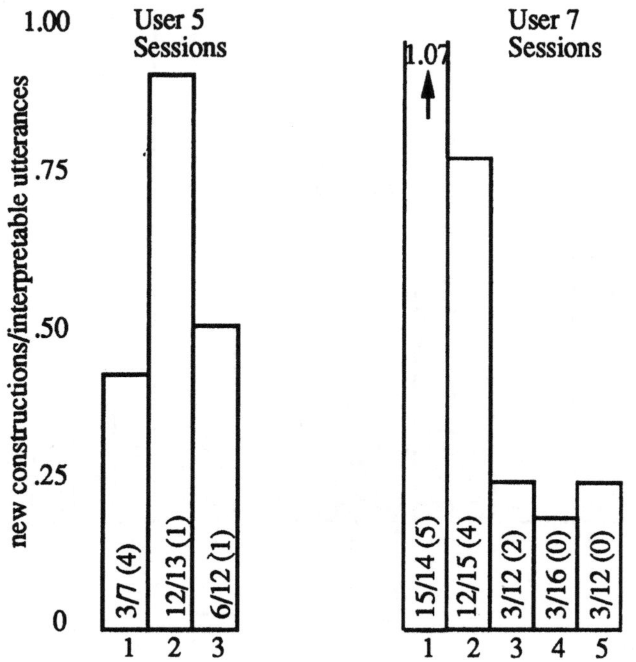

Figure 3-4: Self-limiting behavior in the Adapt/Echo condition measured by number of new constructions/number of interpretable sentences.

Reprinted with permission of Springer-Verlag

experience did, however, conform well with a broader interpretation of Slator's claims and replicated the experiences of Good *et al.* [24] and Cobourn [14]: there is a strong assumption on the part of users that whatever the system can generate it can also parse. Although neither user in the Adapt/Echo condition chose to integrate the command language provided, many of the users displayed idiosyncrasies that were clearly based on the system's output. User 7, for example, came to construct most instances of the schedule command (and only this command) using minor variations of the template: <start-time> - <end-time> <date> <meeting or meal> <other cases>, as in:

"12:00 - 1:30 June 11 lunch with Andy."

These utterances were learnable with respect to the grammar current at the time of use. Moreover, they closely conform to the template I used as hidden operator to seek confirmation of an interpretation:

Do you want:
12:00-1:30 lunch, Andy

A second set of experiments (described in Chapter 9) demonstrated that the tendency to assume that the system understands what it produces will persist despite explicit instructions to the contrary.

To illustrate what we mean by a self-limiting grammar, the evolution of User 2's referring phrase for a time interval is shown in Figure 3-2. The five forms she uses to refer to an interval are given in the left portion of the figure. The actual use of a form in each session is shown as a fraction of the total number of interval references that session. Initially, the grammar contains only the system form labelled SF. Using the general recovery actions, the experimenter equates the user forms (labelled with UF) as they appear. Note the transience of UF1 and UF2 as well as the eventual reliance on the relatively terse SF and the terser user derivative (UF3). The tendency towards abbreviated forms is symptomatic of movement toward a virtual, user-specific command language.

Forms	**Session**								
	1	*2*	*3*	*4*	*5*	*6*	*7*	*8*	*9*
SF: from <time> to <time>	-	2/6	-	5/9	4/4	2/3	-	6/6	1/3
UF1: from <time> till <time>	2/4	-	-	-	-	-	-	-	-
UF2a: beginning at <time> and ending at <time>	2/4	3/6	6/7	-	-	-	-	-	-
UF2b: beginning at <time> ending at <time>	-	1/6	1/7	-	-	-	-	-	-
UF3: <time> to <time>	-	-	-	4/9	-	1/3	1/1	-	2/3

Table 3-2: Self-Limiting behavior as shown by the evolution of two preferred forms for references to a time interval in User 2's grammar.

Reprinted with permission of Springer-Verlag

Figure 3-5 displays the results for the No-Adapt condition. Recall that the purpose of this variation was to study the claim that people adapt well enough to obviate the need for system adaptation. User adaptation in this condition is measured by categorizing each utterance by the minimum number of deviations required to interpret it. If the user is adapting to the limitations of the system we should see a general increase in interpretable sentences (those containing zero, one or two deviations). Further, grammatical utterances (zero deviations) should come to dominate. The latter conjecture is based on the belief that slower response time and more work are negatively reinforcing. Since the interpretation of utterances with one or two deviations took longer and had to be confirmed by the user, forms in the kernel grammar should have been preferred.

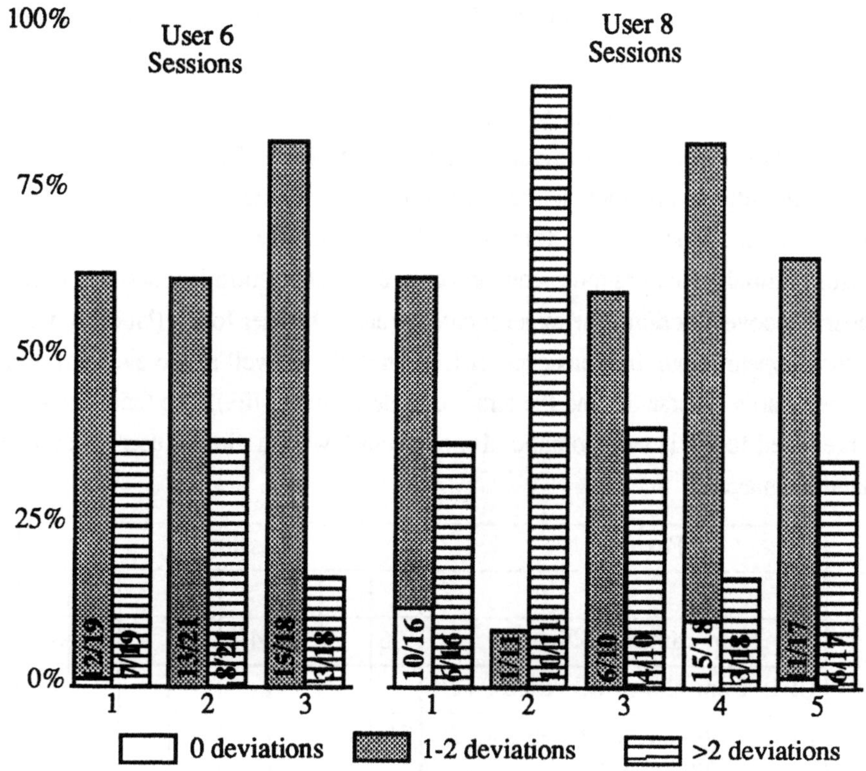

Figure 3-5: The No-Adapt Condition, Users 6 and 8: percentages of interpretable (0, 1, or 2 deviations) and uninterpretable (>2 deviations) utterances by session.

The graph for User 6 shows a clear increase in interpretable sentences. Her behavior is interesting in two respects. First, it is reminiscent of User 1's behavior: User 6's grammar was fairly close to the kernel, especially with respect to vocabulary, and she tended to rely on terse forms. As a result, there were, in general, few loci for deviation. Like the users in the adaptive conditions, User 6 relied on those forms that had worked in the past. When an utterance did meet with failure, her next try was usually a minor variation that almost always succeeded. In short, User 6 performed successfully in the No-Adapt condition, but relatively little adaptation was required of her. A second point of interest is that only one of her 54 sentences was without deviation, a fact that seems to disconfirm the conjecture that grammatical utterances would be sought. The conjectured pressure to seek grammatical forms relies implicitly on the user recognizing that response time could be faster, however. Since only one of her utterances was without deviation, it is possible that User 6 did not realize that her ungrammatical forms were causing the additional interactions. Instead she may have believed that the extra steps taken to confirm an interpretation were part of the system's normal function and not under her control.

Figure 3-5 also displays the results of analyzing User 8's performance in the No-Adapt condition. There is no pattern of improvement in User 8's data; her success at adapting to the interface's subset of English was extremely limited. We defer further discussion of User 8 until we have examined two additional measures of performance: Table 3-3 shows the number of subtasks completed by each user in each session, Table 3-4 shows the related metric of time taken per subtask. With respect to the former measure, users other than User 8 generally managed to effect the changes in each subtask they tried.[11] They rarely required more than three attempts per subtask in the initial sessions and averaged only slightly more than one attempt per subtask in later sessions.

A general decrease in task time is a predictable result of practice. In this experiment, however, the decrease in task time is also attributable to the users' self-limiting behaviors. Users in the adaptive conditions accomplish the task in less time as the grammar of the simulated system comes to reflect their own and more sentences are judged parsable rather than learnable. When the supplementary instructions are given (Adapt condition only) the users are implicitly encouraged to employ simpler, terser forms. As a result, task times increase as the new forms are learned. When these forms stabilize, response times fall to new lows because the shorter forms take less time to check against the grammar. User 6 shows the same general trend in time spent as those in the adaptive conditions both because her initial grammar conformed so closely to the kernel and because she is consistent in her use of what worked in the past.

User 8 shows neither consistent decline in the time taken each session nor in the number of uninterpretable sentences (see Figure 3-5). Both her work experience and the content of her utterances lead to the conclusion that little of her behavior can be attributed to task misunderstanding. Put simply, she was unable or refused to adapt.

Her linguistic style, like that of User 3, can be characterized as verbose. In response to a typical utterance, the system would tell her which segments it could

---

[11]There were four sessions in which a user skipped all or part of one or more subtasks (indicated by a bracketed superscript in Table 3-3). In these cases no utterance relating to the subtask appears in the log file. Half a subtask may be skipped if, for example, a value was to be changed and the old value was removed but the new value was not added.

Experimental Condition	Session (Total Number of Subtasks Possible)								
	1 (10)	*2 (11)*	*3 (12)*	*4 (10)*	*5 (10)*	*6 (10)*	*7 (11)*	*8 (10)*	*9 (11)*
Adapt									
User 1	7[1]	11	12	10	10	8[2]	11	10	11
User 2	10	11	12	10	10	10	11	10	11
User 3	8	11	12	10	10	10	11	10	11
User 4	10	11	12	10	10	10	11	9.5[.5]	10.5[.5]
Adapt/Echo									
User 5	6.5	9	12						
User 7	10	11	12	10	10				
No-Adapt									
User 6	10	11	12						
User 8	7	1	4.5	5	6				

Table 3-3: The number of completed subtasks, arranged by user and session ("[#]" indicates number of subtasks skipped).

parse and ask her to try again. She would then try typing exactly those segments just echoed, with no connecting text. When the terse form met with failure she would gravitate back to overly explanatory sentences.

User 8's performance in session two was so poor (in 31 minutes she produced one learnable sentence with two deviations), and her frustration so great, that she was given hints about how to use the system more effectively prior to beginning session three.[12] Although the help appeared to improve her performance in sessions three and four, in session five there is still a preponderance of unparsable forms. Contrast this with the behavior of users in the other conditions, most of whom had reduced their number of unparsable utterances to zero by session five. Finally, note User 8's low values for the number of tasks completed. The low values were due largely to the fact that she never managed to find a parsable form for an entire class of subtasks (those involving the **change** action). Although User 8 did rely on the few forms that

[12]Specifically, she was told to try to type simple, but fully grammatical sentences and to think of the system as someone to whom she was writing instructions. She was the only user who was given this aid.

Experimental Condition	Session								
	1	*2*	*3*	*4*	*5*	*6*	*7*	*8*	*9*
Adapt									
User 1	5.5*	3.0	2.5	2.8	1.7+	2.4	1.6*	2.1*	1.0
User 2	5.0	3.5	2.0	3.5	2.2	2.1	2.2+	1.3	1.3
User 3	6.3	3.2	2.7	3.3	1.7	2.3	1.6+	2.0	1.0
User 4	3.4	3.3	1.7	2.1	1.1+	1.6	1.5	1.5	1.1
Adapt/Echo									
User 5	8.5	5.3	3.3						
User 7	4.7	3.8	2.5	3.3	1.5				
No-Adapt									
User 6	4.3	3.7	2.0						
User 8	6.3	31.0	7.1	5.0	5.3				

Table 3-4: The average number of minutes per subtask, by user and session ("*" indicates approximate value due to damage to log files "+" indicates instructions to work quickly given this session).

had worked in the past, taken as a whole her performance must be seen as a strong counterargument to the notion that everyone finds it natural or easy to adapt to a system's linguistic limitations.

The purpose of the experiments described in this chapter was to establish certain behavioral characteristics of frequent users which, in turn, guarantee the conditions necessary for an adaptive interface to benefit user performance. The behavior of the users in the adaptive conditions demonstrates the self-limiting, idiosyncratic language use predicted by the Regularity and Deviation Hypotheses. As a result, we may assume that the conditions of within-user consistency and across-user variance will be met, making single-user, adaptive interfaces a practical and desirable alternative to a monolithic interface design. In the broader view, our empirical results demonstrate that self-bounded linguistic behavior is a natural by-product of frequent use. Phrased differently: we have shown that idiosyncratic style can be viewed as a dependable source of constraint.

The experimental results validate the Adaptability Hypothesis as well. Although we cannot guarantee that a particular user will find adaptation to an interface's limitations difficult, User 8 serves as a dramatic example of the kind of limited user adaptability we must be prepared to encounter. Further, a comparison of User 6 and User 8 supports Watt's argument [72] that the ease with which a user adapts to a rigid interface depends significantly on a fortuitous correspondence between the user's natural language and the sublanguage provided by the interface designer. More importantly, the performance of the users in the adaptive conditions demonstrates that an initial lack of correspondence can be overcome by system adaptation.

Having proven our conjectures about user behavior, we return to our single conjecture concerning system behavior in an adaptive environment: (H3) the Fixed Kernel Hypothesis stated in Section 2.3. Its basic claim is that the adaptation model of Section 2.2 in conjunction with a small kernel grammar creates an interface design responsive to the frequent user's needs. In order to validate the Fixed Kernel Hypothesis we now turn our attention to a particular implementation of the model we call CHAMP.

Chapter 4

System Architecture and Knowledge Representation

In Chapter 2 we considered adaptation as a general solution to the problem of natural language interface design. The model we presented was adequate to pinpoint certain implicit assumptions in our approach and to generate a number of testable hypotheses. At the same time, however, the model left many important components underspecified and many practical issues unresolved. In Section 3.2, for example, we noted that without a specific generalization method, multiple ways of integrating a derived form into the grammar were possible. As a result, the hidden operator simply chose an appropriate representation for the derived form without considering the limitations a particular generalization method would create. Similarly, the algorithm for categorizing an utterance (also presented in Section 3.2) required only that some minimally deviant correspondence between input and grammatical form be found; the algorithm did not take into account the computational complexity of finding it.

Because the simulation was being performed by a person who understood the utterances, the "system" usually behaved both correctly and efficiently when the model underspecified the action to be taken. A derived form, for example, was represented in the most useful way possible given the structure and contents of the grammar at that moment. Thus, the conjectures about user behavior were validated by experiments in which an "ideal" system was being simulated. To validate our remaining conjecture, the Fixed Kernel Hypothesis, we must address the creation of an actual adaptive parser and determine whether its behavior can be sufficiently close to the ideal along relevant dimensions. We have implemented the model as an adaptive interface named CHAMP.[13] Of course any implementation of a model forces the designer to make specific what was previously abstract. The particular set of choices embodied in CHAMP, as well as the implications of those choices and their behavior in a running system, are the subjects addressed in the remainder of this book.

---

[13]The system is written in Common LISP and currently runs on an IBM RT. The acronym stands for CHAMeleonic Parser.

Figure 2-2 presented a simple schematic diagram of the components and processes of the adaptation model in Chapter 2. Figure 4-1 represents the same components and processes as they have been realized in CHAMP.

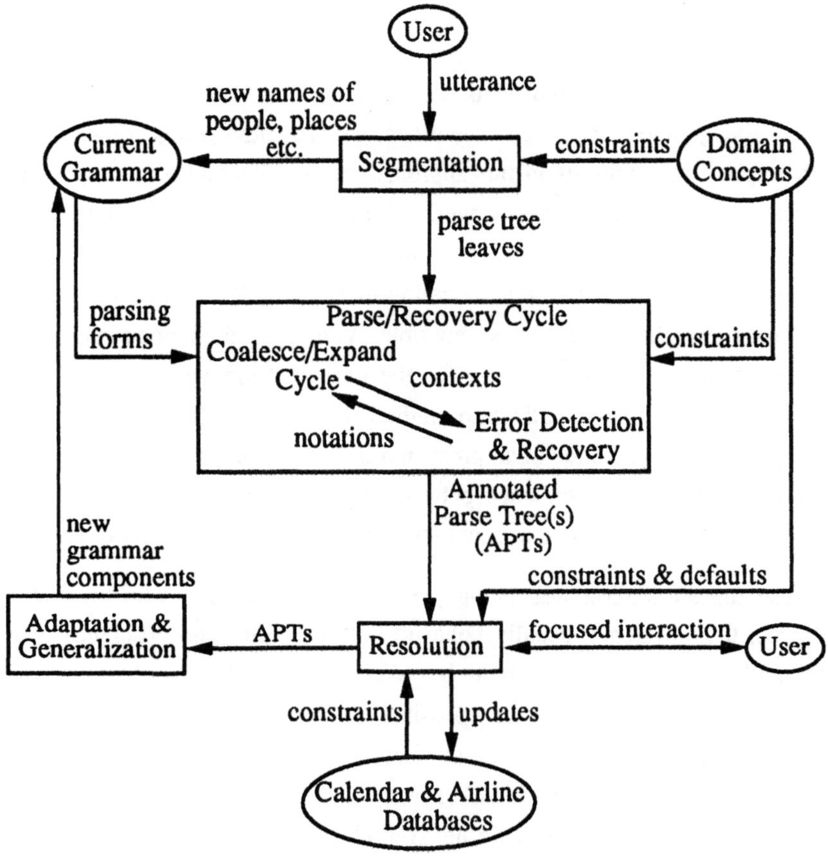

Figure 4-1: Schematic representation of CHAMP's knowledge & control (knowledge sources are enclosed in ovals, processes in rectangles).

A comparison of Figures 2-2 and 4-1 shows that the original two-step understanding process has been decomposed into four distinct phases: Segmentation, the Parse/Recovery Cycle (which is made up of the Coalesce/Expand Cycle and Error Detection & Recovery), Resolution, and Adaptation & Generalization. Considered as a distinct unit (see Chapter 5), Segmentation and the Coalesce/Expand Cycle comprise a bottom-up parser capable of learning new instances of known extendable classes. When we embed the Coalesce/Expand Cycle inside the Parse/Recovery Cycle, however, we create a least-deviant-first parser by integrating Error Detection

& Recovery into the Expand phase of the bottom-up algorithm (see Chapter 6). Error Detection & Recovery has the dual responsibilities of catching violated expectations in a candidate grammatical constituent (called a *context*) and augmenting the parse tree with *recovery notations*.

When the Parse/Recovery Cycle produces more than one annotated parse tree (APT) we consider the set of APTs as competing explanations of the utterance. Resolution (Chapter 7) is responsible for selecting the intended meaning from this set and performing the user's requested action. To accomplish resolution CHAMP may require guidance from the user, or may need nothing more than the additional constraints provided by the entries in the databases.

Once a meaning has been assigned to a deviant utterance, the system is ready to adapt the grammar so that the previously unknown form can be recognized directly in the future as a way of referring to the semantic structure. Since it is unlikely that any particular utterance will reappear repeatedly, word for word, memorization would be of little use. Instead, we need the changes to the grammar to reflect an appropriate degree of generalization. In addition, any successfully understood utterance (deviant or not) may contain information that can help eliminate prior generalizations that were incorrect. Once Adaptation & Generalization (Chapter 8) has been accomplished, the system is ready for the next interaction.

Although the decomposition of processing steps has changed, the ovals in the figure show that CHAMP contains the same four sources of knowledge present in the model: the User (at two points), Current Grammar, Domain Concepts, and Databases (specifically, the Calendar and Airline Databases from the experiments described in the previous chapter). The knowledge structures associated with database interaction are discussed in the context of Resolution, in Chapter 7. The representations chosen for the grammar and the domain concepts are discussed in the remaining sections of this chapter.

4.1. Representing knowledge in CHAMP

Considered from the system's point of view, CHAMP performs two tasks. The first is to aid in the duties of an executive assistant to a professor/entrepreneur. These duties consist of helping to maintain a schedule of meetings and events, and helping to arrange airline reservations when events require travel. CHAMP's second and less visible task is to extend its grammar to understand more effectively the idiosyncratic language of a particular user. Because the tasks are distinct, it is useful to distinguish between two types of knowledge in CHAMP: the application-related structures that organize the domain concepts and databases, and the learning-related structures that comprise the grammar. This division is not one of syntax versus semantics—both types of structures contain what is usually thought of as syntactic and semantic information. The important distinction is between what can and cannot change as a result of adaptation. As a consequence of the Fixed Domain Assumption (Section 2.3), only those structures that make up the grammar can be the target of learning.

To help the user schedule events, the number of general actions and object types the system must know about (the Domain Concepts in Figure 4-1) is fairly small (about fifty). On the other hand, the number of specific objects, such as particular individuals and locations, is unconstrained via the use of extendable classes. In keeping a calendar, CHAMP limits the available actions to viewing some portion of the current schedule or adding, deleting, or changing the value of an entry. Objects that can be referred to include meetings, seminars, specific times of day, time intervals, types of locations (businesses, buildings, rooms), participants, and topics, to name a few. To schedule travel events (which may be by car or plane) the four actions remain the same, but objects such as the airline schedule, flight numbers, cities, and arrival and departure times must be added.[14]

Although the number of types of actions and objects that can be referred to is small, the possible number of ways of referring to them is not. In other words, the size of the domain has little effect upon the degree of linguistic complexity CHAMP might encounter. Consider, for example, possible initial variation between different users expressing the same request:

User A: Schedule a 2:00 - 3:00 meeting with the Robotics Group.
User B: Add a Robotics Group meeting from 2 p.m. to 3 p.m.

User A: Show me the plane schedule leaving NY and arriving in Pittsburgh.
User B: Display flight information for flights from New York to Pittsburgh.

User A: Cancel my 3 o'clock appointment.
User B: Delete the meeting beginning at 3:00 p.m.

User A: Reschedule the meeting at 4 to 10 am.
User B: Change the starting time of the 4 p.m. meeting to 10 a.m.

---

[14]In order to demonstrate the generality of the system, CHAMP's knowledge structures were originally developed for the calendar task without trip scheduling—the "calendar domain." After a complete working version of the system had been built, structures for the travel concepts and travel grammar were written as if scheduling the professor/entrepreneur's trips was an independent task—the "travel domain." As a result, CHAMP can be run with the calendar domain, the travel domain, or both.

User A: Change the 10 am meeting's location to John's office.
User B: Change the location of the meeting at 10 am to John's office.

We know from the experiments described in Chapter 3 that even for a single user reference to the same events may change over time. User A's language, for example, might develop as follows:

Day 1: Schedule a 2:00 - 3:00 meeting with the Robotics Group.
Show me the plane schedule leaving NY and arriving in Pittsburgh.
Cancel my 3 o'clock appointment.
Reschedule the meeting at 4 to 10 am.
Change the 10 am meeting's location to John's office.

Day 14: Schedule 2-3 Robotics Group
Show flights from NY to Pittsburgh
Cancel @ 3
Reschedule @ 4 to @ 10 am
Relocate to John's office

Day 28: Sc Robotics Group 2-3
flights NY to Pgh
C 3
Res 4 to 10 am
Rel John's ofc

The implementation of the understanding and adaptation processes in CHAMP is independent of any particular domain. Thus, to understand or to learn to understand these kinds of utterances, CHAMP must be given information about how the user may refer to the actions and objects meaningful to the task, as well as information about the actions and objects themselves. Because we assume that the domain remains fixed once loaded (except for extendable classes), only the forms of reference can be changed by adaptation. The structures that capture forms of reference (and new instances of known classes) comprise the system's grammar. Specifically, learning-related knowledge is organized by a lexicon and a Formclass Hierarchy, both described in the next section. Information about the actions and objects themselves, information that cannot be changed and is independent of any particular form of reference, is organized by the Concept Hierarchy, described in Section 4.3.

4.2. Learning-related knowledge

The best way to understand the organization of a grammar in CHAMP is by examining part of such a grammar. Although two separate kernel grammars have been implemented, we use examples taken primarily from the calendar domain in the discussion that follows. The upper portions of the figures that introduce the next three subsections (Figures 4-2, 4-5, and 4-8) display a small portion of the calendar kernel as it is organized in CHAMP's case frame representation [18]. The representation in the figures has been simplified for expositional purposes; both kernels are presented in the exact representation used by CHAMP in [46]. The reader is encouraged to examine Figures 4-2, 4-5, and 4-8 briefly before continuing.

The figures show that the grammar is created from the following five types of components:

- **Formclass**: the component that organizes all the syntactically distinct ways of referring to a concept that are recognized by the grammar.
- **Form**: the component that represents a particular way of referring to a concept.
- **Wordclass**: the component that organizes all the lexically distinct ways of referring to a concept that are recognized by the grammar.
- **Step**: the component of a form that assigns a formclass or wordclass to a subsegment in the utterance. Each step reflects a unique usage of the formclass or wordclass in the grammar.
- **Lexical definition**: the component that ties a particular word or phrase to one or more wordclasses.

Each of these types of component is discussed fully in the subsections that follow this overview. It is clear from the figures that the grammar is composed primarily of semantic categories, although there are a few classes (such as **m-intervalforms** which represents a time interval marked by a preposition) that reflect syntactic distinctions.

To establish a frame of reference, the lower portions of Figures 4-2, 4-5, and 4-8 show those aspects of the case frame grammar that can be expressed using standard BNF notation. Although we will study both representations in detail, a high-level comparison reveals that a form is comparable to a non-terminal whose expansion is to be matched against the utterance. The steps taken by a form to recognize a segment of the utterance correspond to looking for the constituent wordclasses and formclasses in the expansion. A wordclass is like a non-terminal that expands to only terminals; recognizing a wordclass means matching actual words and phrases in the lexicon. A formclass, on the other hand, is like a non-terminal that expands to the names of forms; recognizing a constituent formclass means using a form in the constituent class to recognize a subsegment.[15]

Do the two sets of structures—case frames and BNF rules—recognize the same language? Not exactly. As we examine each of the five types of components in CHAMP's grammar in turn, we will find that five of the fields in CHAMP's case frames have no BNF correlates. Two of these, the instance generator (*ig*) that may be associated with a formclass and the *def* field that may be associated with a lexical definition, facilitate the recognition task without changing the language recognized. On the other hand, the *concept* and *active* fields associated with a formclass and wordclass, and the *bindvar* field associated with a step allow CHAMP to apply context-sensitive constraints during parsing. As a result, CHAMP recognizes a more semantically consistent language than a context-free BNF grammar permits. Our comparison of the two representations will also uncover the significant reduction in grammar size afforded by a form's *unodes*, *mnodes*, and *rnode* fields.

4.2.1. The formclass

actionforms	**addforms**	**m-intervalforms**	**u-intervalforms**
isa root	isa actionforms	isa root	isa root
members (addforms)	members (ACT1)	members (INT0)	members (INT1 INT2)
locations *root*	locations *root*	locations (702)	locations (206)
agenda-level 8	agenda-level 7	agenda-level 2	agenda-level 1
active t	active t	active t	active t
concept action	concept add	concept interval	concept interval
ig ig-act			ig ig-act

<actionforms> ::= <addforms>
<addforms> ::= <act1>
<m-intervalforms> ::= <int0>
<u-intervalforms> ::= <int1> | <int2>

Figure 4-2: Examples of formclass definitions from the calendar domain displayed in CHAMP's case frame representation and those portions of the case frames expressible in standard BNF notation.

A *formclass* is a grammatical component that organizes all the syntactically distinct ways of referring to a concept that are recognized by the grammar. The upper

[15]Few natural language systems use a simple context free grammar exclusively, though most systems do have such a grammar embedded within them (see, for example, [65, 66, 75]). Like CHAMP, most formalisms add explicit mechanisms to overcome many of the shortcomings of CFGs shown here. Thus, although the contrastive analysis between CHAMP and CFGs offered in this section does not serve to compare CHAMP directly to other, more complex formalisms, it does provide a basis for such a comparison by explicating CHAMP's advantages with respect to their common denominator.

portion of Figure 4-2 shows that a formclass may have associated with it seven pieces of information. The first, given by the *isa* field, is the parent formclass. In the portion of the kernel displayed, only **addforms** stands in a hierarchical relationship with another class (**actionforms**). The other formclasses shown (**actionforms, m-intervalforms,** and **u-intervalforms**) are roots of some of the subtrees that comprise the Formclass Hierarchy (discussed below). The second piece of information in a formclass definition is *isa*'s inverse: *members*. Thus, **addforms** *isa* **actionforms** just as the *members* field of **actionforms** includes **addforms**. These inverse relations holds across different types of components in CHAMP: formclass and formclass, formclass and form (note ACT1 *isa* **addform** in Figure 4-5), and wordclass and lexical definition (see Figure 4-8). In the lower portion of Figure 4-2 the *isa* and *members* relations are captured in BNF.

The value in a formclass's *locations* field is simply the union of all the step numbers that may assign that formclass to a subsegment in the utterance. A formclass's *locations* field participates in an inverse relation with the *class* field of a form's steps. Figures 4-2 and 4-5, for example, show that the set of *locations* associated with **m-intervalforms** contains step 702 which, in turn, has **m-intervalforms** as its *class*. These relations are left implicit in the BNF notation. We will see in Chapter 5 that the *locations* field holds information used to expand partial parse trees.

The next field, the *agenda-level*, ties a formclass into the partial ordering of all formclasses called the Formclass Hierarchy. The purpose of the hierarchy is to organize the search for constituents during parsing. Thus, the structure of the hierarchy is derived from the relative embeddedness of constituents in the grammar. Strictly speaking, CHAMP's grammar is a forest of trees defined by the *isa* fields of the formclasses and forms (formclasses without parent classes serve as the roots of the trees). Relative embeddedness is particularly easy to see in the BNF rules: since <addforms> expands to <act1> (Figure 4-2), and <act1>'s expansion contains <m-intervalforms> (Figure 4-5), <m-intervalforms> must be lower in the hierarchy than <addforms>. Figure 4-3 demonstrates that to recover the same information from the case frame representation we must follow the relevant *isa* relations and replace the step numbers in a form's *steps* list with the *class* assigned by the step. Thus, step 702 in ACT1's steps list indicates that ACT1 may contain as a constituent a member of **m-intervalforms.** Alternatively, we say that step 702 "seeks" an **m-intervalform.** Since ACT1 *isa* **addform** and ACT1 contains step 702, **m-intervalforms** is lower in the Formclass Hierarchy than **addforms**; in a bottom-up parser we must recognize marked intervals before we try to recognize references to actions. Similarly, the formclass **u-intervalforms** is lower than the formclass **m-intervalforms** because part of recognizing a marked interval involves recognizing an unmarked interval (step 206 of INT0).

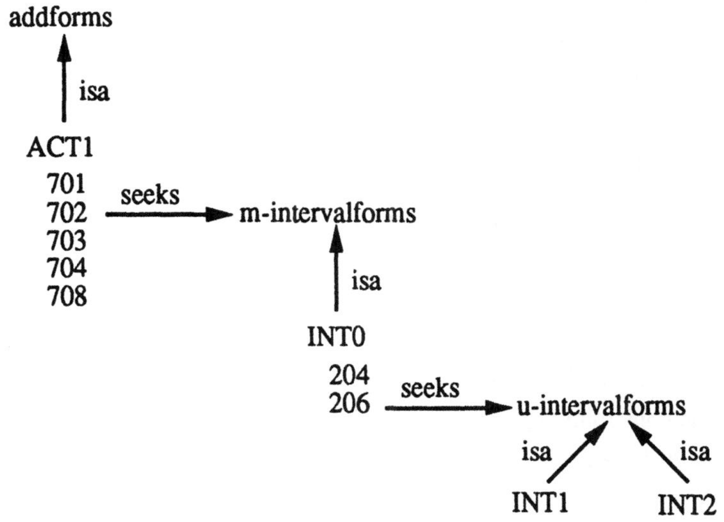

Figure 4-3: An example of the relationships among grammatical components that define the Formclass Hierarchy.

The final three fields in a formclass case frame contribute to the application of context-sensitive constraints during parsing. The role of the *active* field is explained when we discuss segmentation in Section 5.1. The *concept* field is a connection between learning-related knowledge and application-related knowledge. Any information that might help recognize a reference to the **add** action or the **interval** object, but that cannot be changed by adaptation, is accessible through the token **add** or **interval**, respectively. For example, the **interval** concept contains the knowledge that the starting hour of an interval must be strictly less than the ending hour. This prevents CHAMP from interpreting the segments "5 to 3" and "5 to 5" as time intervals even though the BNF rule for <u-intervalforms> permits such interpretations. Note that both the classes **m-intervalforms** and **u-intervalforms** point to the same concept; what is true about intervals is true regardless of the presence or absence of a preposition.

The *ig* field (short for "instance generator") contains the name of a LISP function. The purpose of an ig is to create a canonical value for a segment in the formclass.

Ig-hour, for example, tries to convert the segment of the utterance recognized as a **u-hourform** into a number between zero and 2400. In this way, each of "12:00 p.m.," "12 pm," and "noon" becomes the same canonical value, **1200.** If the information in the segment is incomplete, **ig-hour** produces as its canonical value a number with a question mark (such as **(1200 ?)** for "12:00"). Thus, a canonical value distills the important information in a constituent into a convenient form. Some igs (such as **ig-hour)** are invoked during the Expand phase of the Coalesce/Expand Cycle, others are invoked during the Resolution phase in order to help convert an annotated parse tree (APT) into the canonical form expected by the database functions (see Chapter 7.

Figure 4-4 demonstrates how a canonical value can facilitate the application of semantic constraints. The ig for **u-intervalforms**, for example, uses the canonical values previously generated by **ig-hour** for its **starthour** and **endhour** to represent the interval in terms of a twenty-four hour clock. Once this has been done, the semantic constraint that assures that the **starthour** precedes the **endhour** can be applied (the constraint application process is explained in Section 4.3). In Figure 4-4 the constraint is satisfied because **ig-int** creates the interval **(1500 1630)**. Checking the constraint requires only a simple test because the relevant information is represented in a way that is independent of the actual referring phrases.

Utterance: "Schedule an AI seminar from 3 p.m. to 4:30 on June 5"

IG	Argument Bindings	Canonical Form Result
ig-hour	hr=3, minutes=0, dnbit=pm	1500
ig-hour	hr=4, minutes=30, dnbit=nil	(430 ?)
ig-int	starthour=1500, endhour=(430 ?)	(1500 1630)

Figure 4-4: The role of instance generators in providing canonical values for constraint application during parsing.

The main purpose of a formclass is to organize the information that applies to all its members. Although a formclass's *members* may be other formclasses (see **actionforms** in Figure 4-2), most of the time the *members* are forms, the grammatical component we examine next.

4.2.2. The form and its steps

```
ACT1
isa addforms
steps
701: class m-hourforms
702: class m-intervalforms
703: class m-dateforms
704: class addwd
708: class m-i-ggforms
mode (704 708)
unodes ((701 702 703))
mnodes ((701 702))

INT0
isa m-intervalforms
steps
204: class ivlmkr
     bindvar marker
206: class u-intervalforms
     bindvar (ivl divl)
mode (204 206)

INT1
isa u-intervalforms
steps
107: class u-hourforms
     bindvar starthour
108: class ehrmkr
     bindvar emarker
109: class u-hourforms
     bindvar endhour
mode (107 108 109)

INT2
isa u-intervalforms
steps
110: class intervalwd
     bindvar instance
mode (110)

<addforms> :: = <act1>
<act1> ::= ([[<m-hourforms> | <m-intervalforms>] [<m-dateforms>]] |
          [[<m-dateforms>] [<m-hourforms> | <m-intervalforms>]]) <addwd> <m-i-ggforms>
<m-intervalforms> ::= <int0>
<int0> ::= <ivlmkr> <u-intervalforms>
<u-intervalforms> ::= <int1> | <int2>
<int1> ::= <u-hourforms> <ehrmkr> <u-hourforms>
<int2> ::= <intervalwd>
```

Figure 4-5: Examples of form & step definitions from the calendar domain displayed in CHAMP's case frame representation and those portions of the case frames expressible in standard BNF notation.

A form is a declarative structure that is interpreted by the system as an algorithm (recognizer) for detecting references to its formclass's concept. The upper portion of Figure 4-5 displays some of the kernel forms that are members of the formclasses in Figure 4-2. The steps that make up the algorithm are given in the second field. Steps are implemented as distinct structures so that they may be shared among strategies; each step constitutes a unique usage of its class within the grammar. We see in the next chapter how sharing steps helps eliminate redundant search during a parse. The lower portion of Figure 4-5 shows those portions of the case frames that can be expressed in BNF.

To understand the correspondence between a form and its BNF representation we must first understand the role of the step. The purpose of a step is to assign a *class* to a constituent that may span a number of contiguous segments in the utterance. The process of assigning a class to a set of contiguous segments is similar to that of substituting a non-terminal for its expansion in a context-free parser. Thus, in Figure 4-5, it is not until each of steps 107, 108, and 109 is satisfied by a portion of the input that an instance of **u-intervalforms** has been found by INT1. Similarly, finding <u-hourforms>, <ehrmkr>, and another <u-hourforms> tells us we have found <int1>. At this point, however, the differences in the information available from each of the representations changes the nature of the understanding process. As we saw in Figure 4-4, in CHAMP the *concept* **interval** associated with the class **u-intervalforms** imposes semantic constraints on candidate intervals. The tokens in a step's *bindvar* field are used in the definition of those semantic constraints. In this way the predicate associated with **interval** can enforce the relation **starthour** < **endhour.** Of course, no processing of this kind occurs in a context-free parser.

Expanding our view from the step to the form itself, let us first compare INT0 and <int0>. INT0's *steps* list contains two entries: 204 followed by 206. The step's definitions indicate that step 204 is satisfied by finding a member of the wordclass **ivlmkr** in the utterance, while step 206 seeks a member of the formclass **u-intervalforms.** Since both steps are in the *rnode* field of the INT0 form, they are both required if we are to be certain we have found a marked interval. In other words, we have found an **m-intervalform** using the steps in INT0 if we can find an **ivlmkr** followed by a **u-intervalform** in the sentence. In BNF we capture the same idea by writing:

<m-intervalforms> ::= <int0> and <int0> ::= <ivlmkr> <u-intervalforms>.

In general we say that a form succeeds if all the steps are satisfied by contiguous portions of the utterance occurring in the given step-order. Exceptions to this rule are expressed by the annotation nodes: the *rnode* stands for "required," the *unode* for "unordered," and the *mnode* for "mutually-exclusive." More precisely, the *rnode* field overrides the need for all steps to be satisfied; a form may still succeed as long as those steps on the *rnode* list are matched. Similarly, the *unodes* field overrides the ordering of the steps list; steps in a unode's sublist may be satisfied by any permutation of corresponding contiguous segments in the utterance. The *mnodes* field demands that steps in its sublists be considered mutually-exclusive—only one of the set may appear.[16] As an example of the interpretation of annotation nodes within a parsing form, let us consider ACT1. Figure 4-6 displays the variation in utterances recognized by the form. We can summarize the algorithm represented by ACT1 as follows:

1. If there are contiguous references to the marked forms of a date, an hour, or a time interval, they are part of the reference to the concept **add**. Any order is permitted among the introductory adverbial phrases, but only one of **m-hourforms** or **m-intervalforms** may be present.

[16] There is one more type of annotation node which is not shown in Figure 4-5: the *snode*. It is discussed in the context of the Coalesce/Expand Cycle, in Section 5.2.

2. Regardless of the presence or absence of a date, hour, or interval, an **addwd** must be present. If any of the introductory adverbial phrases are present, they must precede the **addwd**.
3. A group-gathering marked by an indefinite article (**m-i-ggforms**) must be found following the **addwd**.

Form	Steps	Annotations
ACT1	701 m-hourforms	mutually-exclusive with 702, unordered with 703
	702 m-intervalforms	mutually-exclusive with 701, unordered with 703
	703 m-dateforms	unordered with 702 and 701
	704 addwd	required
	708 m-i-ggforms	required

Examples of Directly Recognizable Utterances:

- "On June 4 at 5 p.m. schedule lunch with John."
- "From noon to 1:30 on June 7 schedule a speech research meeting."
- "On June 12 add a seminar in Room 5409 from 3 to 4."
  (the marked interval is picked up by m-i-ggforms in step 708)

Examples of Utterances Requiring Recovery:

- "Schedule on June 4 a meeting with Alice."
  (steps 703 and 704 out of order)
- "On June 7 at 5 p.m. [add] a natural language interfaces seminar."
  (required step 704 omitted)
- "At 6 from 6 to 7 p.m. schedule dinner with dad."
  (mutually-exclusive steps 701 and 702 both present.)

Figure 4-6: The **addform** ACT1 considered as a parsing algorithm: examples of non-deviant utterances it recognizes directly, and deviant utterances it fails to recognize without error recovery.

At first glance it seems trivial to capture the "required," "unordered," and "mutually-exclusive" relations in BNF. Square brackets indicate optionality and therefore, indirectly, those elements that are required. The Kleene star permits both optionality and permutation by matching zero or more elements from a set in any order. The vertical bar represents mutual-exclusion among elements that may fill the same position in the production. Unfortunately, the ways in which the "unordered" and "mutually-exclusive" relations are manifested in natural language makes a trivial translation from *unodes* and *mnodes* to star and bar impossible.

Consider the single *unode* associated with ACT1; it says that the hour, date, and interval may occur in any order. Implicit, however, is that only one of each constituent may be present. Thus, translating the *unode* using the Kleene star is inappropriate because the star allows, by its definition, multiple dates, hours, and intervals to be matched in the input. To avoid an overly general production but still capture the meaning of the *unode* in ACT1, we must explicitly include in the BNF all the permissible orderings of the unordered steps in the case frame representation. The *mnode* relation between the hour and interval means that the true number of constituents in the unordered set is two. In general, if there are *n* unordered constituents then there are *n!* terms in the disjunct representing the permissible orderings. Figure 4-7 shows that the appropriate translation from ACT1 to <act1> results in a disjunct with two terms.

In the case of ACT1 and <act1> the mutual-exclusivity relation between **m-hourforms** and **m-intervalforms** could be expressed in BNF using the vertical bar because the two non-terminals play the same role in the same position in the production. Expressed differently, there are no constraints between **m-hourforms** and the other non-terminals that are not identical for **m-intervalforms**. In English, however, there are common mutual-exclusion relations that do not have this property. Subject-verb agreement is an example where the mutual-exclusion relation holds over non-terminals playing different roles. To capture the idea that "single/plural subject requires single/plural verb" in BNF, we cannot write

<sentence> ::= (<singlesubj> | <pluralsubj>) (<singleverb> | <pluralverb>).

Instead, we must enumerate the pairings:

<sentence> ::= (<singlesubj> <singleverb>) | (<pluralsubj> <pluralverb>).

Expressing the mutual-exclusion between prenominal and postnominal instances of the same modifying case is another requirement for understanding English. This time the discontiguity of non-terminals playing the same role causes the enumeration. MEETING1 and <meeting1> in Figure 4-7 demonstrate the problem. The definition of MEETING1 says that if the location of a meeting is included, it may be given prenominally ("AISys meeting"), or postnominally ("meeting at AISys"), but not both. The expansion of <meeting1> expresses the same idea by enumerating the possible positions for the modifying case relative to the head noun. If we ignore the question of case order for a moment, then the number of disjuncts required to capture *n* modifying cases that may occur either prenominally or postnominally is given by:

$$\sum_{k=0}^{n} \binom{n}{k} \binom{n}{n-k}$$

```
ACT1
  steps (m-hourforms m-intervalforms m-dateforms addwd m-i-ggforms)
  rnode (addwd m-i-ggforms)
  unodes ((m-hourforms m-intervalforms m-dateforms))
  mnodes ((m-hourforms m-intervalforms))

<act1> ::=
  [[[<m-hourforms> | <m-intervalforms>] [<m-dateforms>]] |
   [[<m-dateforms>] [<m-hourforms> | <m-intervalforms>]]]
  <addwd> <m-i-ggforms>

MEETING1
  steps (u-locationforms meetingwd m-locationforms)
  rnode (meetingwd)
  mnodes ((u-locationforms m-locationforms))

<meeting1> ::=
  [<u-locationforms>] <meetingwd> | <meetingwd> [<m-locationforms>]

FULLMEETING
  steps (u-hourforms u-intervalforms u-dateforms u-locationforms u-subjectforms
         u-participantforms meetingwd m-hourforms m-intervalforms m-dateforms
         m-locationforms m-subjectforms m-participantforms)
  rnode (meetingwd)
  unodes ((u-hourforms u-intervalforms u-dateforms u-locationforms
            u-subjectforms u-participantforms)
           (m-hourforms m-intervalforms m-dateforms m-locationforms
            m-subjectforms m-participantforms))
  mnodes ((u-hourforms m-hourforms u-intervalforms m-intervalforms)
            (u-dateforms m-dateforms) (u-participantforms m-participantforms)
            (u-subjectforms m-subjectforms) (u-locationforms m-locationforms))

<fullmeeting> ::= 3840 terms
```

Figure 4-7: A comparison of CHAMP's grammar and BNF viz. capturing the complex ordering and mutual-exclusivity relations common in English.

In other words, all *n* modifiers may appear to the left of the head noun, or any one of the modifiers may appear on the left with the remaining *n-1* on the right, and so forth.

The reality, of course, is that we cannot ignore case ordering. It should not be surprising, however, that the size of a grammar in BNF grows quickly when discontiguity and mutual-exclusivity interact with freedom of ordering. FULLMEETING in Figure 4-7 shows the actual definition for a meeting in CHAMP—each of the six modifying cases may occur prenominally or postnominally (but not both) in any order. The general formula for determining the number of BNF disjuncts required under these circumstances is:

$$\sum_{k=0}^{n} \frac{n!\ \ n!}{(n-k)!k!}$$

which is at least *n(n!)* (because *(n-k)! >= 1* for all *k*). As a result, the BNF equivalent of FULLMEETING requires 3840 disjuncts ($n = 5$ because the four time modifiers are all mutually-exclusive). The shorthand afforded by the annotation nodes in CHAMP's case frame representation clearly leads to a more compact grammar.

A formclass represents all the ways of referring to a concept that are recognized by the grammar while each form represents a particular way of referring to the concept through its steps and annotation nodes. The *class* field of a step may assign either a formclass or a wordclass to a subsegment of the utterance. Having discussed formclasses above, we turn our attention now to the wordclass.

4.2.3. The wordclass and the lexical definition

addwd members (add schedule) locations (704) active t concept add	**ivlmkr** members (from) locations (204) active t concept none	**ehrmkr** members (to) locations (108) active t concept none	**intervalwd** members (lunch) locations (110) active t concept none
add isa addwd **schedule** isa addwd	**from** isa sourcemkr isa ivlmkr	**to** isa ehrmkr isa targetmkr	**lunch** isa mealwd (isa intervalwd def (1200 1300))

<addwd> ::= add | schedule
<ivlmkr> ::= from
<ehrmkr> ::= to
<intervalwd> ::= lunch

Figure 4-8: Examples of wordclass and lexical definitions from the calendar domain displayed in CHAMP's case frame representation and those portions of the case frames expressible in standard BNF notation.

As explained in Section 4.2.1, the Formclass Hierarchy is recursively defined through the *isa* fields of forms and formclasses and through the *class* fields of the step definitions. At the bottom of the hierarchy are the *wordclasses*, some of which are shown in the top portion of Figure 4-8. The fields in a wordclass definition are a subset of those in a formclass definition and carry the same general meaning. The *concept* field contains a pointer into application-related knowledge if there are semantic constraints that are signalled by the presence of member of a wordclass in the utterance. If, for example, the word "add" is present in the utterance and only the kernel definition for "add" is in the lexicon, then knowledge in the **add** concept turns off the *active* fields for **deleteforms**, **deletewd**, **changeforms**, **changewd**, and so forth. In other words, if the only way in which "add" can be understood is as a referent to the **add** action, then we may eliminate from the search space all paths that cannot contribute to that interpretation. The *members* of a wordclass are the actual words and phrases in the lexicon. As the lower portion of Figure 4-8 demonstrates, wordclasses in CHAMP correspond to non-terminals that expand to only terminals in a BNF representation.

The middle portion of Figure 4-8 shows that lexical definitions provide entry into the Formclass Hierarchy through the wordclass in the *isa* field. CHAMP allows both word and phrase entries in the lexicon. The system also permits multiple definitions for each entry (see, for example, "from"). In addition to the *isa* field, an entry may contain a *def* field that associates a canonical value with the usage of a word. When "lunch" is used as an **intervalwd**, for example, the *def* of "lunch" is **(1200 1300)**—the canonical value for the interval noon to 1 p.m. Instance generators, which have the task of producing canonical representations that aid in constraint application and database search, also have the responsibility of recovering the value in a *def* field. Figure 4-9 demonstrates how the mechanism works. In the example, the second definition of "lunch," which reflects usage of the word as a modifier indicating time, leads to a successful parse. INT2 seeks the wordclass for this definition (**intervalwd**) in its sole step (110). Thus the presence of the word "lunch" is adequate to satisfy INT2 and invoke the instance generator for the class **u-intervalforms**. The special token **instance** in the *bindvar* field of the step directs the ig to recover the canonical value from the lexical definition rather than to compute it. In this way the canonical form of the default lunch interval, **(1200 1300)**, is bound to each of **ivl** and **divl** in step 206.

4.3. Application-related knowledge

By basing forms and formclasses on semantic categories, CHAMP's learning-related structures contain some language-independent knowledge about the domain. A formclass ties together different ways of expressing the same concept. In turn, the fixed number of formclasses limits the user to a fixed number of meaningful actions and objects; we organize these domain concepts into a Concept Hierarchy. It is not surprising that the structure of the Concept Hierarchy largely parallels that of the

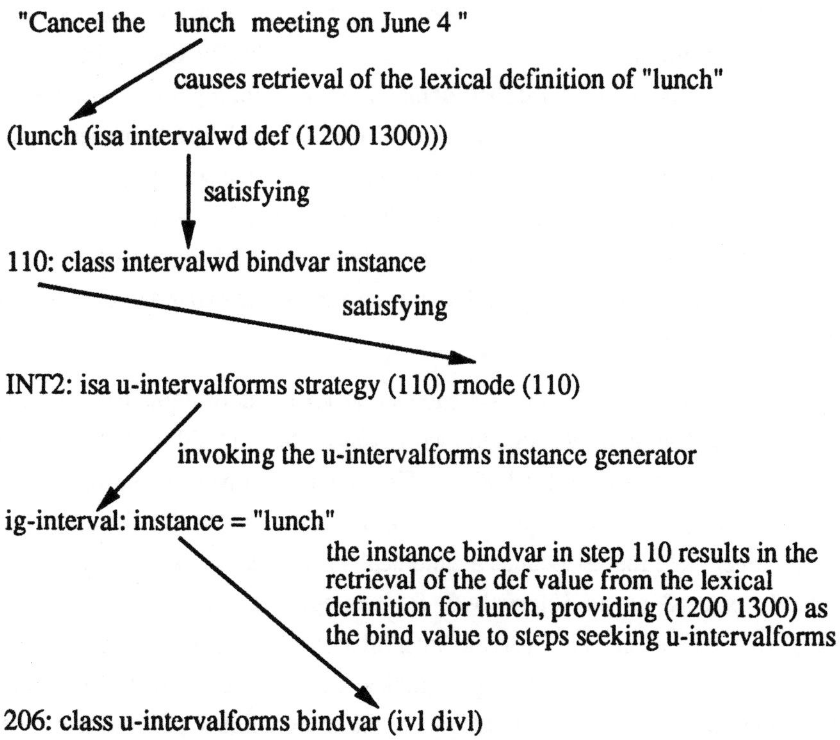

Figure 4-9: Providing canonical values through the interaction of **instance** *bindvars* and lexical *def* fields.

Formclass Hierarchy—the former organizes information about meaningful referents, the latter organizes information about meaningful references. The two hierarchies can be thought of as densely connected within but sparsely connected between. We have already seen that connections between the hierarchies are limited to the wordclass's and formclass's *concept* and *active* fields and the step's *bindvar* field.

If all we knew about domain concepts were their names and categories, it would be unnecessary to build a separate structure to organize them. Fortunately, we can say more than just what constitutes a meaningful referent. Specifically, what we mean by a "domain concept" is precisely that collection of invariant information that defines an action or object within an application. In this section we examine how the information associated with concepts and *conceptclasses* can help to constrain search and facilitate user interaction. Figure 4-10 displays both kinds of knowledge for a portion of the calendar Concept Hierarchy. Like the representation of the grammar, the representation of domain concepts has been simplified in our examples for expositional purposes—the exact representation can be seen in [46]. In CHAMP, a Concept Hierarchy must be hand-coded for each domain in terms of the primitive fields *isa*, *seg*, *bind*, *exp*, *rec*, *default*, and *extend*. To the extent that different domains share concepts, the application knowledge coded for one may be used in the other. CHAMP shares action concepts, time concepts, and some location concepts between its two domains. As in the previous section, most of our examples are taken from the calendar domain.

add
isa action
seg (opponents showwd showforms...)

hr
isa root
bind (<= 1 !value 12)

interval
isa root
exp (lambda (starthour endhour)...)
rec ((no-del interval starthour endhour) (no-trans (marker interval)..)))

meal
isa object
default ((location (* office)))

lunch
isa meal
default ((starthr 1200))

Figure 4-10: Examples of application-related knowledge from the calendar domain.

Search control is aided by the four types of constraint information found in the fields labelled *seg*, *bind*, *exp*, and *rec*. CHAMP takes an integrated approach to controlling search [64], applying each type of constraint as early and as often in the understanding process as possible. Thus, the four kinds of constraint information correspond to the four points in processing at which constraining knowledge can be brought to bear.[17]

At *seg*mentation-time we may use the presence of a word or phrase that is unique to a wordclass or domain to eliminate large portions of the search space. Thus, if the utterance contains the word "add" and our grammar contains no definition for "add" other than the kernel definition (*isa* **addwd**), we know that we may ignore those portions of the grammar that are incompatible with an **add** action. We eliminate the incompatible paths in the search space by turning off the *active* fields

[17]Actually, there are five points in processing at which we apply constraining knowledge. We have postponed any discussion of the constraints imposed by the database until Chapter 7, when we examine the resolution process.

of the wordclasses and formclasses found in the *opponents* subfield. The uses of the *seg* and *active* fields are discussed further in Section 5.1.

At *bind*-time we apply predicate constraints to the values associated with a *bindvar*. In Figure 4-10, for example, we see that a strategy step whose *bindvar* list contains the token **hr** can be satisfied only by a number between one and twelve. Bind-time constraints are also discussed further in Section 5.1.

*Exp*and-time constraints are applied during the Expand phase of the Coalesce/Expand Cycle (Section 5.2). At that time we consider the limiting effects of intercase constraints. In Figure 4-10 the concept **interval** carries a constraint of this type on the cases **starthour** and **endhour**. Each case is recognized by a step seeking a **u-hourform** (see the definition of INT1 in Figure 4-5). The expand-time predicate accesses the canonical values bound to **starthour** and **endhour** and prevents further search down any path in which the **starthour** is later than the **endhour**. As an example, consider the sentence

"Change the meeting from 5 p.m. to 3 p.m."

In this case, the interval constraint prevents the segment "5 p.m. to 3 p.m." from being parsed as an interval (and, consequently, prevents "from 5 p.m. to 3 p.m." from being parsed as a marked interval). The concept definition for a source-target pair, on the other hand, demands only that the classes of the source and target be compatible. Thus, our sample sentence is correctly understood as a command to change the starting time of a particular meeting.

*Rec*overy-time constraints occur, naturally enough, during error recovery (Chapter 6). These constraints block error corrections otherwise permitted by the model. Let us consider the recovery constraints associated with the conceptclass **subject**. A **subject** is referred to by any word or phrase that acts as the specific topic of a meeting or seminar (for example, the phrase "Non-monotonic Logics" in "Schedule an AI seminar about Non-monotonic Logics"). Figure 4-11 summarizes CHAMP's knowledge about the concept. As shown, the form SUBJ0, a member of **m-subjectforms**, is made up of a marker and a member of **u-subjectforms**. The recovery constraint in the corresponding concept definition **(no-del subject)** prevents the recovery mechanism from deleting step 214 whose *bindvar* list contains the token **subject**. In other words, the constraint prevents us from considering as a reference to a **subject** any segment that does not actually contain a subject. Similarly, **(no-trans (marker subject))** prevents recovery from transposing steps 213 and 214; what makes a marker a marker (in English) is that it introduces what it marks. Although they do not apply to **subject, no-sub** constraints may also be specified. The concept **date**, for example, contains the recovery constraint: **(no-sub day year)**. This entry prevents substitution of non-numbers in steps with the *bindvar* symbol **day** or **year**. The fourth type of error recovery, insertion, has no corresponding constraint—insertions are always permitted.

```
From the Formclass Hierarchy                From the Concept Hierarchy
SUBJ0                                       subject
isa m-subjectforms                          rec ((no-del subject)
mode (213 214)                                   (no-trans (marker subject)))
steps                                        extend (subject subjname)
   213: class sbjmkr bindvar marker
   214: class u-subjectforms bindvar subject
```

Figure 4-11: A portion of CHAMP's knowledge about subjects.

Since recovery constraints are clearly tied to the form of a reference, it is reasonable to ask why they are contained in the Concept Hierarchy. In part, the reason is that these constraints help insure that a new form of reference is meaningful. More important, however, is that recovery constraints are like other pieces of application-related knowledge—they are part of the fixed assumptions about the domain. Since they are not truly language-independent, recovery constraints may affect the language the system can learn. Why, then, do we add them? In general we include a constraint because we believe it will eliminate unnecessary search. Recovery constraints generally eliminate search down paths that correspond to nonsensical explanations of deviant utterances. By adding the recovery notation **(no-del subject)**, we choose not to entertain the notion that the existence of a preposition that may introduce a subject is, by itself, adequate to hypothesize that the subject has been deleted. Similarly, **(no-trans (marker subject))** means we will not accept that the word following a recognized subject may be a legitimate substitution for a missing marker (because we expect markers to appear before what they mark). Although it cannot be guaranteed that the search eliminated by these constraints is unnecessary, when used carefully the possibility of eliminating the user's intended meaning is slight, and the savings in search increases at each deviation-level.

In addition to constraining search, information organized in the Concept Hierarchy may facilitate user interaction. Knowledge of this type is located in the *default* and *extend* fields. If explicit default values are provided for a concept, CHAMP may use them to compensate for user omissions. Consider the sentence

"Schedule lunch with John on June 4."

which indicates neither where the participants will eat nor at what time. Under these circumstances, CHAMP uses the reference to lunch to provide a default time and location. The former value is given explicitly in the definition of the concept **lunch**, while the latter is inherited from **meal** through lunch's *isa* field (see Figure 4-10). In general, default reasoning by the system prevents interactions perceived as unnecessary by the user. We will have a great deal more to say about default reasoning and inference when we discuss resolution in Chapter 7.

The *extend* field supplies class extendability information. The how's and why's of learning new instances of known classes are discussed in full in Section 5.1.3. Here we recall only that the conceptclasses that are to be considered extendable are fixed. Figure 4-11 shows that **subject** is one such class. As a result, when CHAMP encounters an unknown segment in a context that permits a **subjectform** constituent, it tries, with the user's help, to resolve the segment as a new subject. In this way, the system learns about new topics, people, and places as the user's experience dictates. The price paid for relaxing the Fixed Domain Assumption in this limited sense is additional (but focused) user interactions. The benefits include reduced search, fewer future interactions, and the ability to learn even when presented with an ultimately unparsable sentence.

One of the main challenges in building an adaptive interface is designing knowledge structures that are (1) general enough to support grammar growth in unanticipated directions, and (2) specific enough to constrain search to reasonable limits. The decomposition of a grammar based on semantic categories into the components of a Formclass Hierarchy gives CHAMP the flexibility to capture the user's idiosyncratic language by adaptation at the appropriate level of representation. The combination of formclasses, forms, wordclasses, and lexical entries is robust enough to learn new sentential, phrasal or lexical references, with the latter including both synonyms and new instances of extendable classes. At the same time, the use of shared steps and of the invariant constraints, defaults and extendability information in the Concept Hierarchy help control the search for an effective meaning. Thus the knowledge structures discussed in this chapter appear to meet the design challenge imposed by (1) and (2), above. In the next chapter we begin our examination of how these knowledge structures are used in the understanding and adaptation processes.

Chapter 5
Understanding Non-Deviant Utterances

The knowledge representations introduced in the previous chapter guide the parser's search for a meaning structure. In CHAMP, the meaning of an utterance is represented by an *annotated parse tree* (APT). A grammatical sentence—one with no deviations—produces an APT with no recovery notations (or more than one unannotated tree if the sentence is ambiguous). We call such a tree an *explanation* of the utterance. Note that explanations are produced at Deviation-level 0 by definition. If the sentence requires error recovery, an APT with notations is produced at Deviation-level 1 or higher; we call an APT of this type a hypothetical explanation, or *hypothesis*. This chapter discusses the bottom-up parsing process by which APTs and their constituent parse nodes are constructed (for an example of an APT see Figure 5-26, page 93). To simplify the exposition, we consider here only Deviation-level 0 search, creating explanations. In the next chapter we extend our discussion to creating hypotheses.

Figure 5-1 presents an overview of the parsing process for non-deviant utterances; the figure extracts from Figure 4-1 those aspects of CHAMP required for parsing without error recovery. The first step in parsing is the segmentation of the utterance into the words and phrases found in the system's lexicon. As shown in the figure, the resolution of unknown segments as new instances of extendable classes is also accomplished at this time.

When segmentation has been completed, CHAMP has access to the leaf nodes in the parse tree for the utterance. CHAMP constructs the remainder of the APT in a bottom-up manner, building larger and larger subtrees (constituents) via the interactions of the Coalesce/Expand Cycle (shown in Figure 5-1) and a data structure called the *Agenda* (not shown in the figure). The purpose of the Agenda is to impose on the search process the partial ordering of constituents given by the Formclass Hierarchy. Each level of the Agenda corresponds to a level in the Hierarchy. Thus, the number of Agenda-levels is domain-dependent rather than implementation-dependent, reflecting the degree of embedding inherent in a particular grammar. CHAMP's basic parsing algorithm progresses bottom-up, level-by-level through the

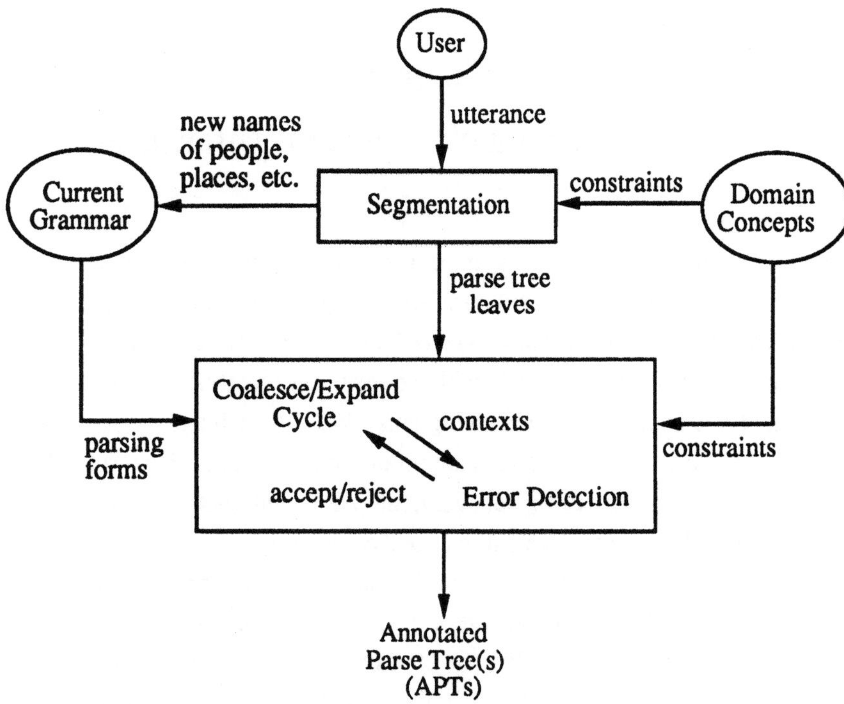

Figure 5-1: The components for parsing at Deviation-level 0 extracted from Figure 4-1.

Agenda coalescing previously constructed subtrees into new constituents, then expanding the new constituents to higher levels of the Agenda. The process is essentially a variant of semantic chart parsing [38, 20].

If we consider only non-deviant utterances, parsing in CHAMP is analogous to bottom-up parsing in a context-free grammar. A form's step list performs the same role as a production, dictating which constituents may coalesce at the form's *agenda-level* in the same way that the right-hand side of a production dictates which of the existing terminals and non-terminals should be matched. Expanding the coalesced set of constituents to a higher Agenda-level is analogous to replacing the set of matched terminals and non-terminals with the non-terminal on the left-hand side of the production. One significant difference between the two parsing methods, however, is that during both segmentation and the Coalesce/Expand Cycle, CHAMP may apply semantic search constraints that are external to the grammar.

In the remainder of this chapter we examine in detail how each phase of parsing is implemented in CHAMP by following a non-deviant utterance

"Cancel the 3 p.m. speech research meeting on June 16"

through the parsing process. The output from CHAMP used in the examples below reflects the work done at Deviation-level 0 with both the calendar and travel domains loaded. Where appropriate, the descriptions of CHAMP's algorithms have been simplified to specify only Deviation-level 0 behavior; the full algorithms are given in Chapter 6.

5.1. Segmentation

The purpose of segmentation is to create the leaf nodes in an APT. As shown in Figure 5-2, the process is divided into five parts: (1) converting the input string to tokens, (2) partitioning the tokens into meaningful segments, (3) trying to resolve unknown segments as instances of extendable classes, (4) applying segmentation-time constraints, and (5) seeding the Agenda. We examine each subprocess in turn.

```
SEGMENT (string)
Convert the string to tokens                                          (1)
FOR each token in the utterance, DO                                   (2)
  IF a token has no definition
  THEN apply spelling correction
  ELSE create an unknown pnode
  FOR EACH definition of the token as part of a phrase, DO
    IF the whole phrase is present and maximal in length             (2a)
    THEN create a pnode for that definition spanning the phrase
    ELSE IF there is no definition for that word by itself           (2b)
            THEN create a partof pnode for that definition
    IF the token was not part of a complete phrase                   (2c)
    THEN FOR EACH non-phrasal definition, create a pnode
IF contiguous pnodes are unknown OR partof different phrases          (2d)
THEN combine the pnodes into one unknown
IF a pnode is partof an extendable class
THEN try resolve it as an abbreviation of the phrase
ELSE make it unknown
IF a pnode is unknown                                                 (3)
THEN try to resolve it as a new instance of an extendable class
Apply segmentation-time constraints                                   (4)
FOR EACH pnode with an active wordclass, DO                           (5)
  FOR EACH active step that seeks the pnode's class, DO
    IF the pnode satisfies the step's bind-time constraints
    THEN create a pc for that step and pnode and place it on the Agenda
```

Figure 5-2: The SEGMENT algorithm at Deviation-level 0.

5.1.1. Creating tokens

Since CHAMP expects a string as input, the first step in the segmentation process converts the input string to tokens recognizable in the grammar. Three kinds of changes to the utterance occur during this stage: capitalization is removed ("John Smith" creates the tokens (john smith)), spaces are inserted around punctuation marks and numbers ("June 14th" becomes (june 14 th)), and punctuation marks are converted to an internal form ("3:00-4:00" becomes (3 %colon 0 %hyphen 4 %colon 0)). The conversion of our sample input produces the tokens: (cancel the 3 p %period m %period speech research meeting on june 16).

5.1.2. Partitioning tokens into segments

Once the string has been converted to tokens, the tokens must be partitioned into the discrete words and phrases in the lexicon. CHAMP does this by creating *pnodes*. A *pnode* assigns a class to a subsegment of the utterance using three values: the starting and ending positions of the phrase in the input and the name of a class. In our sample sentence, for example, the token **cancel** causes the creation of the pnode: (0 0 deletewd).

During the experiments described in Chapter 3, if any segmentation of the input could be found that made the utterance parsable, that segmentation was chosen. The need to implement segmentation in CHAMP, however, revealed the computational complexity of achieving this ideal behavior. There were essentially three issues to be addressed:

1. If both a phrase and a word within the phrase have definitions, do we explore both? In other words, do we explore only the maximal defined subsegment (for example, "University of Chicago"), or all defined subsegments ("University," "of", and "Chicago") as well?
2. If an unknown segment spans more than one token, do we assume a single grammatical function for the phrase, or do we explore multiple functions? The problem is demonstrated by contrasting the sentence "Schedule a seminar with John speaking about AI" when neither **John** nor **speaking** are known and "Schedule a seminar with John Smith about AI" when neither **John** nor **Smith** are known. In the latter case the unknowns form a single functional unit while in the former case they do not.
3. How do we treat the appearance in the utterance of portions of a phrase in the lexicon: as unknown segments, or as indications of abbreviation? If we know "Columbia University" is a school, do we assume "Columbia" refers to the same place? Do we make the same assumption for "University"? Are the rules different if we know "show me" but the utterance contains only "show"? Only "me"?

CHAMP's segmentation algorithm resolves these questions in an interrelated fashion. Complete phrases of maximal length are preserved over any shorter, embedded complete phrases ((2a) in Figure 5-2), over incomplete phrases (2b), and over the definitions of individual words within a phrase (2c). Thus, even if each of "university of chicago," "university," "of," and "chicago," appears in the lexicon, only "university of chicago" is assigned a pnode during segmentation.

Addressing the question raised by multi-word unknown segments, the algorithm incorporates:

- **The Single Segment Assumption**: contiguous unknown tokens are considered to perform a single function in the utterance.

This assumption avoids the combinatoric cost of exploring multiple functions within a segment at the price of rendering sentences that violate the assumption unparsable.[18] Thus, SEGMENT behaves correctly when given "Schedule a seminar with John Smith about AI" by considering "John Smith" as a single segment; the algorithm behaves incorrectly, however, when given "Schedule a seminar with John speaking about AI" by considering "John speaking" as a single segment as well.

The third question concerned the status of incomplete phrases. The SEGMENT algorithm says that if only a portion of a phrase is present in the utterance, its status depends upon what else is in the sentence and what is in the lexicon. If all of the words within the incomplete phrase can be defined independently of the phrasal definition, the phrasal definition is ignored ((2b) and (2c)). Even if a subsegment of the utterance can be explained only as a partial phrase, the subsegment may still lose its assignment to the phrase's class if it is surrounded by unknown segments or other incomplete phrases (2d). This merging of contiguous unknowns and partial phrases enforces the Single Segment Assumption.

The final status of a subsegment that remains identified as a partial phrase after (2d) depends upon whether or not the class associated with that phrase is extendable. If the class is extendable the chance to establish an abbreviation is offered to the user

---

[18]Each of the learning programs discussed in Section 2.5 (prior research) makes the same assumption in a more restrictive way by guaranteeing *a priori* that the input contains exactly one unknown segment performing exactly one function. That guarantee enables the systems' designers to avoid most of the questions we have posed as integral to the complex issue of segmentation. In designing CHAMP to handle real utterances that contain multiple unknowns requiring different kinds of resolution, we were forced to face the issue directly. Our solution was the algorithm presented and the Single Segment Assumption. Unfortunately, the evaluation of our experimental data in Chapter 9 clearly demonstrates that the assumption is sometimes violated in real user input. Equally unfortunate, however, is the performance degradation that would accompany the relaxation of the assumption. We postpone further discussion to Chapter 11.

(for an example, see Figure 5-5, page 75)). If the abbreviation is refused, or if the phrase's class is not extendable, the pnode is assigned to the class **unknown**. Thus, either of "Columbia" or "University" would signal a possible abbreviation (because **schoolname** is an extendable class) but "me" would be considered unknown (because **showwd** is not extendable). In the next section we examine how unknown segments are treated as candidate new instances of extendable classes (not as candidate abbreviations for a known phrase).

Figure 5-3 shows the effect of the first two steps of SEGMENT on the conversion of the tokens in our sample sentence into pnodes. Each token leads the system to kernel lexical definitions which, in turn, dictate the partitioning of tokens into segments. The pnode marks the bounds of the segment within the utterance and assigns to the segment the grammatical role of the definition that created it. Notice the different ways in which **speech** and **on** are treated. Both tokens have phrasal and non-phrasal definitions. In the sample sentence, however, the phrasal definition for **speech** can be completed while the phrasal definitions for **on** cannot. Thus, (2a) identifies **speech research** as the name of a subject (by looking up the completed phrase in the lexicon) and the alternative meaning of **speech** (as a projectname) is ignored in (2c). In contrast, **on** falls through (2a) because its phrases are incomplete, allowing (2c) to create a pnode for each of **on**'s uses as marker of two semantically distinct kinds of dates.

5.1.3. Recognizing new instances of extendable classes

Since our sample sentence does not contain unknown segments or incomplete phrases, it is unaffected by the portions of SEGMENT that cover abbreviation and extension ((2d) and (3) of the algorithm in Figure 5-2). Let us suppose, however, that the words "speech" and "research" have no definition in the kernel lexicon. A strict interpretation of the Fixed Domain Assumption (Section 2.3) requires that an unknown segment correspond to a new way of referring, not to a new referent. While the Fixed Domain Assumption is a powerful mechanism for controlling search, it seems, at the same time, to be an unreasonable limitation for an adaptive interface. Following Kaplan [37], we would prefer a system in which the types of objects that could be referred to could not change, but the particular instances of those types could. To accomplish this limited relaxation of the Fixed Domain Assumption in CHAMP, we designate certain conceptclasses to be extendable (see Sections 2.3 and 4.3). In particular, the conceptclasses for participants, locations, subjects, general

Tokens	Kernel Lexical Definitions	Segments	Pnodes
cancel	deletewd	cancel	(0 0 deletewd)
the	defmkr	the	(1 1 defmkr)
3	<no entries>	3	(2 2 number)
p	(1 (p %period m %period))	(p %period	(3 6 nightwd)
%period	(2 (p %period m %period))	m %period)	
	(4 (p %period m %period))		
	(2 (a %period m %period))		
	(4 (a %period m %period))		
	eosmkr		
m	(3 (p %period m %period))		
	(3 (a %period m %period))		
%period	(2 (p %period m %period))		
	(4 (p %period m %period))		
	(2 (a %period m %period))		
	(4 (a %period m %period))		
	eosmkr		
speech	(1 (speech research))	speech research	(7 8 subjname)
	projectname		
research	(2 (speech research))		
meeting	meetingwd	meeting	(9 9 meetingwd)
on	(2 (arriving on))		
	(2 (departing on))		
	datemkr	on	(10 10 datemkr)
	departdatemkr	on	(10 10 departdatemkr)
june	monthwd	june	(11 11 monthwd)
16	<no entries>	16	(12 12 number)

Figure 5-3: The pnodes created during segmentation of the tokens from "Cancel the 3 p.m. speech research meeting on June 16."

topics, hours, time intervals, and dates are extendable.[19] Thus, "speech research," if unknown, would be a candidate new instance for these classes.

Assuming we wish the introduction of new instances to be possible, why not treat the occurrence as a new type of deviation? The justification for distinguishing between deviations and new instances is simple: we expect the former to become increasingly infrequent but not the latter. The model predicts (and our experiments confirm) that as the adapted grammar comes to more closely reflect the user's actual

[19]The inclusion of hours, time intervals, and dates in the list may seem odd since the number of hours in a day and days in a year are fixed. We make hours extendable so that words can come to designate particular hours (for example, "tea time" or "lunch time"). Similarly, the user may wish to nominalize particular intervals ("happy hour"). We make dates extendable in order to be able to designate particular days (for example, John's birthday).

grammar, the number of deviant utterances approaches zero. On the other hand, we cannot assume the same monotonic decrease in the number of new people met, places traveled, or topics discussed. Over time, then, we expect that unknown phrases will, with increasing likelihood, correspond to new instances rather than new ways of referring. As a consequence, we want to explore that correspondence early in the understanding process—before embarking on the comparatively lengthy search for a deviant explanation. Thus, the reason for detecting new instances at Deviation-level 0 is to guarantee a more responsive interface in the long run.[20]

There are three reasons why we try to resolve unknown phrases specifically at segmentation-time rather than during parsing at Deviation-level 0. First, assigning a segment to a particular wordclass enables us to eliminate search during the parse whenever the class triggers the application of segmentation-time constraints (as discussed in the next section). Since most of the extendable categories in CHAMP index such constraints, it is in our best interest to identify them *before* parsing begins. The second and third reasons for resolving unknowns during segmentation are interrelated; early resolution enables us to detect one kind of unparsable sentence quickly and to increase the system's knowledge despite the fact that the sentence is unparsable. Observe that if, after segmentation, the number of still unresolved segments is greater than the maximum number of deviations permitted by the system (two in CHAMP), the parse must ultimately fail. Thus, the user can be asked to rephrase her request immediately rather than after a potentially lengthy search that cannot succeed. At the same time, the new names and places learned during segmentation are available without further interaction when the rephrased request is entered.

CHAMP's method for detecting new instances requires user interaction. In general there is a trade-off between user effort and user satisfaction—the more the system requires of the user the less useful the system is perceived to be. This is especially true if the required interaction appears unnecessary or confusing to the user. Since confusion can come from misinterpreting a user's response, CHAMP maintains tight control over the interaction by asking only yes/no or multiple choice questions. The course of the interaction is dictated by the knowledge in the *extend* fields of the conceptclasses (see Section 4.3) and by the user's responses. Figure 5-4 shows a typical interaction that might result from our sample sentence given the assumption that both "speech" and "research" are unknown. Note that since the tokens are both contiguous and unknown they are considered as a single segment.

---

[20]The same reasoning explains why spelling correction is implemented during segmentation rather than as part of deviation detection and recovery (see step (2) of the SEGMENT algorithm).

next> cancel the 3 p.m. speech research meeting on June 16

Trying to understand (SPEECH RESEARCH). Does it refer to a/an:
(0) DATE, (1) TIME-INTERVAL, (2) SINGLE-TIME, (3) PARTICIPANT,
(4) LOCATION, (5) SUBJECT, (6) GENERAL-TOPIC,
(7) none of these? [give number]: 5
Ok, adding new definition.

Figure 5-4: Resolving "speech research" as a new instance of **subjname**.

When the pnode created for "speech research" has its class defined as **unknown**, CHAMP searches the Concept Hierarchy for extendable classes in the current domain. Part of the information found in the *extend* field for a concept is a discrimination tree of arbitrary depth that translates into a focused clarificational dialogue during the interaction. In the case of the concept **subject**, the *extend* field requires no further discrimination. The result of the user's choice of SUBJECT is the addition of a definition of "speech research" as a member of **subjname** to the lexicon.

The interaction proceeds slightly differently if the pnode has been identified by SEGMENT as **partof** a phrase. Let us assume that "speech research" has been successfully added to the dictionary as a result of the interaction in Figure 5-4. Now suppose that the user asks CHAMP to: "Schedule a speech meeting on June 20 at noon." Although "speech" by itself has no definition in the lexicon, it is present as part of the defined phrase "speech research." The interaction in Figure 5-5 shows the kind of extremely focused question posed by the system when abbreviation is correctly suspected.

next> Schedule a speech meeting on June 20 at noon.

Is SPEECH short for (SPEECH RESEARCH)? [y or n] y
Ok, adding new abbreviation.

Figure 5-5: Introducing "speech" as an abbreviation for "speech research."

In contrast, the interaction in Figure 5-6 shows how the system's behavior changes when an abbreviation is incorrectly suspected—the user's rejection causes the segment to be treated as an unknown. As an unknown, the word "speech" must be offered to the user as a candidate instance of the full set of extendable categories. In the figure, the user chooses to assign the word to the category **participant**. This forces one level of further clarification in which the user identifies "speech" as the name of a project. The example demonstrates how the additional definition of "speech" as a **projectname** in Figure 5-3 could be introduced into the lexicon.

next> Schedule a speech meeting on June 20 at noon.

Is SPEECH short for (SPEECH RESEARCH)? [y or n] n

Trying to understand SPEECH. Does it refer to a/an:
(0) DATE, (1) TIME-INTERVAL, (2) SINGLE-TIME, (3) PARTICIPANT,
(4) LOCATION, (5) SUBJECT, (6) GENERAL-TOPIC,
(7) none of these? [give number]: 3

Is SPEECH the name of a:
(0) STUDENT, (1) PROFESSOR, (2) FAMILY-MEMBER, (3) GROUP,
(4) BUSINESS, (5) PROJECT,
(6) none of these? [give number]: 5
Ok, adding new definition.

Figure 5-6: Introducing "speech" as a member of the wordclass **projectname.**

5.1.4. Applying segmentation-time constraints

Once we have assigned segments to wordclasses we may have access to a great deal of information constraining the possible meanings of the utterance. The relevant information is available through the *seg* fields of the concepts pointed to by the wordclasses. As shown in Figure 5-7, our sample sentence contains three segments that provide the constraints called for in step (4) of the SEGMENT algorithm.

The algorithm that applies segmentation-time constraints is straightforward. Any pnode with a class that appears in the *pointers* list of a concept's *seg* field acts as evidence for that concept. Evidence is considered conclusive if all the pnodes covering that segment act as pointers to consistent concepts and no pnode exists uniquely covering some other segment and having a class in the concept's *opponents* list. In other words, evidence is conclusive if every explanation of some segment refers to a set of consistent concepts and no other segment can be explained only by an inconsistent concept. If a concept is voted for conclusively the classes in its *opponents* list have their *active* fields set to false—if we know that some segment must be explained as a reference to a particular concept then we need never generate interpretations inconsistent with that reference. We shall see in the next section (and Section 5.2) that only active classes may contribute constituents to an annotated parse tree.

Tokens	Wordclass	Concept
cancel	deletewd	delete
the	indefmkr	
3	number	
p %period m %period	nightwd	
speech research	subjname	groupgathering
meeting	meetingwd	groupgathering
on	datemkr	
	departdatemkr	
june	monthwd	
16	number	

Concept Definitions:
delete
isa action
seg (pointers deletewd)
    (opponents addwd addforms gowd changewd indefmkr...)

groupgathering
isa object
seg (pointers meetingwd classwd seminarwd mealwd buildingname...)
    (opponents tripwd flightforms departdatemkr poundsymb...)

Figure 5-7: Segmentation-time constraints provided by segments in "Cancel the 3 p.m. speech research meeting on June 16."

Let us consider the effect of segmentation-time constraints on our example. Since the token **cancel** is a **deletewd** it indexes the segmentation-time constraints for the concept **delete**. As there is no alternative referent for **cancel** and no opposing reference among the other pnodes, all the wordclasses and formclasses that are inconsistent with a delete action are made inactive for the duration of the parse. The classes turned off are those unique to the other actions recognized by the system: add, change, and show.

Both **speech research** and **meeting** index the **groupgathering** concept through **subjname** and **meetingwd**, respectively. Neither segment has an alternative definition but there does appear to be an opponent pnode: one definition for **on** is as a **departdatemkr**, a wordclass in **groupgathering**'s *opponents* list. The evidence for **groupgathering** is considered conclusive, however, because **on** has an alternative definition (as a **datemkr**) that is not inconsistent with the **groupgathering** concept. Thus, the wordclasses and formclasses pertaining to flights and trips are also made inactive.

Note that the application of segmentation-time constraints depends on both the values in the *pointers* and *opponents* lists (which are fixed) and the lexical definitions indexed by the tokens in an utterance (which may vary as the lexicon grows through adaptation). As a result, a word may provide constraint at one point in the evolution of a grammar but lose that constraining property if it gains a definition that points to an opposing concept. If enough lexical ambiguity enters the grammar it is possible for an utterance to introduce no constraints from the Concept Hierarchy during segmentation.

5.1.5. Seeding the Agenda

The final step of CHAMP's segmentation algorithm places the possible leaf constituents for an APT onto the Agenda. The pnodes we have constructed contain only some of the information required. To fully specify a constituent parse node we must turn each pnode that contains an active class into one or more *pclones* (*pcs*, for short). A *pc* is the full representation of a grammatical constituent in an annotated parse tree. A *pc* is specified by the values in five fields:

Pc Field	Description
step	associates a segment of the utterance interpreted as a member of a grammatical class with a particular step that seeks that class.
pnode	assigns a segment to a grammatical class. The class in the pnode is always the same as the class sought by the *step*. Pcs with different steps but the same class may share a pnode (thus, the "clone" in "pclone").
subs	lists the pcs that are the roots of the subtrees of the current pc. Equivalently, the pcs representing embedded constituents. Leaf nodes have no *subs*.
forms	lists the names of the parsing forms that contain the steps of all the pcs in the *subs* field. In other words, the forms by which the subconstituents may coalesce to create a member of the class. Leaf nodes also have no *forms*.
dlevel	records notations during error recovery and keeps track of the amount of deviance in the subtree rooted at the current pc.

Figure 5-8 shows a constituent from the APT for our example sentence (the full APT appears at the end of the chapter). The figure introduces the notation used to display pcs: the *step* field is given first, followed by the contents of the *pnode*, *forms*, *subs*, and *dlevel* fields. In future figures, we suppress fields with nil or zero values.

Figure 5-9 demonstrates how the steps contained in a wordclass's *locations* field are used to convert a pnode to one or more pcs. The figure illustrates step (5) of the pc25: 316 (10 12 m-dateforms) (DATE0) (8 22) 0

pc field	value	comments
step	316	marked date as part of a **groupgathering**
pnode	(10 12 m-dateforms)	assigns "on June 16" to **m-dateforms**
subs	(8 22)	pc8 is the **datemkr**, pc22 is the **u-dateform**
forms	(DATE0)	form allowing pc8 and pc22 to combine
dlevel	0	"on June 16" is a non-deviant marked date

Figure 5-8: The pc representing "on June 16" as a marked date in the APT for "Cancel the 3 p.m. speech research meeting on June 16."

SEGMENT algorithm applied to the token **16** in our example sentence. The pnode for the token **16** contains the class **number** which, in turn, can be found at eight different step locations in the grammar.

Pnode: (12 12 number)
Token at position (12 12) in the utterance: **16**
Step locations for the wordclass **number**: (4 6 11 12 14 102 105 353)

step	forms	active	bindvar	bind-time constraint
4	HR1, HR2	T	hour	1 <= hour <= 12
6	HR2	T	minutes	0 <= minutes <= 59
11	LOC6	T	roomnum	roomnum >= 4000
12	CLNUM1	T	class-level	15 <= class-level <= 18
14	CLNUM1	T	class-id	700 <= class-id <= 800
102	DATE1	T	day	1 <= day <= 31
104	DATE1	T	year	year >= 1980
353	FL2	F	flightnum	(member *flightlist*)

Conversion produces:
pcx: 6 (12 12 number)
pcy: 12 (12 12 number)
pcz: 102 (12 12 number)

Figure 5-9: Cloning a pnode.

Figure 5-9 shows that not every pc that can be created for a pnode is placed on the Agenda; both segmentation-time and bind-time constraints can affect the process of conversion. As an example of the former, consider step 353 which seeks a member of the class **number** to act as a flight number. Recall that the presence of the token **meeting** previously turned off all references to flights. In particular, the formclass **flightforms** was made inactive. Since step 353 occurs only in FL2's steps list and FL2 is a member of the inactive formclass **flightforms**, step 353 is also inactive and no pc is created for its meaning of **number**.

As an example of bind-time constraints, consider step 4 which seeks a number to act as an hour designator. Since **16** does not meet the requirement of falling between one and twelve, no pc is created for this interpretation either. Thus, although a number may play eight distinct roles in the grammar, context-sensitive constraints eliminate all but three interpretations for the token **16** in our sample sentence: **16** as a day (step 102), as a class-level (step 12), and as minutes (step 6). To place these interpretations on the Agenda, we trace back through the steps' forms to find their formclass' *agenda-level* fields. As an example, pc*x* sharing a step must have the same *agenda-level*). contains step 6 which is found in form HR2, a **u-hourforms**; the *agenda-level* field for **u-hourforms** places pc*x* at Agenda-level 0.

In total, the *location* fields of the wordclasses indexed by the segments for our sample utterance suggest twenty-four interpretations of those segments. Segmentation-time and bind-time constraints prune the twenty-four to twelve. Figure 5-10 shows the complete set of pcs corresponding to potential leaf nodes in the APT for our sample sentence, arranged by Agenda-level. If we compare this figure to Figure 5-3 we find that only one pnode, (7 7 departuredatemkr), created no pcs (because its wordclass was made inactive during the application of segmentation-time constraints).

Agenda-level	pc: step (pnode)	Comments
7:	pc0: 705 (0 0 deletewd)	**delete**
6:		
5:		
4:	pc1: 401 (1 1 defmkr)	**the**
3:	pc7: 309 (9 9 meetingwd)	**meeting**
2:	pc8: 201 (10 10 datemkr)	**on**
1:	pc4: 102 (2 2 number)	**3** interpreted as day
	pc6: 129 (7 8 subjname)	**speech research**
	pc9: 101 (11 11 monthwd)	**June**
	pc12: 102 (12 12 number)	**16** interpreted as day
0:	pc2: 4 (2 2 number)	**3** interpreted as hour
	pc3: 6 (2 2 number)	**3** interpreted as minutes
	pc5: 16 (3 6 nightwd)	**p %period m %period**
	pc10: 12 (12 12 number)	**16** interpreted as class-level
	pc11: 6 (12 12 number)	**16** interpreted as minutes

Figure 5-10: Possible APT leaf nodes created during segmentation of "Cancel the 3 p.m. speech research meeting on June 16".

The relationship between a pnode and its pcs supports the design decision to make steps into distinct structures that can be shared. A pnode assigns a segment to a class;

one pnode must be created for every class to which the segment could belong. A pc assigns a pnode to a step; one pc must be created for every step seeking the pnode's class. Consider the forms from CHAMP's kernel represented in Figure 5-11. Each of ACT1, ACT2, ACT3, and ACT7 allows an introductory adverbial phrase to designate the date on which the action occurred (step 703). If each form seeking a constituent of a particular class (in this case **m-dateforms**) is given a unique step seeking that class, then the number of pcs created for every pnode is equal to this number of unique steps (in this case, four). When a member of the class is present in the utterance, each step is satisfied and in turn creates a distinct search path. If, on the other hand, steps are implemented as structures that can be shared across forms (as shown in the figure), then the number of pcs created for every pnode can be reduced to the number of unique ways in which a class is used in the grammar (Figure 5-11 shows a single use). Since every pc represents a unique path through the grammar, redundant search is eliminated. As long as two or more forms occupy the same level of the Formclass Hierarchy, there need be only one copy of any steps they have in common. In this way only one pc need be created per distinct usage at each level, rather than one pc per virtual location (this is especially important as the grammar expands through adaptation and the number of virtual locations increases).

5.2. The Coalesce/Expand Cycle

When segmentation has been completed, the Agenda from Figure 5-10 becomes available to the Coalesce/Expand Cycle. The bottom-up parsing algorithm, shown in Figure 5-12, is quite simple. Explicit in the algorithm is the implementation choice to consider only maximally coalescable sequences; if a constituent can be JOINed to others, it is. This decision makes CHAMP's search heuristic rather than exhaustive (thus, we refer to the design choice as the *Maximal Subsequence Heuristic*). In general the decision is a good one—paths containing EXPANDed non-maximal subsegments usually fail because segments that should have JOINed are left dangling, unable to JOIN with higher level constituents. Although it depends on the particular utterance and adapted grammar, experiments with CHAMP have demonstrated that an exhaustive search produces about three times as many nodes as

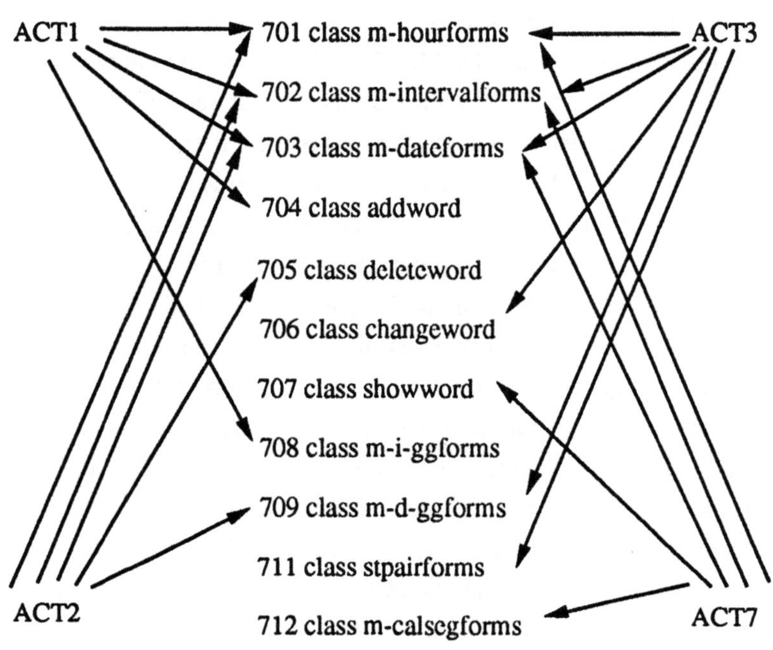

Figure 5-11: The components for parsing at Deviation-level 0 extracted from Figure 4-1.

a heuristic search based on maximal subsequences.[21]

If we use a heuristic search we must ask what effect the heuristic has on the language recognized by the parser. With maximal subsequences, two distinct problems arise. The first problem occurs whenever two constituents that can JOIN may also be used independently at a higher Agenda level. As an example, consider what happens to the sentence

"Change the time of the meeting from 3 to 4"

---

[21]The estimate of a three-fold increase is based on a version of the system with exhaustive search. The system was run on the sentences of four users from the experiments described in Chapter 3. The estimate is an average; the actual values depend on the stage of development of the grammar, the particular tokens in the utterance, and the level of deviation required by the parse. Under one set of circumstances, the node count was six times higher under exhaustive search. Although the increase is given as a constant, the impact of that constant on an IBM RT running Common LISP is pronounced once memory limitations are approached. In fact, because of the almost continuous need to garbage collect and swap to the disk as more nodes are produced and retained and memory limits are reached, one sentence required more than 17 hours using the exhaustive search but only 5 minutes with the heuristic. In two of the four grammars tested, parsing a two-deviation sentence using exhaustive search usually took more than an hour after a certain point in the development of each idiosyncratic grammar. Even Deviation-level 1 sentences were, in general, too slow for the interface to be evaluated on-line.

<u>The Coalesce/Expand Cycle</u>

FROM Agenda-level 0 TO the highest Agenda level, DO (1)
  FOR EACH pair of nodes, pc1 and pc2, DO
    IF pc1 and pc2 are COALESCABLE
    THEN JOIN them AND add the new pc to the current Agenda-level (1a)
    ELSE IF pc1 is maximal for its class at this Agenda-level
        THEN EXPAND pc1 to higher Agenda-levels (1b)

Figure 5-12: CHAMP's bottom-up parsing algorithm: behavior of the Coalesce/Expand Cycle at Deviation-level 0.

in Figure 5-13. Recall that parsing proceeds bottom-up. At Agenda-level 1, the individual constituents for "3," "to," and "4" JOIN as an unmarked time interval. At Agenda-level 2, the unmarked interval becomes marked. At Agenda-level 3 the pc for "meeting" can coalesce with the marked interval; JOINed, the two subtrees EXPAND to an instance of the class of **meetingforms.** By the time the Coalesce/Expand Cycle finishes Agenda-level 3, however, two different interpretations have been given to the segment "from 3 to 4": one as a marked interval and the other as the source and target of a source-target pair. At Agenda-level 4 the **meetingform** picks up its marker. Independently, the source and target JOIN to become a source-target pair. When processing reaches Agenda-level 5, the **slotform** cannot JOIN with the required source-target pair because the segment "from 3 to 4" is already embedded in the marked **meetingform.** Since the source-target pair of a **slotform** carries a **no-delete** recovery constraint, the parse ultimately fails.

To overcome this problem a fourth type of annotation node for forms was introduced. The *snode* explicitly instructs the parser to independently EXPAND a portion of a maximal subsegment. The kernel **meetingform** includes on its *snode* list the step that seeks a member of **m-intervalforms.** Thus, when the system sees that "meeting" and "from 3 to 4" can coalesce, it EXPANDs both the JOINed node (as shown) and a separate node covering "meeting" alone. Both **meetingform** nodes become marked **groupgatherings** at Agenda-level 4. At Agenda-level 5, however, a pc representing "the meeting" is now available to JOIN with pcs representing "time," "of" and, most important, "from 3 to 4" interpreted as a source-target pair. The subtree produced by that JOIN also produces a successful parse.[22]

[22]The best way to implement the snode solution would have been through a dynamic analysis of interdependencies in the grammar. In CHAMP, however, the snode lists are hand-coded.

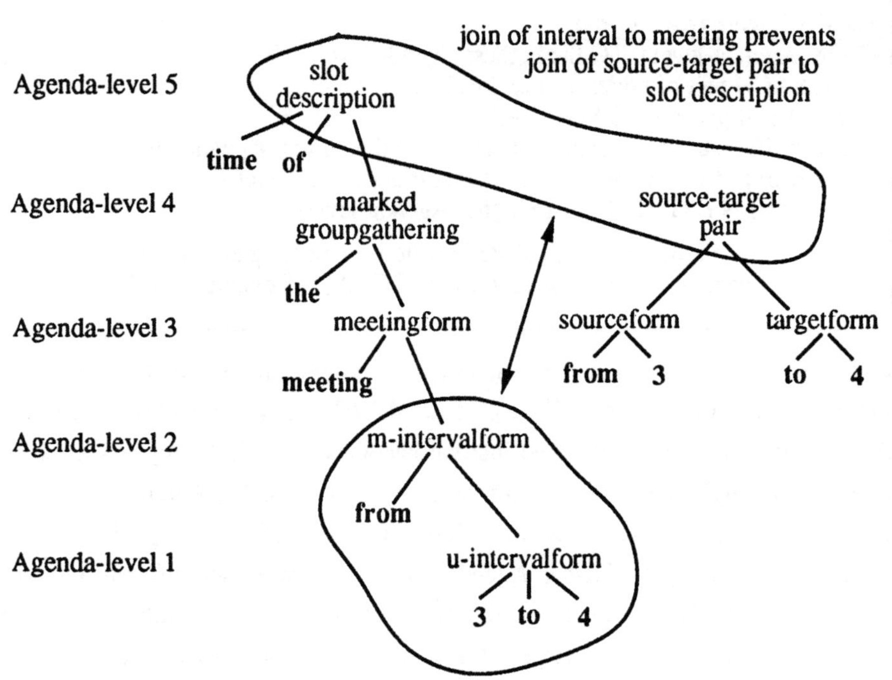

Figure 5-13: One problem with maximal coalesced sequences: JOINing nodes needed by higher level constituents in the grammar.

The second problem with maximal subsequences is an inherent interaction between using the heuristic and using a bottom-up parsing algorithm. Figure 5-14 illustrates a different way in which a maximal subsequence may prevent the expansion of a correct interpretation and cause the parse to fail. After segmenting "Schedule a June 4 10 p.m. meeting with John," the token **4** is represented by a number of pcs. One of those pcs correctly interprets **4** as the day portion of an unmarked date. A different pc uses **4** to satisfy the hour step of HR2. HR2 seeks an hour, a colon, minutes, and a **daywd or nightwd.** Although the colon is missing, the other steps can be filled if we use the interpretation of **10** as minutes. In this way the segment "4 10 p.m." is JOINed as a candidate **u-hourforms.** Even though this pc fails to expand at Deviation-level 0 for the kernel grammar (because the colon is required and missing), it prevents expansion of the embedded segment "10 p.m." as a **u-hourform.**[23]

[23]In this particular example, the problem would be solved if we removed from the Agenda those JOINed nodes that fail to EXPAND. Unfortunately the solution does not work in general; the problem would still exist if, for example, the user's grammar included a derived form in which the colon was no longer required.

The example in Figure 5-14 seems contrived because it is extremely difficult to find instances of the problem. In fact, of the 657 utterances from the six users in the adaptive conditions of the experiments described in Chapter 3, not one was rejected by CHAMP because of the Maximal Subsequence Heuristic. The gain in speed seems worth the slight possibility of eliminating the correct parse.

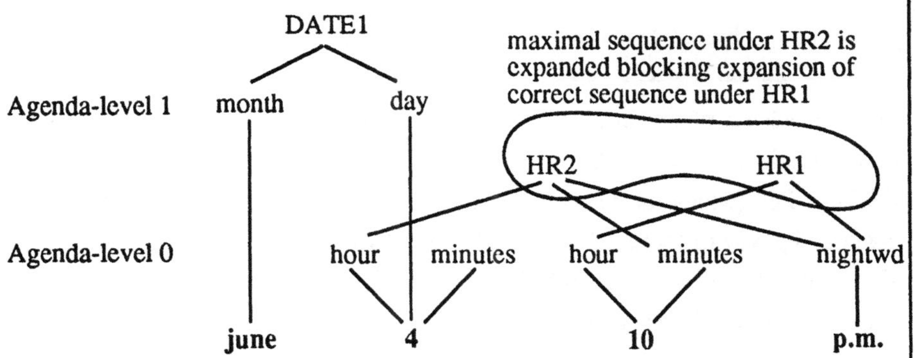

Figure 5-14: Another problem with maximal coalesced sequences: JOINing that masks the correct interpretation.

The Coalesce/Expand Cycle relies primarily on the predicate COALESCABLE and the two functions JOIN and EXPAND. The five criteria under which two nodes are considered COALESCABLE at Deviation-level 0 are shown in Figure 5-15.

<u>COALESCABLE (pc1 pc2)</u>
Pc1 and pc2 represent contiguous segments of the utterance AND (1)
Neither pc's class is **unknown** AND (2)
There is at least one active form containing the steps in both nodes AND (3)
No step is represented twice AND (4)
No mutually-exclusive steps (sharing an mnode) are present. (5)

Figure 5-15: The behavior of COALESCABLE at Deviation-level 0.

The JOIN function is shown in Figure 5-16. JOINing two COALESCABLE nodes preserves some of the work done by the predicate in the pc fields *subs* and *forms*. Recall that *subs* is used to record co-constituent nodes while *forms* is used to record the forms that parse the *subs*.

<u>JOIN (pc1 pc2)</u>
IF pc1 is already a JOIN node (1)
THEN add pc2 to pc1's *subs* field
    let pc1's *forms* field include only the active forms parsing all the *subs*
ELSE create a new JOIN node (2)
    let its *subs* field contain pc1 and pc2 AND
    let its *forms* field contain the active forms that parse both subnodes

Figure 5-16: The behavior of JOIN at Deviation-level 0.

of the Coalesce phase on Agenda-level 0 for our sample sentence, "Cancel the 3 p.m. speech research meeting on June 16." Only two node pairs are COALESCABLE. Pc2 (which interprets "3" as an hour) and pc5 (representing "p.m.") can coalesce by way of forms HR1 and HR2. Pc3 (which interprets "3" as minutes) can also coalesce with pc5, but only by way of HR2. Pc10 and pc12 do not coalesce because they are discontiguous with the other nodes at the Agenda-level.

Agenda-level 0	Pcs Created by JOIN
pc2: 4 (2 2 number)	
pc3: 6 (2 2 number)	pc13: nil (2 6 join) (HR1 HR2) (2 5)
pc5: 16 (3 6 nightwd)	pc14: nil (2 6 join) (HR2) (3 5)
pc10: 12 (12 12 number)	
pc12: 6 (12 12 number)	

Figure 5-17: The JOIN nodes produced by coalescing Agenda-level 0 for "Cancel the 3 p.m. speech research meeting on June 16."

JOINing nodes together creates virtual grammatical constituents. EXPAND's responsibility is to create the actual higher level pcs and place them on the Agenda. The algorithm accomplishing this is presented in Figure 5-18. The process of EXPANDing a set of co-constituents is essentially the same as that of converting a pnode to a set of pcs. Just as we created one pc for each step seeking the pnode's class, so we want to create one pc for each step seeking each formclass represented by a maximal set of co-constituents.

To create each higher level pc we must fill its five fields: *step*, *pnode*, *subs*, *forms*, and *dlevel*. Two of the values we need are immediately available: the *dlevel* of a pc is always zero at Deviation-level 0 and the *subs* field is simply the *subs* in a JOIN node or the pc itself if it is maximal (step (1) in Figure 5-18).

The value to fill the *forms* field of the higher level pcs also seems to be immediately available until we consider that a set of subconstituents may violate a

```
EXPAND (pc)
IF the pc is a JOINed node                                               (1)
THEN let the forms = the forms field
        let the subnodes = the subs field
ELSE let the forms = the active locations of the pc's step
        let the subnodes = the pc itself
FOR EACH form, DO                                                        (1a)
   IF the subnodes violate no expectations for that form
   THEN consider the form successful
Partition the successful forms into classes by their isa fields          (2)
FOR EACH class, DO                                                       (3)
   IF the subnodes satisfy all expand-time constraints for this class
   THEN create a pnode for this class that spans the subnodes
           IF there is an expand-time ig for this class
           THEN invoke it AND cache the canonical value for this pnode
   FOR EACH active step that seeks the pnode's class, DO                 (4)
     IF the step has a bind-time constraint AND the pnode satisfies it
     THEN create a pc for the step, pnode, subnodes, and forms and
              place it on the appropriate level of the Agenda
```

Figure 5-18: The behavior of EXPAND at Deviation-level 0.

form's expectations. COALESCABLE only guarantees that a set of constituents can be explained by a set of *forms*, not that they can be explained without deviation. Step (1a) of the EXPAND algorithm performs the error detection. As discussed in Chapter 2, a violated expectation corresponds to an insertion, deletion, transposition or substitution with respect to the context established by a form. In Figure 5-17, for example, the attempt to EXPAND pc14 fails because of a violated expectation in HR2. HR2 expects an hour, colon, minutes and day or night marker. Since only the minutes and night marker are bound, the time is incompletely specified. Two deletions would be required to explain "3 p.m." using HR2, causing a failure along this path at Deviation-level 0.

It is possible that the forms that remain after error detection fall into more than one formclass. Since a pnode assigns a unique class to a segment, the next step in expansion (step (2)) partitions the forms into distinct formclasses. Step (3) demonstrates that we create a pnode for a formclass only if the coalesced subconstituents satisfy the class's expand-time constraints. Expand-time constraints were introduced in Section 4.3; they correspond to intercase dependencies. Although the constituents in our sample sentence do not invoke any expand-time constraints, a source-target pair, for example, must satisfy the constraint that the value bound to the **source** is compatible with the value bound to the **target**. Thus, the constraint accepts interpretations that change a meeting from one location to another or from one time interval to another, but rejects interpretations that try to change a location to a time interval.

Step (3) also shows the point at which **exp**-type instance generators are invoked. The canonical value produced by the generator is computed once for a set of subnodes and a class; by tying the canonical value to the pnode, all the pcs that share that pnode also share the value.

Pcs that share a pnode are nevertheless distinguished by the values in their *step* fields. The steps seeking the formclass in each pnode are available through the formclass's *locations* field. Note that the fourth step in EXPAND is the same as the last step of SEGMENT (Figure 5-2); bind-time constraints are applied during expansion as well.

We now have all the information needed to create a set of higher level pcs from the constituent passed to EXPAND. One pc is created for each step seeking each formclass represented by one or more forms that parsed the maximal subsegment. Figure 5-19 shows the result of EXPANDing pc13, the node representing "3 p.m."

Maximal subsegment	Pcs created by expansion
pc13: nil (2 6 join) (HR1 HR2) (2 5)	pc15: 113 (2 6 u-hourforms) (HR1) (2 5)
	pc16: 107 (2 6 u-hourforms) (HR1) (2 5)
	pc17: 109 (2 6 u-hourforms) (HR1) (2 5)
	pc18: 302 (2 6 u-hourforms) (HR1) (2 5)

Figure 5-19: The result of applying EXPAND to pc13.

The versions of SEGMENT, COALESCABLE, JOIN, and EXPAND described in this chapter define the behavior of a bottom-up parser that uses context-sensitive constraints to reduce search. In the next chapter we examine how to modify and generalize these algorithms to produce a least-deviant-first parser whose output acts as a source of new grammatical components. Before extending the system's capabilities, however, we conclude our description of the basic bottom-up parser by following our sample sentence through the rest of the Coalesce/Expand Cycle at Deviation-level 0.

5.3. A detailed example: the Coalesce/Expand Cycle for "Cancel the 3 p.m. speech research meeting on June 16."

After the Coalesce phase, Agenda-level 0 contains seven nodes (the original 5 plus the two JOIN nodes, pc13 and pc14). The fate of each node during expansion is shown in Figure 5-20. Although only one node (pc13) can be EXPANDed, it produces four new pcs: one pc for each location of **u-hourforms** that is still active in the grammar. Since **u-hourforms** has an associated expand-time instance generator, the canonical representation of "3 p.m.," **1500**, is shared by pcs 15 through 18.

Agenda-level 0	New pcs or reason for non-expansion
pc2: 4 (2 2 number)	not maximal (sub of pc13)
pc3: 6 (2 2 number)	not maximal (sub of pc14)
pc5: 16 (3 6 nightwd)	not maximal (sub of pc13 and pc14)
pc10: 12 (12 12 number)	requires 2 deletions in CLNUM1
pc12: 6 (12 12 number)	requires 2 deletions in HR2
pc13: nil (2 6 join) (HR1 HR2) (2 5)	pc15: 113 (2 6 u-hourforms) (HR1) (2 5)
	pc16: 107 (2 6 u-hourforms) (HR1) (2 5)
	pc17: 109 (2 6 u-hourforms) (HR1) (2 5)
	pc18: 302 (2 6 u-hourforms) (HR1) (2 5)
pc14: nil (2 6 join) (HR2) (3 5)	requires 2 deletions in HR2

Figure 5-20: Results from EXPANDing Agenda-level 0 for "Cancel the 3 p.m. speech research meeting on June 16."

The last step in EXPAND places the new pcs onto the Agenda; pc15, pc16, and pc17 are placed at Agenda-level 1, and pc18 is placed on Agenda-level 3, in accordance with the position of their steps' forms in the Formclass Hierarchy. Once expansion is over at Agenda-level 0, the Coalesce/Expand Cycle returns to the Coalesce phase to process the next level of the Agenda.

Figure 5-21 shows the results from processing Agenda-level 1. "June" and the interpretation of "16" as a day first JOIN (pc19, in the left-hand column of the last row) then EXPAND to create the unmarked dates sought by step 203 and step 303. In addition, "speech research" (pc6) becomes a member of the class **u-subjectforms** via the form IFSUBJ which requires only a **subjname** for success. The remaining pcs at this level all have interpretations only as subconstituents: pc4 represents part of an unmarked date (in particular, the day), pc15 represents the hour portion of a marked hour, pc16 represents the starting hour in an unmarked interval, and pc17 tries to use the same segment in the utterance to fill the ending hour. Without their co-constituents, these pcs cannot EXPAND at Deviation-level 0.

Agenda-level 1	New pcs or reason for non-expansion
pc4: 102 (2 2 number)	requires a deletion in DATE1
pc6: 129 (7 8 subjname)	pc20: 214 (7 8 u-subjectforms) (IFSUBJ) (6)
	pc21: 307 (7 8 u-subjectforms) (IFSUBJ) (6)
pc9: 101 (11 11 monthwd)	not maximal (sub of pc19)
pc12: 102 (12 12 number)	not maximal (sub of pc19)
pc15: 113 (2 6 u-hourforms) (HR1) (2 5)	requires a deletion in HR0
pc16: 107 (2 6 u-hourforms) (HR1) (2 5)	requires 2 deletions in INT1
pc17: 109 (2 6 u-hourforms) (HR1) (2 5)	requires 2 deletions in INT1
pc19: nil (11 12 join) (DATE1) (9 12)	pc22: 203 (11 12 u-dateforms) (DATE1) (9 12)
	pc23: 303 (11 12 u-dateforms) (DATE1) (9 12)

Figure 5-21: The Coalesce/Expand Cycle applied to Agenda-level 1 for "Cancel the 3 p.m. speech research meeting on June 16."

Figure 5-22 shows the effect of the Coalesce/Expand Cycle on Agenda-level 2 where the unmarked date produced at Agenda-level 1 picks up its marker (pc8 + pc22 produce pc24). The unmarked **subjectform** produced at Agenda-level 1 has two interpretations in the kernel grammar: one as part of a postnominal marked subject and the other as a prenominal modifier (pcs 20 and 21, respectively in Figure 5-21). Agenda-level 2 sees the demise of the marked interpretation because there is no marker to support it.

Agenda-level 2	New pcs or reason for non-expansion
pc8: 201 (10 10 dtmkr)	not maximal (sub of pc24)
pc20: 214 (7 8 u-subjectforms) (IFSUBJ) (6)	requires a deletion in SUBJ0
pc22: 203 (11 12 u-dateforms) (DATE1) (9 12)	not maximal (sub of pc24)
pc24: nil (10 12 join) (DATE0) (8 22)	pc25: 316 (10 12 m-dateforms) (DATE0) (8 22)
	pc26: 703 (10 12 m-dateforms) (DATE0) (8 22)

Figure 5-22: The Coalesce/Expand Cycle applied to Agenda-level 2 for "Cancel the 3 p.m. speech research meeting on June 16."

Activity at Agenda-level 3 (Figure 5-23) is interesting for three reasons. First, we see another example of the *snode* annotation's effects. Two pcs are produced during the JOINing of "3 p.m.," "speech research," "meeting," and "on June 16" because step 316 of pc25 is on GG1's snode list: pc29 advances the segment with the date, while pc28 advances the segment without it.

As a second point of interest, Agenda-level 3 gives us the opportunity to introduce the concept of a *critical difference* between forms:

- **Critical Difference**: a form, X, contains a critical difference with respect to another form, Y, if X and Y contain the same steps with different ordering constraints, or if X and Y differ by at least one step.

The JOIN node produced by coalescing "3 p.m." and "speech research" is pc27

Agenda-level 3	New pcs or reason for non-expansion
pc7: 309 (9 9 meetingwd)	not maximal (sub of pc28)
pc18: 302 (2 6 u-hourforms) (HR1) (2 5)	not maximal (sub of pc28 and pc29)
pc21: 307 (7 8 u-subjectforms) (IFSUBJ) (6)	not maximal (sub of pc28 and pc29)
pc23: 303 (11 12 u-dateforms) (DATE1) (9 12)	requires 1 deletion in GG1-GG4
pc25: 316 (10 12 m-dateforms)(DATE0) (8 22)	not maximal (sub of pc29)
pc27: nil (2 8 join) (GG4 GG1) (18 21)	not maximal (masked by pc28)
pc28: nil (2 9 join) (GG1) (18 21 7)	pc31: 403 (2 9 meetingforms) (GG1) (18 21 7)
pc29: nil (2 12 join)(GG1)(18 21 7 25)	pc30: 403 (2 12 meetingforms)(GG1) (18 21 7 25)

Figure 5-23: The Coalesce/Expand Cycle applied to Agenda-level 3 for "Cancel the 3 p.m. speech research meeting on June 16."

which contains GG4 and GG1 in its *forms* field. In creating pc27 we do not know if the combined segment is a reference to a meeting (GG1) or a meal (GG4) because steps 302 and 307 are shared by the two forms. By coalescing "meeting" with "3 p.m. speech research," step 309 reduces the set of possible forms to GG1 (see pc28). Thus, we say that step 309 is a *critical difference* between GG1 and GG4 because the satisfaction of step 309 by a segment in the utterance is enough to eliminate GG4 from further consideration. Critical differences between forms are an important factor in controlling search. We will have more to say about them in the next chapter.

Our final observation about Agenda-level 3 also involves pc27 and the segment "3 p.m. speech research." Note that it is not EXPANDed because it is masked by the maximal segment in pc29 (pc28 is EXPANDed despite being non-maximal because it was created by an *snode* annotation). It is masked by pc29 because pc29 and pc27 share a form (GG1) in the same formclass (**meetingforms**)—interpreting "3 p.m. speech research" as part of a **meetingform** via GG1 enables the system to create a larger segment than interpreting the same portion of the utterance as a **mealform** via GG4. By not EXPANDing the alternate interpretation of "3 p.m. speech research," the potential reference to a **mealform** is lost. In an exhaustive search we would have had to preserve that interpretation because it is distinct from the interpretation of the segment as a **meetingform**. Although pc27 would have failed to EXPAND at Deviation-level 0 (because the required head noun is missing), it would have EXPANDed had the parse proceeded to Deviation-level 1. Once created, that fragment would progress up the Agenda creating spurious interpretations at each level—interpretations that fail globally for this utterance. The Maximal Subsequence Heuristic prevents the unnecessary work; regardless of the deviation-level, a smaller segment is always masked by a larger one if they share a form.

At Agenda-level 4 (Figure 5-24), each of the **meetingforms** produced at Agenda-level 3 picks up its definite article. Pc34 and pc35 reflect the use of the noun phrase

Agenda-level 4	New pcs or reason for non-expansion
pc1: 401 (1 1 defmkr)	not maximal (sub of pc32 and pc33)
pc30: 403 (2 12 meetingforms)(GG1)(18 21 7 25)	not maximal (sub of pc33)
pc31: 403 (2 9 meetingforms) (GG1) (18 21 7)	not maximal (sub of pc 32)
pc32: nil (1 9 join) (DGG1) (1 31)	pc34: 709 (1 9 m-d-ggforms) (DGG1) (1 31)
pc33: nil (1 12 join) (DGG1) (1 30)	pc35: 709 (1 12 m-d-ggforms) (DGG1) (1 30)

Figure 5-24: The Coalesce/Expand Cycle applied to Agenda-level 4 for "Cancel the 3 p.m. speech research meeting on June 16."

as the subject of the sentence. If segmentation-time constraints had not turned off all the constituents in the grammar associated exclusively with **changeforms**, the marked group-gatherings would also be EXPANDed to permit embedding of the noun phrase in a slot description ("location of the 3 p.m. speech research meeting") at Agenda-level 5. The **slotform** would then have a chance to pick up its marker at Agenda-level 6. In our example, however, Agenda-levels 5 and 6 are empty, and the Coalesce/Expand cycle continues processing at Agenda-level 7 (Figure 5-25).

Agenda-level 7	New pcs or reason for non-expansion
pc0: 705 (0 0 deletewd)	not maximal (sub of pc39)
pc26: 703 (10 12 m-dateforms) (DATE0) (8 22)	not maximal (sub of pc38)
pc34: 709 (1 9 m-d-ggforms) (DGG1) (1 31)	not maximal (sub of pc36)
pc35: 709 (1 12 m-d-ggforms) (DGG1) (1 30)	not maximal (sub of pc37)
pc36: nil (0 9 join) (ACT2) (0 34)	not maximal (masked by pc37)
pc37: nil (0 12 join) (ACT2) (0 35)	pc39: *ROOT* (0 12 deleteforms)(ACT2) (0 35)
pc38: nil (0 12 join) (ACT2) (0 34 26)	requires 1 transposition in ACT2

Figure 5-25: The Coalesce/Expand Cycle applied to Agenda-level 7 for "Cancel the 3 p.m. speech research meeting on June 16."

Agenda-level 7 shows the ultimate fate of the extra pc produced by the *snode* annotation during expansion of Agenda-level 3 (pc31). JOINed with pc1 at Agenda-level 4, pc31 reaches Agenda-level 7 as part of pc34. Pc34 represents a marked **meetingform** that does not contain the marked date "on June 16." Pc26, contiguous with pc34, appears to make the marked date available. However, since pc26 actually captures a segment of the utterance after the verb and ACT2 expects an introductory adverbial phrase, pc34 and pc26 may coalesce but may not EXPAND due to the violated ordering expectation. Of course, pc0 and pc35 do not have this problem because the date has already been explained as a postnominal modifier; they coalesce and EXPAND to produce pc39.

When all of the words in an utterance have been explained, one or more APTs with the special step *ROOT* are placed by EXPAND at Agenda-level 8. The APT for our sample sentence, rooted at pc39, is given in Figure 5-26 in both CHAMP's internal form and in a more conventional tree form. In the internal form we indicate the subtree relationship by indentation. The tree structure in the figure demonstrates that in addition to capturing the meaning of the utterance, the APT provides a virtual trace of the parse through the *step* and *forms* fields. By following these fields we can replay the successful path through the search space: apply steps 705 and 709 from ACT2, followed by steps 401 and 403 from DGG1, followed by step 302 from GG1, steps 4 and 16 from HR1, and so on.

```
39: *ROOT* (0 12 deleteforms) (ACT2)
   0: 705 (0 0 deletewd)
   35: 709 (1 12 m-d-ggforms) (DGG1)
      1: 401 (1 1 defmkr)
      30: 403 (2 12 meetingforms) (GG1)
         18: 302 (2 6 u-hourforms) (HR1)
            2: 4 (2 2 number)
            5: 16 (3 6 nightwd)
         21: 307 (7 8 u-subjectforms) (IFSUBJ)
            6: 129 (7 8 subjname)
         7: 309 (9 9 meetingwd)
         25: 316 (10 12 m-dateforms) (DATE0)
            8: 201 (10 10 datemkr)
            22: 203 (11 12 u-dateforms) (DATE1)
               9: 101 (11 11 monthwd)
               12: 102 (12 12 number)
```

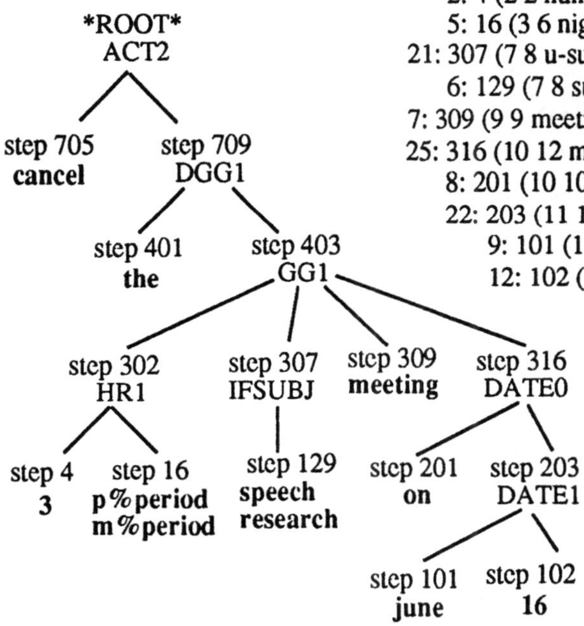

Figure 5-26: The APT for "Cancel the 3 p.m. speech research meeting on June 16" in CHAMP's internal form and tree form.

Producing a *ROOT* for an APT signals the end of parsing but not the end of the understanding process. The explanation (or explanations if the sentence is ambiguous with respect to the current grammar) produced at Deviation-level 0 must still be checked for consistency against the state of the application databases. This is done during Resolution (see Chapter 7). If the explanation makes sense in the current state of the world, then the user's request is carried out without further interaction. As the final stage of understanding, an APT (even one produced at Deviation-level 0) is examined by the adaptation functions to see if it contains information for removing overgeneralizations in the adapted kernel (see Chapter 8).

As an adapted kernel grows to include a user's preferred forms of expression, the majority of utterances the system encounters will be directly recognizable by the process described in this chapter. It is imperative, therefore, that an adaptive interface understand non-deviant input efficiently. CHAMP accomplishes this goal by controlling the number of paths followed at each stage of the bottom-up parse. Controlling search takes three forms during segmentation: the Single Segment Assumption limits the number of interpretations given to unknown segments, segmentation-time constraints may turn off whole areas of the search space, and bind-time constraints may eliminate the interpretation of a segment as a member of a particular formclass. During the Coalesce phase of the Coalesce/Expand Cycle, search is controlled by gathering only maximal sequences of co-constituents in active classes, as well as by the effects of incorporating critical differences into the kernel forms. During the Expand phase both bind-time and expand-time constraints may be applied to candidate constituents in active classes. More importantly, during expansion at Deviation-level 0, a path is terminated if a violated expectation is discovered.

A different aspect of performing well in the long run demands that categories like names and topics be extendable. Even after the user's grammar has stabilized she is likely to continue to meet new people and discuss new subjects. Given an adapted kernel that captures the stabilized grammar, it will be the case that an unknown segment is a new instance of an extendable class most of the time. Recognizing this fact, CHAMP attempts to resolve unknown segments as new instances *before* proceeding with a lengthy search through the space of deviation hypotheses.

Of course unknown segments cannot always be resolved as new instances of known classes and user utterances cannot always be explained within the current grammar. In the next chapter we see how the framework we have constructed for understanding non-deviant utterances can be extended to perform error recovery as well.

Chapter 6

Detecting and Recovering from Deviation

What are the changes that will transform the basic bottom-up parsing algorithm described in Chapter 5 into one that tolerates deviant input? By comparing Figures 5-1 and 6-1, we see that the key lies in extending the error detection mechanism to include error recovery. We know that error detection is the discovery of violated expectations in the context provided by a form and a set of co-constituents. When we were considering only Deviation-level 0, error detection was a yes-or-no proposition; either a set of subnodes satisfied a form or they did not. If the answer was "yes" then we considered the form successful and EXPANDed the co-constituents as an instance of the recognized formclass. If the answer was "no" the search path represented by the context was simply terminated—at Deviation-level 0 no violated expectations are tolerated. It follows that to understand deviant utterances within this framework we must be willing to relax a form's expectations in a principled way without losing sight of what constitutes a good explanation. Following the model presented in Chapter 2, we have implemented the general recovery actions as our principled method of relaxing expectations. As a result, we define the best explanation of a deviant utterance as the one that requires the fewest recovery actions. Finding the best explanation is accomplished by a least-deviant-first search using the current grammar and successive applications of the recovery actions. Thus, if a deviant utterance can be explained by performing only one recovery action we say that it succeeds at Deviation-level 1, or, alternatively, that the utterance requires one deviation. An utterance requiring two deviations succeeds at Deviation-level 2 and has no less deviant explanation within the current grammar.

Figure 6-1 also reminds us that CHAMP's basic control structure is the Parse/Recovery Cycle which is made up of the Coalesce/Expand Cycle and the Error Detection & Recovery mechanism. Figure 6-2 shows that the Parse/Recovery Cycle is implemented in CHAMP's READLOOP through successive invocations of the Coalesce/Expand Cycle at increasing deviation-levels. Each time through the cycle, paths that failed at the previous deviation-level may be extended by a recovery action, reflecting increasing deviance in the partial APTs constructed. When describing our model of deviation and recovery in Section 2.2 we defined "Deviation-

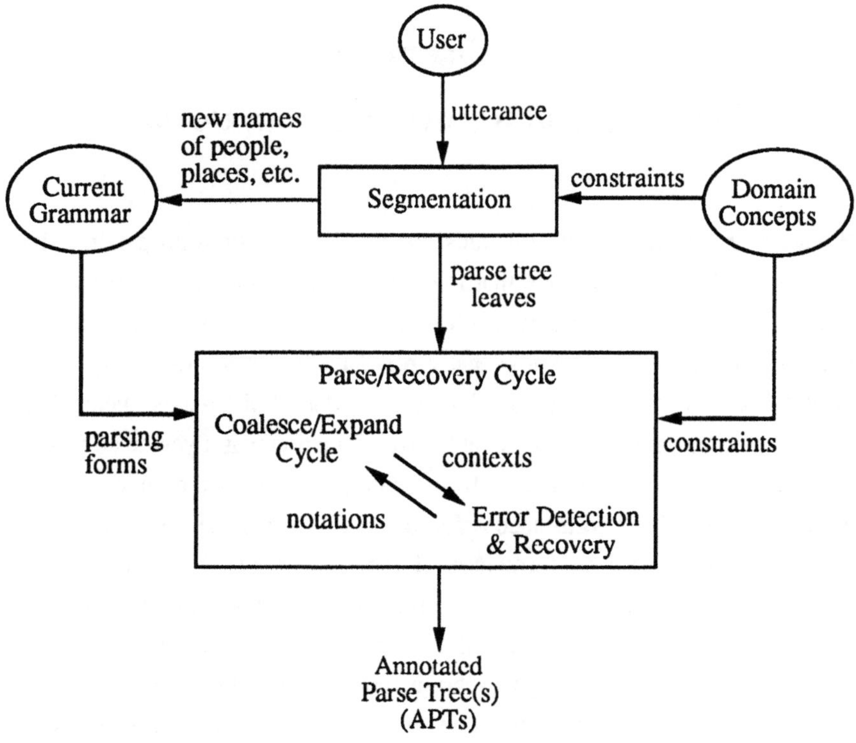

Figure 6-1: Making the transition from bottom-up to least-deviant-first parsing by adding error recovery (detail of Figure 4-1).

level'' to be ''a value that indicates the number of deviations permitted at a given point in the search for a meaning structure.'' Rephrasing the definition in terms more specific to the implementation, we redefine

- **Deviation-level**: the total number of recovery actions permitted along a search path during the current Parse/Recovery cycle. Equivalently, the total amount of deviance that may accumulate in any partial APT during the current cycle.

The algorithm in Figure 6-2 also introduces

- **Maximum Deviation-level**: the largest number of recovery actions permitted along every search path before the parse is considered to have failed. In CHAMP this number is fixed at two, partly to keep the system's response-time reasonable, and partly to control the quality of the explanations produced.[24]

[24]Note, however, that the restriction to two deviations in an utterance is a limitation of the implementation, *not* the model. In addition, the implementation accepts the Maximum Deviation-level as a parameter—with one exception CHAMP is actually designed to work for an arbitrary maximum deviation limit. The exception is in the recovery mechanism's decomposition of cases (see Section 6.5).

READLOOP ()
UNTIL the end of the session, DO
  Set the Deviation-level to 0 (1)
  Get the next utterance (2)
  SEGMENT the utterance (3)
  IF the number of unknown segments > the Maximum Deviation-level (4)
  THEN consider the utterance unparsable
  ELSE UNTIL Deviation-level > Maximum OR *ROOT* appears, DO (5)
      Run the Coalesce/Expand Cycle
      Increment the Deviation-level

Figure 6-2: CHAMP's READLOOP without adaptation
(The Parse/Recovery Cycle is Step (5))

In the next section we examine how the parsing process must be changed to accommodate deviant input. Specifically, we reexamine most of the algorithms presented in the previous chapter, describing how to generalize them to function at any deviation-level. Once we understand the parsing phase of the Parse/Recovery Cycle, we will turn our attention to the related processes of error detection (Section 6.3) and error recovery (Section 6.5).

6.1. Parsing as least-deviant-first search

If our goal is to be certain that we have found the best explanation for an utterance, then we must not accumulate more deviance along a search path than is permitted by the value of the deviation-level during the current cycle. To accomplish our goal is to generalize the parsing process described in Chapter 5 to create a least-deviant-first search. We begin by making a single alteration to CHAMP's SEGMENT algorithm, previously introduced in Figure 5-2. Figure 6-3 gives the actual algorithm used for segmentation. The only difference between the algorithms occurs in step (5). Throughout this chapter differences between old and new versions of an algorithm are marked by boldface step numbers.

The new version of step (5) creates pcs with a *dlevel* of one for unknown segments. We call such a pc *unresolved* because the segment it represents has yet to be assigned a meaningful wordclass and step. Recall that the *dlevel* field of a pc keeps track of the amount of deviance accumulated in the subtree rooted at that node. Since an unresolved pc must be explained via a substitution or insertion recovery, an unresolved pc has a *dlevel* of one by definition.

<u>SEGMENT (string)</u>
Convert the string to tokens (1)
FOR each token in the utterance, DO (2)
  IF a token has no definition
  THEN apply spelling correction
  ELSE create an **unknown** pnode
  FOR EACH definition of the token as part of a phrase, DO
    IF the whole phrase is present and maximal in length (2a)
    THEN create a pnode for that definition spanning the phrase
    ELSE IF there is no definition for that word by itself (2b)
        THEN create a **partof** pnode for that definition
    IF the token was not part of a complete phrase (2c)
    THEN FOR EACH non-phrasal definition, create a pnode
IF contiguous pnodes are **unknown** OR **partof** different phrases (2d)
THEN combine the pnodes into one **unknown**
IF a pnode is **partof** an extendable class
THEN try resolve it as an abbreviation of the phrase
ELSE make it **unknown**
IF a pnode is **unknown** (3)
THEN try to resolve it as a new instance of an extendable class
Apply segmentation-time constraints (4)
FOR EACH pnode with an active wordclass, DO (5)
  IF the pnode is **unknown**
  THEN create an unresolved pc with step=0 and dlevel=1 AND
      place it on Agenda-level 0
  ELSE FOR EACH active step that seeks the pnode's class, DO
    IF the step has a bind-time constraint AND the pnode satisfies it
    THEN create a pc for that step and pnode and place it on the Agenda

Figure 6-3: CHAMP's SEGMENT algorithm
(Figure 5-2 generalized to enforce a least-deviant-first search).

The generalized Coalesce/Expand Cycle (Figure 6-4) differs from its predecessor by including the partitioning steps that used to be in EXPAND (see Figure 5-18). Recall that the purpose of the partitioning is to separate by class the higher level grammatical constituents to which a set of pcs may be EXPANDed. Figure 6-5 demonstrates: the JOINed node (pcz) contains co-constituents (pc*x* and pc*y*) that are sought by GG1, GG2, GG3, and GG4. Since each form explains a higher level constituent belonging to a different class, each form creates a distinct partition that, in turn, defines a different

- **Context**: a candidate grammatical constituent. A context is represented by a list of subnodes and a list of forms. The subnodes are co-constituents that define members of the higher candidate class, the forms recognize members of the higher class by those co-constituents. Thus, all the forms within a context recognize the same candidate class.

The Coalesce/Expand Cycle

```
FROM Agenda-level 0 TO the highest Agenda level, DO                        (1)
  FOR EACH pair of nodes, pc1 and pc2, DO
    IF pc1 and pc2 are COALESCABLE
    THEN JOIN them AND add the new pc to the current Agenda-level          (1a)
     ELSE CASE                                                             (1b)
          pc1 is unresolved:
            move pc1 to the next Agenda-level
          pc1 is a JOINed node:
            let forms = the forms field
            let subnodes = the subs field
          pc1 is neither JOINed nor unresolved:
            let forms = the active locations of the pc's step
            let subnodes = the pc itself
         Partition the forms by formclass
         FOR EACH partition, DO
           EXPAND the context to higher Agenda-levels
```

Figure 6-4: CHAMP's Coalesce/Expand Cycle
(Figure 5-12 generalized to enforce a least-deviant-first search).

Each context, therefore, corresponds to a different path in the search space by explaining a particular segment as an instance of a particular class. A path that succeeds locally at Deviation-level *i* may still fail to produce a global parse. At the end of this section we will see that partitioning candidate constituents into contexts *before* EXPANDing them helps CHAMP pinpoint exactly which search paths should be extended each time through the Parse/Recovery Cycle.

Utterance: "Change the 3 pm June 11 [meeting] to 4 pm."

During The Coalesce Phase:

pc*x* created from **3 + pm**
pc*y* created from **June + 11**
pc*z*: nil (2 5 join) (GG1 GG2 GG3 GG4) (pc*x* pc*y*)

Before EXPAND:

Four contexts created from pc*z*:
1: [(pc*x* pc*y*) (GG1)] explains "3 pm June 11" as part of a **meetingform**
2: [(pc*x* pc*y*) (GG2)] explains "3 pm June 11" as part of a **seminarform**
3: [(pc*x* pc*y*) (GG3)] explains "3 pm June 11" as part of a **classform**
4: [(pc*x* pc*y*) (GG4)] explains "3 pm June 11" as part of a **mealform**

Figure 6-5: Distinguishing search paths by creating contexts during the Coalesce/Expand Cycle.

To insure a least-deviant-first search, the components of the Coalesce/Expand Cycle must also be generalized. Specifically, each of COALESCABLE, JOIN and EXPAND must be altered to insure that the amount of deviance along a search path does not exceed the current deviation-level. The *dlevel* field of a pc keeps track of the amount of deviance accumulated in the subtree rooted at that node. Similarly, we define the *dlevel* of a context to be the sum of the *dlevels* of its subnodes.

To provide for the effect of a subtree's *dlevel* on search, CHAMP's COALESCABLE predicate is changed from the algorithm in Figure 5-15 to the one in Figure 6-6. Step (2) of the original algorithm prevented coalescing an unresolved pc—representing an unknown or incomplete phrase—with one or more resolved pcs. Step (2) of Figure 6-6 generalizes this idea; it prevents the coalescing of any two pcs whose combined deviance is greater than that permitted in the current cycle.

COALESCABLE (pc1 pc2)	
Pc1 and pc2 represent contiguous segments of the utterance AND	(1)
The sum of the *dlevels* of the nodes <= the current deviation-level AND	**(2)**
There is at least one active form containing the steps of both nodes AND	(3)
No step is represented twice AND	(4)
No mutually-exclusive links (sharing an mnode) are present.	(5)

Figure 6-6: CHAMP's COALESCABLE Predicate
(Figure 5-15 generalized to all deviation-levels).

To see the effect of the true COALESCABLE predicate on processing, consider the sentence

"Change the 3 pm seminar June 4 to rm 7620"

which contains two deviations with respect to the kernel: a deletion of the required **datemkr** in the postnominal date, and a substitution of the token **rm** for a recognizable token of the class **roomwd**. Figure 6-7 shows COALESCABLE's uniform effect at different deviation-levels. The figure arranges the results of processing by increasing deviation-level. The leftmost column at each deviation-level shows some of the maximal sets of co-constituent subtrees. The middle column shows whether or not the subtrees can JOIN. The rightmost column explains what happens to the candidate context during expansion. The last row of Deviation-level 0 shows, for example, that a previously constructed, non-deviant unmarked hour (u-hour@0) may JOIN with the token **seminar** and EXPAND via GG2 to a subtree representing a non-deviant **seminarform**.

Utterance: "Change the 3 pm seminar [on] June 4 to *rm* 7620"

Coalesce/Expand Cycle at Deviation-level 0:

Subtrees	COALESCABLE	EXPAND
3 + pm	yes	u-hour@0, HR2
June + 4	yes	u-date@0, DATE1
rm@1 + 7620	no	
u-date@0	maximal	fails (missing marker)
u-hour@0 + seminar	yes	seminar@0, GG2

Coalesce/Expand Cycle at Deviation-level 1:

Subtrees	COALESCABLE	EXPAND
u-date@0	maximal	m-date@1, DATE0
rm@1 + 7620	yes	room@1, LOC6
to + room@1	yes	stpair@1, STP1
seminar@0 + m-date@1	yes	seminar@1, GG2
the + seminar@1	yes	m-d-gg@1, DGG1
change + m-d-gg@1+stpair@1	no	

Coalesce/Expand Cycle at Deviation-level 2:

Subtrees	COALESCABLE	EXPAND
change + m-d-gg@1+stpair@1	yes	change@2, ACT3
change@2	maximal	*ROOT*

Figure 6-7: The incremental progress of a least-deviant-first search via the uniform effect of COALESCABLE's step (2) across Deviation-levels.

Also at Deviation-level 0 we see that although the pcs for **June** and **4** can coalesce and EXPAND via DATE1 to produce an unmarked date (u-date@0), the subtree containing that unmarked date cannot EXPAND because its position in the utterance demands that it be marked by a preposition. The subtrees for **rm** and **7620** cannot even coalesce at Deviation-level 0 because **rm** is represented by an unresolved pc and, therefore, has a *dlevel* of one (rm@1).

At Deviation-level 1, each of the previously failed paths is advanced: the subtree for "June 7" as an unmarked date (u-date@0) becomes a marked date by compensating for the deletion in DATE0. Meanwhile, rm@1 and **7620** JOIN and then successfully EXPAND using a substitution in LOC6. The resulting subtree is represented by room@1. Of course, each of the new subtrees has a *dlevel* of one because each new subtree contains an explained violated expectation. As long as the subtrees containing the deviant marked date and the deviant room do not try to coalesce, higher level constituents can be constructed at the current deviation-level (for example, seminar@1). To parse the sentence, however, the two subtrees must eventually be JOINed—COALESCABLE's step (2) blocks the action until the deviation-level is incremented because no less deviant explanation could be found. When the extra deviation point becomes available, the subtrees coalesce and a *ROOT* is produced.

To see how COALESCABLE's step (2) may interact with adaptation to make the understanding process more efficient, Figure 6-8 shows the algorithm's effect on search under a derived grammar. To the kernel we add a single derived form, DATE0', that recognizes marked dates in which the marker has been omitted. Such a form would have been created, for instance, after CHAMP confirmed its interpretation of the utterance in Figure 6-7 (the definition of "rm" as a **roomwd** would have been added to the lexicon as well, but we ignore that to simplify the comparison).

Utterance: "Change the 10 am class June 9 to *rm* 7620"
Derived Form: (DATE0'
isa m-dateforms
steps (203: class u-dateforms)
rnode (203))

Coalesce/Expand Cycle at Deviation-level 0:

Subtrees	COALESCABLE	EXPAND
10 + am	yes	u-hour@0, HR2
June + 9	yes	u-date@0, DATE1
rm@1 + 7620	no	
u-date@0	maximal	m-date@0, DATE0'
u-hour@0 + class + m-date@0	yes	class@0, GG3
the + class@0	yes	m-d-gg@0, DGG1

Coalesce/Expand Cycle at Deviation-level 1:

Subtrees	COALESCABLE	EXPAND
rm@1 + 7620	yes	room@1, LOC6
to + room@1	yes	stpair@1, STP1
change + m-d-gg@0 + stpair@1	yes	change@1, ACT3
change@1	maximal	*ROOT*

Figure 6-8: The uniform effect of COALESCABLE's step (2) over time (least-deviant-first search in a derived grammar).

The utterance in Figure 6-8 is structurally identical to the sentence in Figure 6-7. CHAMP uses DATE0' to find the explanation of the new sentence at Deviation-level 1 rather than Deviation-level 2. Although the subtree for "rm 7620" still has a *dlevel* of one, the subtree for "June 9" as a marked date has a *dlevel* of zero, via the derived form. Thus when step (2) of the COALESCABLE predicate is reached at

Deviation-level 1, the two subtrees are permitted to JOIN. As a result, a *ROOT* node appears on the Agenda, and no further invocations of the Parse/Recovery Cycle need occur. COALESCABLE's judgment that the previously ungrammatical segment has a non-deviant interpretation is made possible by the existence of DATE0' which was constructed in response to the prior interaction.

Figures 6-7, 6-8, and 6-9 demonstrate that when two subtrees JOIN their *dlevels* are combined. Thus the implementation, like the model, contains only a simple notion of deviance: every recovery action compensates for the same "amount" of deviation and the amount of deviance along a path is additive. In Chapter 11 we discuss briefly the advantages of a more complex approach to measuring deviation.

```
JOIN (pc1 pc2)
IF pc1 is already a JOIN node                                              (1)
THEN add pc2 to pc1's subs field
        let pc1's forms field include only the active forms parsing all the subs
        add pc2's dlevel to pc1's dlevel                                   (1a)
ELSE create a new JOIN node                                                (2)
        let its subs field contain pc1 and pc2 AND
        let its forms field contain the active forms that parse both subnodes
        let its dlevel be the sum of the dlevels of the two nodes          (2a)
```

Figure 6-9: CHAMP's JOIN Algorithm
(Figure 5-16 generalized to all deviation-levels).

COALESCABLE and JOIN comprise the Coalesce phase of the Coalesce/Expand Cycle, leaving the task of generalizing EXPAND to work at non-zero deviation-levels. Although the function in Figure 6-10 looks radically different from the one in Figure 5-18, there are only two important changes. The most important, of course, is that EXPAND now takes a context as an argument rather than a pc—the Coalesce/Expand algorithm does the actual expansion to and partitioning of the parent classes that used to be done in EXPAND. The second difference is that EXPAND now contains an explicit gateway to the error detection and recovery mechanism in the function CLOSEOFF (step (1)). Notice that by creating unresolved pcs with a *dlevel* of one we guarantee that during error detection and recovery the number of unresolved pcs in a context cannot be greater than the number of deviations currently permitted along a path. The processing in CLOSEOFF and the range of values it can return are the topic of Section 6.5. Here we note only that through CLOSEOFF a context may be modified by the removal of unresolved subnodes, the elimination of forms, or the addition of recovery notations. When control returns to

EXPAND, the changes to the context are incorporated into the new pcs that are added to the Agenda. We look more closely at EXPAND's step (3) when we examine CLOSEOFF in detail (see Figure 6-23).

```
EXPAND (context)
CLOSEOFF the context                                                    (1)
IF CLOSEOFF returned failure                                            (2)
THEN RETURN
ELSE cache "true" for the context
Use the value returned by CLOSEOFF to modify the context and            (3)
  IF the subnodes satisfy all expand-time constraints for the context's class
  THEN create a pnode for the class that spans the subnodes
       IF there is an expand-time ig for the class
       THEN invoke it AND cache the canonical value for the pnode
       FOR EACH active step that seeks the pnode's class, DO            (4)
         IF the step has a bind-time constraint AND the pnode satisfies it
         THEN create a pc for the step, pnode, subnodes, and forms in the
             modified context and place it on the appropriate level of the Agenda
```

Figure 6-10: CHAMP's EXPAND Algorithm (Figure 5-18 generalized to all deviation-levels).

6.2. The cache

CHAMP redoes very little work in increasingly deviant Coalesce/Expand Cycles because the system caches values for JOIN and EXPAND. The only node pairs offered to COALESCABLE each time through the Agenda are those that have not previously JOINed. In addition, every context that successfully EXPANDed in a prior cycle has a cached value of "true" (see step (2) in Figure 6-10). When that value is found, EXPAND need not be reinvoked for the context because all the EXPANDed nodes were placed on the Agenda during the previous cycle. Thus, when Deviation-level *i* is run, only previously unCOALESCABLE node pairs and paths that failed to EXPAND successfully at Deviation-level *i-1* actually produce new work. This is demonstrated by Figure 6-11 for the utterance

"Schedule meeting at 3 pm June 7"

which requires two deviation points in the kernel grammar: one for a deleted article and one for a deleted preposition. The figure shows only a small portion of the search space explored during parsing; a larger portion of the space is examined in Figures 6-13 through 6-15 in the next section.

Each row of Figure 6-11 corresponds to a candidate constituent offered to EXPAND. The rows are divided into groups by increasing *dlevel* for the context. If a candidate constituent in the first column can be CLOSEdOFF without requiring more recovery actions that the current deviation-level allows, then the root node for the EXPANDed subtree is shown in the second column along with any recovery actions applied. If trying to CLOSEOFF the context uncovers an unacceptable degree of deviation, however, then the second column explains the error. Reading down the figure, the first context shows that **3** and **pm** coalesce at Deviation-level 0 to produce an unmarked hour via HR1. **At** then coalesces with the unmarked hour to produce a marked hour. In the third context, **June** and **7** produce an unmarked date via DATE1, but the unmarked date cannot EXPAND to a marked date without its preposition. Since GG1 can take an unmarked date in the prenominal position, u-date@0 can coalesce with **meeting** and m-hour@0 but cannot EXPAND because of a transposition.

The middle section of Figure 6-11 demonstrates that the work done at Deviation-level 1 stems from the two paths that failed to EXPAND at Deviation-level 0. When the path containing u-date@0 is retried with one deviation permitted, the unmarked date becomes m-date@1 with the help of a deletion recovery action. In turn, the marked date contributes to the maximal set of subnodes at Deviation-level 1 that EXPANDs to meeting_1@1. Another path that failed to EXPAND at Deviation-level 0 interprets "meeting at 3 pm June 7" as a maximal subsegment containing an unmarked date. This path can also succeed at Deviation-level 1; in meeting_2@1, the deviation point is used to explain the transposition.[25] Both meeting_1 and meeting_2 fail to EXPAND to marked **groupgatherings** because the utterance is missing the article and no deviation points are left to compensate for the deletion.

Since no *ROOT* appears on the Agenda during the Parse/Recovery cycle for Deviation-level 1, the deviation-level is incremented to two. Again the only work done stems from paths that failed: each of meeting_1@1 and meeting_2@1 is allowed to accrue the additional deviation point required to omit the article. The grammar allows two possibilities in the expansion of each **meetingform**—it may be either the definite or the indefinite article that has been deleted. Because the **add** action expects an object marked by an indefinite article, only the **m-i-ggforms** may coalesce with the pc for "schedule," leading to two *ROOT* nodes each with a *dlevel* of two. The first *ROOT* uses its two deviation points to explain the sentence with a deletion of

[25]Actually, the kernel grammar contains a **no-trans** recovery constraint that prevents steps seeking prenominal modifiers from being transposed with respect to the step seeking the head noun. A similar constraint applies to postnominal modifiers. For demonstrative purposes we assume in this example that the **no-trans** constraint was not placed in the grammar.

Utterance: "Schedule [a] meeting at 3 pm [on] June 7"

Deviation-level 0:

Context	Result of EXPAND
[(3 pm) (HR1)]	u-hour@0
[(at u-hour@0) (HR0)]	m-hour@0
[(June 7) (DATE1)]	u-date@0
[(u-date@0] (DATE0)]	fails due to missing marker
[(meeting m-hour@0 u-date@0) (GG1)]	fails by transpose of u-date

Deviation-level 1:

Context	Result of EXPAND
[(u-date@0) (DATE0)]	m-date@1, DATE0 + deletion
[(meeting m-hour@0 m-date@1) (GG1)]	$meeting_1$@1, GG1
[(meeting m-hour@0 u-date@0) (GG1)]	$meeting_2$@1, GG1 + transpose
[($meeting_1$@1) (IGG1)]	fails by missing indefinite article
[($meeting_1$@1) (DGG1)]	fails by missing definite article
[($meeting_2$@1) (IGG1)]	fails by missing indefinite article
[($meeting_2$@1) (DGG1)]	fails by missing definite article

Deviation-level 2:

Context	Result of EXPAND
[($meeting_1$@1) (IGG1)]	m-i-gg_1@2, IGG1 + deletion
[($meeting_1$@1) (DGG1)]	m-d-gg_1@2, DGG1 + deletion
[($meeting_2$@1) (IGG1)]	m-i-gg_2@2, IGG1 + deletion
[($meeting_2$@1) (DGG1)]	m-d-gg_2@2, DGG1 + deletion
[(schedule m-i-gg_1@2) (ACT1)]	add_1@2
[(schedule m-i-gg_2@2) (ACT1)]	add_2@2
[(add_1@2) (*ROOT*)]	succeeds
[(add_2@2) (*ROOT*)]	succeeds

Figure 6-11: Extending the search space by EXPANDing only contexts that failed at the previous deviation-level.

the date marker and a deletion of the definite article. The second *ROOT* uses its two deviation points to explain the sentence with a deletion of the article and a transposition of the unmarked date.

Turning to the cache before recomputing the value of EXPAND has an important consequence: if a context was successfully CLOSEdOFF at a deviation-level less than *i* then no more deviance is allowed to accrue to that path. In other words, as the space of deviance hypotheses grows it does not grow uniformly. To see why this is a desirable consequence, consider that if a path EXPANDs at Deviation-level *i-1* but no complete parse can be found at that deviation-level then the utterance must require additional recovery actions to be understood. Using the additional deviation points on a path we have already explained cannot make the global parse successful; the partitioning of forms into contexts that was done in the Coalesce/Expand algorithm guarantees that the additional recovery actions will change neither the size of the segment accounted for nor the formclass to which the segment will be EXPANDed. If neither the size of the segment nor its assigned class changes then no new paths have been created. Instead, the higher level constituents produced by EXPAND for the context will simply be more deviant versions of the paths produced at the lower deviation-level. Since no new paths have been created, the global parse must still fail. Thus, for the global parse to succeed the additional deviation points must have been needed by some other context—a context that failed to EXPAND in a prior cycle. These are precisely the contexts for which the cached value of EXPAND is not "true."

At Deviation-level *i*, the generalized parsing functions find sets of co-constituents that have together accrued no more than *i* deviation points. Before the contexts are converted from virtual to actual higher grammatical constituents, CHAMP's cache prevents redundant and provably useless work by allowing the system to weed out those contexts for which less deviant explanations already exist. The remaining contexts must be shown to require no more than a total of *i* deviation points before they can be EXPANDed. Determining the degree of deviance represented by a context is the responsibility of Error Detection, the portion of the system to which we now turn our attention.

6.3. Error detection

Throughout the Parse/Recovery Cycle our strongest search constraint is the detection of violated expectations in the interpretation of a segment as a particular grammatical constituent. Even as we expand the search space to encompass larger and larger sets of deviance hypotheses, the boundary of the space during any given cycle remains rigidly defined by the errors we can explain at the current deviation-level. We have already seen that the violation of a Concept Hierarchy constraint or a condition in the COALESCABLE predicate is adequate to terminate a path at any deviation-level—these errors are *non-recoverable*. Because we want to detect non-recoverable errors as soon as possible, the responsibility for their detection is spread throughout the system. In contrast, the responsibility for detecting *recoverable* errors in CHAMP rests within the Error Detection & Recovery mechanism shown in Figure 6-1, and primarily within the function ISCOMPLETE (Figure 6-12).

<u>ISCOMPLETE (context)</u>
Separate the unresolved nodes (**urs**) from the other subnodes in the context (1)
FOR EACH form in the context, DO (2)
  Find the missing, required steps (**mls**) (2a)
  Find the minimum number of transposed steps (**tls**) (2b)
  IF there are tls AND they violate a no-trans constraint OR (2c)
    there are mls AND no urs AND the mls violate a no-del constraint
  THEN go on to the next form
  Compute the amount of deviance for the subcontext where (2d)
    aod = the *dlevel* of the context + the number of tls +
        max (0, (the number of mls - the number of urs))
  Assign the subcontext to a partition according to its aod
IF the smallest aod <= the Deviation-level (3)
THEN FOR EACH form in the partition (3a)
    RETURN (form mls tls)
  ELSE RETURN (Retry the lowest aod) (3b)

Figure 6-12: CHAMP's ISCOMPLETE predicate for general error detection.

Recall that the *dlevel* of a context is defined to be the sum of the *dlevels* of its subnodes. Expressed in another way, a context is a candidate grammatical constituent that may have already accrued some amount of deviance during the explanation of its sub-constituents. ISCOMPLETE determines whether a particular context can be explained without accumulating a total deviance greater than that allowed by the current deviation-level. Note that the function does not explain any errors; it merely determines whether (and how much of) the context should be passed to Error Recovery. Specifically, ISCOMPLETE tries to pinpoint which *subcontexts* contain the fewest additional violated expectations. A *subcontext* is defined as a pairing of the subnodes in the context with a particular form in the context. For example, if both the **u-hourforms** HR1 and HR2 are forms in a context for pc*x* and pc*y* then each of [(pc*x* pc*y*) (HR1)] and [(pc*x* pc*y*) (HR2)] is a subcontext. By finding the minimally deviant explanation for each context, we guarantee that the least-deviant global explanation is produced first.

From the model in Chapter 2 we know that there are four types of recoverable errors: insertion, deletion, substitution and transposition. In ISCOMPLETE these error types correspond to the values computed for particular variables for a given subcontext. Insertions and substitutions are signalled by the presence of unresolved nodes (**urs**, step (1)), transpositions by transposed steps (**tls**, step (2b)), and deletions by missing, required steps (**mls**, step (2a)). To find the amount of deviance (**aod**) in a subcontext we collect the *step* fields of the subnodes into a list then compare that list with the steps list of the subcontext's form. Using the form's annotation nodes, the comparison allows us to compute the number of **mls** and **tls**. The amount of deviance for the context is then computed according to the formula in step (2d).

Note that the presence or absence of unresolved segments has no effect on the number of **tls**, but can effect whether an **ml** is considered an additional source of deviation or not. If a **ur** is present then it may fill in for the missing step; under these circumstances we do not need to add a deviation point because the projected substitution uses the deviation point made available in the unresolved subnode when it was created with a *dlevel* of one. In other words, if the unknown phrase is to be used as a synonym for a required lexeme then only one expectation has been violated, not two. If there are no unresolved segments, or the number of missing, required steps is greater than the number of nodes available to fill them, then we count one deviation point for every required but unsatisfied step. Observe, however, that ISCOMPLETE neither makes the substitution nor decides whether the substituted step occurs in a permissible order. At the time we compute the amount of deviance in a subcontext, we do not know if the current form will be among those in the least-deviant subset or not, so we leave the additional error detection to the recovery action that performs the substitution.

Once all of the forms in the context have been partitioned by the amount of deviation they add to the subtree, the lowest-valued set is chosen. If the value is less than or equal to the current deviation-level, ISCOMPLETE returns a triple for each form in the set (step (3a)), giving Error Recovery a head start on the information it needs to choose an appropriate recovery action. If, on the other hand, the best explanation that could be offered for the context has an **aod** greater than the current deviation-level, ISCOMPLETE returns a "retry message" that tells recovery the lowest deviation-level required for a subcontext to succeed (step (3b)). Since the cached value for EXPAND is intended to reflect the success of error detection and recovery, we cache "true" if one or more subcontexts are returned, and the retry message otherwise. In this way we retry EXPANDing a failed path only when enough deviation points are available for it to succeed.

6.4. A detailed example: Error detection during the parse of "Schedule a meeting at 3 pm June 7."

Let us now reexamine the search space for the utterance "Schedule meeting at 3 pm June 7" in light of what we know about error detection. Figures 6-13, 6-14, and 6-15 demonstrate how the least-deviant-first search progresses. Each figure shows a subset of the contexts considered at a particular deviation-level. For each context the results of the calls to ISCOMPLETE (ISC) and EXPAND (EXP) are displayed along with the value cached. As in Figure 6-11, when a context fails to EXPAND, the reason for the failure is given in the EXPAND column.

Context	ISC (form mls tls)	EXP/cache
[(3 pm) (HR1 HR2)]	(HR1 – –)	u-hour@0/t
[(June 7) (DATE1)]	(DATE1 – –)	u-date@0/t
[(at u-hour@0) (HR0)]	(HR0 – –)	m-hour@0/t
[(u-date@0) (DATE0)]	(Retry 1)	missing marker/1
[(meeting m-hour@0 u-date@0) (GG1)]	(Retry 1)	transposed u-date/1

Figure 6-13: Error detection at Deviation-level 0 for "Schedule meeting at 3 pm June 7"

Figure 6-13 shows how the paths from Deviation-level 0 of Figure 6-11 failed. In the fourth row the unmarked date is proposed as a candidate marked date using DATE0. Because of the missing preposition, ISCOMPLETE finds one **ml** in the subcontext. Since the deviation-level is zero, the violated expectation cannot be tolerated and ISCOMPLETE translates the single deviation into a message to retry the context at Deviation-level 1. In row five, the same unmarked date is proposed to ISCOMPLETE as a postnominal modifier in GG1 (which expects unmarked cases to occur prenominally). This time ISCOMPLETE detects one **tl** and, again, a retry message is returned.

Figure 6-13 also gives us the opportunity to point out that when more than one form is included in a context, error detection's ability to control search may be augmented by *critical differences* between the forms. In Chapter 5 we defined a

- **Critical Difference**: a form, X, contains a critical difference with respect to another form, Y, if X and Y contain the same steps with different ordering constraints, or if X and Y differ by at least one step.

Under a strict interpretation of the definition, a critical difference exists between forms independent of any utterance. The limiting effect of a critical difference on search, however, is manifested only if the utterance contains the critical constituents. An utterance causes the termination of one or more subcontexts via a critical difference if:

1. The utterance satisfies the ordering constraints in some of the forms but not in others (**ordering**); or
2. The utterance contains a constituent sought by some of the forms but not by others (**presence**); or

3. The utterance does not contain a constituent required by some of the forms but not by others (**absence**).

We saw an example of the second type of termination in Section 5.2; a JOINed node representing prenominal modifiers carried forms for the classes **meetingforms** and **mealforms** in its *forms* field until the word "meeting" was encountered. The word "meeting" manifested the critical differences between the *forms* because only GG1 seeks a **meetingwd**. As a result of the critical difference, the JOINed node built to encompass "meeting" had only GG1 in its *forms* field. Thus, the **presence** of a distinguishing constituent is detected by COALESCABLE, and the winnowing of the search space accomplished by JOIN. The justification for reducing the context is the design decision to EXPAND only maximally coalescable sequences; since some forms can account for the extra token, those subcontexts continue while subcontexts represented by forms that cannot account for the token are terminated.

Like COALESCABLE, ISCOMPLETE may also reduce the context when the forms contain critical differences. The justification in ISCOMPLETE, however, is the need to advance only the least-deviant subcontexts. A difference in **ordering** constraints between two forms translates into **tls** for any utterance that contains the relevant constituents. Since every transposition requires a recovery action, a subcontext that does not need a transposition recovery to explain the segment must be preferred over a subcontext that does.

Mls play a role in the **absence** condition similar to the role played by **tls** in the **ordering** condition. Consider as an example the critical difference between HR1 and HR2 in row one of Figure 6-13. HR1 recognizes times of the form "number [clockwd | daywd | nightwd]," while HR2 recognizes "number colonsymb number [clockwd | daywd | nightwd]." In the subcontext for HR2 and "3 pm," ISCOMPLETE detects the absence of the required constituents (colon and minutes) as two **mls**. Since HR1 requires no recovery actions to explain the segment and HR2 requires two deletions, only HR1 remains in the context at the end of error detection.

Critical differences also play a role in parsing at Deviation-level 1 for our sample sentence. The first row of Figure 6-14 shows how the path for the marked date that failed previously succeeds at Deviation-level 1 by using the available deviation point for the deletion. In turn, $meeting_1$ is created by coalescing the just created m-date@1 with the pcs for "meeting" and "at 3 pm" that still reside on the Agenda. Since the step picking up the marked date is included in GG1's *snode*, $meeting_{1a}$ is also created a this time (row 3). Note that the subtree represented by $meeting_{1a}$ has a *dlevel* of zero because the constituent that contributed deviance to the context has been removed in response to the *snode*. Along a different path, $meeting_2$ is created using the available deviation point to account for the transposition of step 303 (the unmarked date) detected by ISCOMPLETE. In the next six rows, CHAMP tries to EXPAND each of the three **meetingforms** using IGG1 and DGG1—two kernel forms distinguished by a critical difference. IGG1 has required steps seeking an indefinite article and object, while DGG1 seeks a definite article and object. In Figure 6-14, as in Figure 6-11, both contexts fail to EXPAND for $meeting_1$ and $meeting_2$ because neither article is present in the utterance. Both paths succeed for $meeting_{1a}$, however, because that subtree can use the available deviation point to compensate for the **ml** found in each context by ISCOMPLETE. Both contexts succeed because the user's deviation negates the critical difference between the forms.

Although the critical difference between IGG1 and DGG1 is not manifested by the utterance, the critical difference between ACT1 and ACT2 is (last two rows of Figure 6-14). Because the **addform** ACT1 requires an object marked by an indefinite article, only $m\text{-}i\text{-}gg_{1a}$ can coalesce with **schedule**. This path fails to become a *ROOT* node, however, because it does not account for the entire utterance (only "schedule meeting at 3 p.m."), a non-recoverable error. Notice that the cached value for EXPAND under these circumstances is "true" so that the path is never retried. The **deleteform** (ACT2) requires a **deletewd** and an object marked by a definite article. Since $m\text{-}d\text{-}gg_{1a}$ is available but an appropriate verb is not, the global failure of the path for ACT2 is delayed until Deviation-level 2 (see row 7 of Figure 6-15).

Unlike $meeting_{1a}$, $meeting_1$ and $meeting_2$ each have a *dlevel* of one. Both **meetingforms** explain the segment, "meeting at 3 pm June 7." Because this is a different segment than "meeting at 3 pm," (explained by $meeting_{1a}$), $meeting_1$ and $meeting_2$ represent paths distinct from $meeting_{1a}$. In addition, even though $meeting_1$ and $meeting_2$ explain the same segment, they nonetheless represent different subtrees by incorporating different explanations. As different subtrees they are represented by different root pcs which in turn may coalesce with other subnodes to form distinct contexts. Thus, the failure of both $meeting_1$ and $meeting_2$ to EXPAND to either **m-i-ggforms** or **m-d-ggforms** creates four paths to be retried at Deviation-level 2.

The fate of those four paths can be seen in Figure 6-15. Each context reenters ISCOMPLETE with a *dlevel* of one and uses the extra deviation point available at Deviation-level 2 to recover from its missing, required step. Again, the critical difference between IGG1 and DGG1 is not manifested by the utterance, but the

Context	ISC (form mls tls)	EXP/cache
[(u-date@0) (DATE0)]	(DATE0 201 –)	m-date@1/t
[(meeting m-hour@0 m-date@1) (GG1)]	(GG1 – –)	$meeting_1$@1/t
[(meeting m-hour@0) (GG1)]	(GG1 – –)	$meeting_{1a}$@0/t
[(meeting m-hour@0 u-date@0) (GG1)]	(GG1 – 303)	$meeting_2$@1/t
[($meeting_1$@1) (IGG1)]	(Retry 2)	missing indefinite article/2
[($meeting_1$@1) (DGG1)]	(Retry 2)	missing definite article/2
[($meeting_2$@1) (IGG1)]	(Retry 2)	missing indefinite article/2
[($meeting_2$@1) (DGG1)]	(Retry 2)	missing definite article/2
[($meeting_{1a}$@0 (IGG1)]	(IGG1 402 –)	m-i-gg_{1a}@1/t
[($meeting_{1a}$@0 (DGG1)]	(DGG1 401 –)	m-d-gg_{1a}@1/t
[(m-d-gg_{1a}@1) (ACT2)]	(Retry 2)	missing verb/2
[(schedule m-i-gg_{1a}@1) (ACT1)]	(ACT1 – –)	incomplete *ROOT*/t

Figure 6-14: Error detection at Deviation-level 1
for "Schedule meeting at 3 pm June 7"

critical difference between ACT1 and ACT2 is: only the **m-i-ggforms** can coalesce with **schedule**, while the absence of a **deletewd** requires an additional recovery action for the **m-d-ggforms** that have been produced. Thus, each of m-i-gg_1 and m-i-gg_2 produces a valid **addform** that accounts for all the tokens in the utterance. The complete **addforms** become *ROOT* nodes for two APTs.

Context	ISC (form mls tls)	EXP/cache
[($meeting_1$@1) (IGG1)]	(IGG1 402 –)	m-i-gg_1@2/t
[($meeting_1$@1) (DGG1)]	(DGG1 401 –)	m-d-gg_1@2/t
[($meeting_2$@1) (IGG1)]	(IGG1 402 –)	m-i-gg_2@2/t
[($meeting_2$@1) (DGG1)]	(DGG2 401 –)	m-d-gg_2@2/t
[(schedule m-i-gg_1@2) (ACT1)]	(ACT1 – –)	add_1@2/t (*ROOT*)
[(schedule m-i-gg_2@2) (ACT1)	(ACT1 – –)	add_2@2/t (*ROOT*)
[(m-d-gg_{1a}@1) (ACT2)]	(ACT2 705 –)	incomplete *ROOT*/t
[(m-d-gg_1@2) (ACT2)]	(Retry 3)	retry level > maxdev/3
[(m-d-gg_2@2) (ACT2)]	(Retry 3)	retry level > maxdev/3

Figure 6-15: Error detection at Deviation-level 2
for "Schedule meeting at 3 pm June 7"

When a *ROOT* has a *dlevel* greater than zero we call it a hypothetical explanation of the utterance or, more simply, an hypothesis. Although we have found hypotheses at Deviation-level 2 for the example, ISCOMPLETE is clearly a general mechanism capable of performing error detection at higher deviation-levels. Unfortunately, the greater the amount of deviance required to explain an utterance, the greater the chance of constructing multiple hypotheses that differ only in terms of their recovery notations. The correlation occurs because recovery is the process by which we relax the very expectations that distinguish grammatical forms. Figure 6-16 shows that the annotated parse trees built by CHAMP for the example are a case in point.[26]

The figure also gives us the opportunity to distinguish between the actual meaning of an utterance and its

- **Effective meaning:** an interpretation of the utterance in terms of the effect it produces in the task domain. It is possible for sentences that are effectively equivalent to differ in actual meaning (because the difference in meaning cannot be reflected by the actions available to the system). CHAMP, like other natural language interfaces, builds structures to capture an utterance's effective meaning; this reflects the assumption that the system's primary goal is to perform the action intended by the user.

The hypotheses in pc62 and pc63 capture the same effective meaning but differ in their explanations of the user's errors. Pc62 explains the utterance using a deletion of the indefinite article usually sought by step 402 of IGG1 (see the *recovery notation* in pc54) with the transposition of the step seeking an unmarked date in GG1 (see the recovery notation in pc42). Pc63, on the other hand, combines the deletion of the indefinite marker (pc55) with the deletion of the date marker usually required by step 201 of DATE0 (notated at pc35).

After the error detection performed by ISCOMPLETE but before the creation of higher level constituents in EXPAND, a deviant context must be explained. In the remainder of this chapter we examine how that explanation is constructed: where recovery notations come from and how they are incorporated into the APT. We postpone discussion of how to choose among competing hypotheses like those represented by pc62 and pc63 to Chapter 7. How we convert an APT into a set of grammatical components that recognize a deviant form directly is a discussion left to Chapter 8.

---

[26]The format for displaying a pc was introduced in Section 5.1. After the pc identifier comes the step followed by the pnode (the segment's start position, end position, and class). When non-nil, the *forms* field and *dlevel* fields come next. Subnodes are indicated by indentation.

```
62: *ROOT* (0 6 addforms) (ACT1) 2
  0: 704 (0 0 addwd)
  54: 708 (1 6 m-i-ggforms) (IGG1) (2 (DELETE 402))
    42: 403 (1 6 meetingforms) (GG1) (1 (TRANSPOSE pc27))
      1: 309 (1 1 meetingwd)
      24: 315 (2 4 m-hourforms) (HR0)
        2: 111 (2 2 hrmkr)
        14: 113 (3 4 u-hourforms) (HR1)
          4: 4 (3 3 number)
          7: 16 (4 4 nightwd)
      27: 303 (5 6 u-dateforms) (DATE1)
        8: 101 (5 5 monthwd)
        11: 102 (6 6 number)

63: *ROOT* (0 6 addforms) (ACT1) 2
  0: 704 (0 0 addwd)
  55: 708 (1 6 m-i-ggforms) (IGG1) (2 (DELETE 402))
    40: 403 (1 6 meetingforms) (GG1) 1
      1: 309 (1 1 meetingwd)
      24: 315 (2 4 m-hourforms) (HR0)
        2: 111 (2 2 hrmkr)
        14: 113 (3 4 u-hourforms) (HR1)
          4: 4 (3 3 number)
          7: 16 (4 4 nightwd)
      35: 316 (5 6 m-dateforms) (DATE0) (1 (DELETE 201))
        26: 203 (5 6 u-dateforms) (DATE1)
          8: 101 (5 5 monthwd)
          11: 102 (6 6 number)
```

Figure 6-16: The APTs constructed under CHAMP's kernel for "Schedule meeting at 3 pm June 7."

6.5. Error recovery

The model in Chapter 2 gave us four classes of errors: deletion, insertion, substitution and transposition. In the previous section we implemented error detection by creating a fairly simple correspondence between each class and the values computed for the variables **urs**, **tls**, and **mls** within a subcontext. To compensate for an error, the model also gives us four general recovery actions: insertion, deletion, substitution and transposition. Unfortunately, the correspondence between recovery action and the values of implementation variables is more complex than it was for error detection. The difficulties arise from the need to embed a recovery notation at the correct position in an APT that may be only partially constructed. As we examine the implementation of each of the four general types of recovery we will see that, in

CHAMP, choosing the appropriate recovery action for a subcontext depends upon six factors:

1. The number of unresolved subnodes (**urs**).
2. The number of missing, required steps identified by ISCOMPLETE (**mls**).
3. The number of transpositions independent of substitutions identified by ISCOMPLETE (**tls**).
4. The number of additional transpositions if a substitution is made (**atls**).
5. The number of deviation points available (**dpa**) as calculated by: the Deviation-level - the *dlevel* of the subcontext + the number of **urs**.[27]
6. The presence of recovery-time constraints (**rtc**).

We know from the EXPAND algorithm in Figure 6-10 that the gateway to error detection and recovery is the function CLOSEOFF. CLOSEOFF's first step is to call ISCOMPLETE for a preliminary assessment of the violated expectations in the context. The purpose of error recovery is to choose for each subcontext that ISCOMPLETE returns the recovery action that promotes the least-deviant global parse. As a result, one way to view CLOSEOFF is as a large discrimination net. At the leaves of the net are one or more of CHAMP's six general recovery functions: OK, RETRY, DELETE, TRANSPOSE, INSERT, and SUBSTITUTE. In the model, the general recovery action for an insertion error is a deletion and for a deletion error, an insertion. The recovery notation left in an APT, however, is the description of the user error required by the adaptation mechanism. To avoid confusion when reading APTs, we pair the names of the recovery functions with the errors they detect and the notations they produce. Thus, INSERT recovers from insertion errors and leaves an insertion notation, while DELETE recovers from deletion errors and leaves a deletion notation. Because the discrimination logic in CLOSEOFF is a function of the six factors listed above, our discussion of error recovery will be simpler if we proceed "bottom-up," describing the leaf functions first and the root function last. Thus, once we have introduced the individual recovery functions we will conclude the chapter by presenting the CLOSEOFF algorithm and demonstrating how recovery notations are incorporated into an APT.

---

[27]A **ur** carries its deviation point in order to guarantee that during error detection and recovery the number of unresolved pcs in the context is no greater than the number of deviations currently permitted along a path. In other words, a *dlevel* of one is given to a **ur** to reserve for that node the minimum number of deviation points required to explain it. When the deviation-level is high enough for the **ur** to coalesce with other nodes, the reserved deviation point must be contributed to the total number of deviation points available in order to offset the increase in the *dlevel* of the context caused by the **ur**. In this way, a context with one **ur** and a *dlevel* of one, created at Deviation-level 1, nonetheless has one deviation point available for recovery (1 - 1 + 1).

OK and RETRY represent the extreme conditions that may occur during error detection: no violated expectations and too many violated expectations. OK is the function used when no error recovery is required. If the context given to CLOSEOFF contains no unresolved nodes, and the subcontexts returned by ISCOMPLETE contain no missing or transposed steps, then CLOSEOFF simply returns a list of forms names taken from the preserved subcontexts. In columns labelled "ISC" in Figures 6-13, 6-14, and 6-15 subcontexts that are OK look like: (form – –).

At the opposite end of the spectrum, CLOSEOFF may use the function RETRY. When ISCOMPLETE returns a retry message because every subcontext required more additional deviation points than were available, CLOSEOFF passes the retry value back to EXPAND. CLOSEOFF may also produce a retry message on its own—as when, for example, a substitution creates an added transposition but only one deviation point is available. Regardless of which function detects the retry condition, we have seen that the cache remembers the retry value to keep CHAMP from reEXPANDing a failed path before the deviation-level is high enough for the path to progress.

When error recovery may be able to explain a context, ISCOMPLETE (step (3a)) returns a list in which each least-deviant subcontext is represented by a triple: the form name, a value for **mls**, and a value for **tls**. If the context is free of unresolved nodes but the subcontext has missing, required steps, CLOSEOFF responds by invoking DELETE. Similarly, if there are no unresolved nodes but **tls** have been detected, CLOSEOFF creates a recovery notation using TRANSPOSE. Note that under either set of circumstances ISCOMPLETE has already checked for the appropriate type of recovery-time constraints (step (2c)). We have seen examples of the recovery notations produced by each of DELETE and TRANSPOSE in the APT rooted at pc62 in Figure 6-16.

The logic that discriminates between the remaining two recovery functions presupposes that the context passed to CLOSEOFF contains one or more unresolved subnodes. The complexity of response entailed by this one factor can be seen from the example in Figure 6-17. The figure shows a sentence taken from User 1's log file for the experiments described in Chapter 3.[28] The sentence is displayed in string form, as the user typed it, as well as in CHAMP's tokenized form (see Section 5.1).

---

[28]Examples taken from user data are always preceded by a label of the form U*i*S*jk*, where *i* is the user's number, *j* is the session number (which ranges from 1 to 9), and *k* is the number of the sentence within the log file for the session. User numbers 1, 2, 3, 4, 5, and 7 correspond to data for the users in the two adaptive conditions of the hidden-operator experiments described in Chapter 3. User numbers 9 and 10 correspond to data for two new users performing the original experimental task in interactions with CHAMP. The complete list of sentences from all users participating in the adapt conditions of the experiments is given in [46].

```
U1S39: "Cancel June 12th meeting at AISys"
Tokens: (cancel june 12 th meeting at aisys)

DATE1
 isa u-dateforms
 steps
   101: class monthwd bindvar month
   102: class number bindvar day
   103: class commasymb
   105: class number bindvar year
 mode (101 102)

Deviation-level 1:
Context: [(june 12 th@1) (DATE1)]
ISCOMPLETE: aod = dlevel + tls + max(0, mls - urs)
                  aod(DATE1) = 1 + 0 + 0
 returns (DATE1 --)
```

Figure 6-17: The first context in which **th** is available to recovery.

During segmentation the unknown token **th** is not resolvable as a new instance of an extendable class. Hence, during the Parse/Recovery Cycle the token is represented by an unresolved pc with a *dlevel* of one. The first time CLOSEOFF encounters the node is at Deviation-level 1 (otherwise the pc could not have coalesced) and the context represents the segment "June 12th" as a candidate **u-dateform.** The presence of the unresolved node makes the *dlevel* of the context one, but also contributes the one deviation point available during recovery. Using the steps list for DATE1 and the formula from step (2d), ISCOMPLETE finds that DATE1 requires no more than the one deviation point available and returns the subcontext (DATE1 – –). With no missing, required step in the returned subcontext, CLOSEOFF has three alternatives for interpreting the unresolved node:

1. Treat **th** as an insertion in this constituent.
2. Treat **th** as a substitution for a non-required step.
3. Assume **th** is needed by a higher level constituent.

It is not difficult to imagine a segment for which each of these alternatives is the appropriate action following "June 12": the current value of "th," replacing "th" with "nineteen eighty-eight," and replacing "th" with "business" provide justifications for (1), (2), and (3), respectively. Note, however, that the first and second alternatives create almost the same constituents in terms of the global parse; they consume the same amount of input and EXPAND to the same formclass. The difference between (1) and (2) is in their ability to capture the actual meaning of the sentence. Choosing the second alternative may allow us to learn the meaning of the token, but it does so at the cost of additional interactions with the user. Choosing the first alternative requires no additional effort from the user but is likely to produce only the effectively correct meaning. In addition, choosing either of the first two alternatives precludes the possibility of the third—we are not willing to create a distinct path for each interpretation and experience the exponential blow-up caused by the creation of two paths at each level of constituent in the grammar.

The solution implemented in CHAMP is justified by the goal of finding the least-deviant effective meaning of an utterance. Because we are concerned with finding only the effective meaning, we ignore the possibility of substituting the unresolved token for an unrequired step. If we discover a missing, *required* step during error detection, we try to satisfy it using the unknown phrase and the recovery function SUBSTITUTE. If there are no **mls**, however, then the unknown phrase is explained using INSERT if it is embedded, or is passed back, if it is not embedded. In this way, if the unknown phrase *is* required by a higher level constituent, we have made it available and a path that would have failed at the current deviation-level succeeds using substitution. If the unknown phrase is *not* required anywhere, it continues to "bubble up" until it can be captured within a constituent as an insertion.

Figure 6-18 shows the fate of **th** using INSERT. As in Figure 6-17, the **ur** is allowed to coalesce with **june** and **12** at Deviation-level 1. Since the subcontext contains no missing, required steps and **th** is an end subsegment, CLOSEOFF must return the pc for **th** so it can be made available to higher level constituents. The figure shows that when the value returned by CLOSEOFF is not a retry level it is a list of modified contexts. The first position in each modified context is filled with the names of the forms that succeeded via the modifications. The second position is used to pass back **urs** representing end subsegments that were not needed by the context to explain the user's error. The third position indicates the number of additional deviation points charged to the context and the recovery notation that should be included in the EXPANDed nodes. At Agenda-level 1 in our example, error recovery returns DATE1 as the successful form with the modification that the **ur** representing "th" be removed from the context. When EXPAND reduces a context it removes one deviation point for every **ur** removed (the **ur** takes its point away with it).

At Agenda-level 2 the pc for "th" is discontiguous with the other nodes. Since it cannot coalesce it is simply moved up to Agenda-level 3 where it JOINs with other constituents as a candidate **meetingform**. When **th** JOINs with its co-constituents it

U1S39: (cancel june 12 th meeting at aisys)

Coalesce/Expand Agenda-level 1:
EXPAND Context: [(june 12 th@1) (DATE1)], *dlevel* = 1
Error Detection returns: (DATE1 – –)
Error Recovery returns: ([DATE1 (th) –])

Coalesce/Expand Agenda-level 2:
th@1 moved to next Agenda-level (step (1b) of the Coalesce/Expand Cycle)

Coalesce/Expand Agenda-level 3:
EXPAND Context: [(u-date@0 th@1 meeting m-location@0) (GG1)], *dlevel* = 1
Error Detection returns: (GG1 – –)
Error Recovery returns: ([GG1 – (0 (INSERT th))]) via INSERT

Figure 6-18: Bubbling **th** up the Agenda until an insertion is detected for "Cancel June 12th meeting at AISys" at Deviation-level 1.

raises the *dlevel* of the context to one. CLOSEOFF receives the context and passes it to ISCOMPLETE which detects no additional violated expectations. Without a missing, required step, error recovery compensates for the unknown and now embedded subsegment using INSERT. Thus, the modified context created by error recovery has no **urs** to pass back and the deviation point made available by **th** is consumed by the insertion. The recovery notation in the modified context is included in the *dlevel* field of every pc created as a **meetingform** from the context.

The utterance in the example occurs in User 1's protocol after CHAMP has learned that she expresses **m-d-ggforms** without the definite article. Using the derived form, DGG1'[29], the system produces the APT in Figure 6-19 at Deviation-level 1. Although the APT in the figure explains the unknown segment as an insertion in GG1, we will see in Chapter 8 that CHAMP does not truly take such a narrow view—adaptation and generalization of the APT rooted at pc56 creates a grammatical component that treats "th" as an insertion no matter where it appears in the future.

The final recovery function left to describe is SUBSTITUTE. It is invoked when there are both missing, required steps and available unresolved segments to fill them. The function may be invoked, however, only if the missing, required step is not

[29] CHAMP generates non-mnemonic internal symbols for the names of user forms. For the convenience of the reader those symbols have been replaced in the example APTs by names that show the origin of the derived form.

```
56: *ROOT* (0 6 deleteforms) (ACT2) 1
  1: 705 (0 0 deletewd)
  49: 709 (1 6 m-d-ggforms) (DGG1') 1
    44: 403 (1 6 meetingforms) (GG1) (1 (INSERT pc0))
      16: 303 (1 2 u-dateforms) (DATE1)
        2: 101 (1 1 monthwd)
        5: 102 (2 2 number)
      0: 0 (3 3 unknown) nil 1
      6: 309 (4 4 meetingwd)
      22: 317 (5 6 m-locationforms) (LOC0)
        8: 211 (5 5 locmkr)
        19: 212 (6 6 u-locationforms) (IFLOC2)
          9: 114 (6 6 businessname)
```

Figure 6-19: The APT constructed by CHAMP using a grammar with DGG1' for "Cancel June 12th meeting at AISys"

precluded from a substitution by a recovery-time **no-sub** constraint, and if the substitution itself does not create an additional transposition (**atl**). Consider the situation in Figure 6-20 as an example. In the travel domain grammar, CHAMP expects only the word "departing" or the phrase "departing from" as markers for the source location case in a flight object. User 4 consistently preferred the lexeme "leaving." Given the sentence in the example and the kernel grammar for the travel domain, "leaving" appears as an unknown that is not resolved as a new instance of an extendable class. At Deviation-level 0 **Chicago** EXPANDs to an unmarked location but is unable to either coalesce with **leaving** or EXPAND to a marked source location. At Deviation-level 1 EXPAND is called with a context for "leaving Chicago." In turn, ISCOMPLETE detects the missing marker (step 211 in LOC0) and no transpositions. CLOSEOFF finds the unresolved node, then checks to make sure that the unsatisfied step permits substitution and that using "leaving" to satisfy step 211 does not create a transposition (0 **atls**). When all the conditions have been satisfied, SUBSTITUTE is invoked and returns the modified context in the figure.

With the introduction of the SUBSTITUTE action we have exhausted the recovery strategies needed when one deviation point is available to the context. If the available deviation point is contributed by an unresolved node, then a global parse at the current deviation-level must explain that node using either INSERT or SUBSTITUTE. If, on the other hand, there is no unresolved segment left in the utterance, then a global parse at the current deviation-level must require either a DELETE or TRANSPOSE. Table 6-1 summarizes the conditions under which each of the four basic recovery functions is invoked *by itself* from CLOSEOFF. The conditions are

U4S29: "schedule flight #103 on June 13 *leaving* Chicago at 11 p.m. arriving in NY at 2 a.m."
Tokens: (schedule flight %poundsymb 103 on june 13 leaving chicago at 11 p %period m %period arriving in ny at 2 a %period m %period)

Deviation-level 0:
EXPAND Context: [(u-location) (LOC0)], *dlevel* = 0
Error Detection returns: (RETRY 1)
Error Recovery returns: (RETRY 1)

Deviation-level 1:
EXPAND Context: [(leaving@1 u-location) (LOC0)], *dlevel* = 1
Error Detection returns: (LOC0 211 –)
Error Recovery returns: ([LOC0 – (0 (SUBST leaving 211))]) via SUBSTITUTE

Figure 6-20: Identifying **leaving** as a source marker using SUBSTITUTE.

expressed in terms of the six discrimination criteria listed at the beginning of this section (page 116): **dpa** translates as "deviation points available," **urs** is the number of unresolved pcs in the context, **mls** is the number of missing, required steps in the least-deviant subcontext, **tls** is the number of transposed steps in the least-deviant subcontext without substitutions, **atls** is the number of transpositions considering substitutions, and **rtc** stands for "recovery-time constraints." A value of "na" for an entry indicates that the factor does not apply. **Atls**, for example, are pertinent only if a substitution has taken place. The value of "na" is found in the **rtc** entries for DELETE and TRANSPOSE because ISCOMPLETE has already performed the relevant constraint checks.

Recovery Function	**dpa**	**urs**	**mls**	**tls**	**atls**	**rtc**
DELETE	1	0	1	0	na	na
TRANSPOSE	1	0	0	1	na	na
INSERT	1	1	0	0	na	na
SUBSTITUTE	1	1	1	0	0	no-sub

Table 6-1: The four general recovery functions and the values of the six discrimination factors required for their use ("na" indicates the factor does not apply).

An utterance that succeeds at Deviation-level 2 (or higher) may accumulate deviation points along paths representing different constituents (as in Figure 6-19) or within the same constituent. In the latter case the recovery actions taken for a subcontext are composed from the basic recovery functions we have just described. Since the Maximum Deviation-level in CHAMP is two, no more than two recovery actions may be used to explain a single constituent. Thus there should be ten pairs of recovery functions displayed in Table 6-2 (four functions choose two plus the four pairs that invoke the same function twice). The extra pair occurs because TRANS/SUB is considered distinct from SUB/TRANS; the former is employed when a **tl** is detected by ISCOMPLETE independent of the substitution, and the latter is employed when the transposition is caused by the substitution during error recovery.

Recovery Function	dpa	urs	mls	tls	atls	rtc
DEL/DEL	2	0	2	0	na	na
DEL/TRANS	2	0	1	1	na	na
DEL/INS	2	1	1	0	1	no-del
DEL/SUB	2	1	2	0	0	no-del, no-sub
TRANS/TRANS	2	0	0	2	na	na
TRANS/INS	2	1	0	1	na	na
TRANS/SUB	2	1	1	1	0	no-sub
INS/INS	2	2	0	0	na	na
INS/SUB	2	2	1	0	0	no-sub
SUB/SUB	2	2	2	0	0	no-sub
SUB/TRANS	2	1	1	0	1	no-sub, no-trans

Table 6-2: Combinations of recovery functions applicable when two deviation points are available in a context and the values of the six discrimination factors required for their use ("na" indicates the factor does not apply).

Error recovery when more than one deviation point is available differs from error recovery with a single deviation point in three important respects. First, it may be possible for a single context to satisfy the requirements for a composite recovery action in more than one way. This is impossible for a single deviation point and a single recovery action. SUB/SUB and DEL/SUB are the relevant examples at Deviation-level 2. To invoke SUB/SUB there must be two **mls** and two **urs** in the least-deviant subcontext. Each unresolved node must be tried as a substitution for each missing, required step; if both substitutions are free of consequent transpositions, both paths must be returned to EXPAND. In the kernel grammar for each of the two implemented domains it is impossible for both substitutions to be free of transpositions because all required steps are ordered. Through adaptation, however, a derived grammar may be created that permits either ordering. If that happens then each form will succeed using a different binding of **urs** to **mls**, creating distinct paths despite the fact that the effective meanings of the resulting APTs are probably the same. In the case of DEL/SUB there are two **mls** and only one **ur**. It is clear that the unresolved node must be used for a substitution regardless of its position in the segment (otherwise the subcontext would use two deviation points for the two deletions, leaving no points to explain the unresolved node). Yet it is not clear which step should be considered deleted and which substituted. Thus DEL/SUB may produce two paths via a kernel form at Deviation-level 2. As long as neither substitution produces a transposition, both paths must be EXPANDed.

The second difference when more than one deviation point is available, is that a single subcontext may satisfy the conditions for more than one composite recovery action. Again, this was impossible for one deviation point and one recovery action—the basic recovery actions are mutually exclusive. Figure 6-21 demonstrates, however, that any time a SUB/TRANS is possible, a DEL/INS explanation must succeed as well (providing there is no **no-del** recovery time constraint). The utterance is similar to the one in Figure 6-18 except that a head noun, required in the kernel calendar grammar, is missing. At Deviation-level 1 **th** coalesces with each of **june 16**, **on june 16**, and **at aisys** but is passed back each time. The **ur** becomes embedded at Agenda-level 3. At that time, contexts for **meetingform**, **seminarform**, **classform**, and **mealform** are all EXPANDed, although only **meetingform** (recognized via GG1) is shown in the figure. In each case the required head noun is absent but the token **th** is in the wrong position to substitute. Thus each subcontext results in a retry message.

At Deviation-level 2, the four subcontexts are retried and each results in two paths. On the first path the two available deviation points are used for the substitution of **th** as the head noun in a transposed location. On the second path, it is assumed that the user has deleted the head noun and that **th** is an insertion. In all, eight APTs are created as competing hypothetical explanations for the utterance.

When one subcontext can be explained in two ways, either by different bindings within a single composite recovery action or by satisfying the discrimination conditions of different actions, it is possible, indeed likely, that effectively equivalent meanings are created along the EXPANDed paths. If the meanings are equivalent, why do we produce more than one? We will see in Chapter 8 that different hypotheses lead to different derived forms in the adapted grammar. By producing all

Utterance: (cancel 3 pm on june 16 th at aisys)

Deviation-level 1:
EXPAND context: [(u-hour m-date th@1 m-location) (GG1)], *dlevel* = 1
Error detection returns: (GG1 309 –)
Error recovery returns: (RETRY 2)

Deviation-level 2:
EXPAND context: [(u-hour m-date th@1 m-location) (GG1)], *dlevel* = 1
Error detection returns: (GG1 309 –)
Error recovery returns:
([GG1 – (1 (SUBST th 309) (TRANS th))] via SUB/TRANS
[GG1 – (1 (DELETE 309) (INSERT th))]) via DEL/INS

Figure 6-21: Equivalent hypotheses for "Cancel 3 pm on June 16th at AISys" via SUB/TRANS and DEL/INS using a grammar with DGG1'.

explanations at the lowest possible deviation-level we avoid unecessarily biasing the outcome of the learning algorithm.

The third point we need to raise with respect to composite recovery functions concerns a hidden inconsistency. Consider a sentence containing two deletion errors in separate constituents and only one unresolved segment. The least-deviant explanation for such an utterance contains one deletion and one substitution. Depending upon the boundaries between the constituents present in the utterance, it is possible that the unresolved segment sits on the end of two subsegments, each representing one of the constituents with a deletion (for an example, see Figure 8-15 in Chapter 8). Moreover, one constituent may be embeddable inside the other in the Formclass Hierarchy. At Deviation-level 1, the lower level context will EXPAND successfully using SUBSTITUTE. As a result the **ur** is unavailable to the higher context and only the explanation reflecting a deletion in the outer constituent and a substitution in the embedded constituent is produced. Given that the subsegment was on the end of the outer constituent as well, it should have been possible to interpret the sentence with an outer substitution and an embedded deletion.We compensate for the inconsistency by having CLOSEOFF return two modified contexts when the substituting node is an end segment. The first modified context reflects the substitution, as in Figure 6-20. The other modified context looks like: [form (**ur**) (1 (DELETE **ml**))]. This context represents one step down a path that requires two deviation points to succeed—one for the deletion and another for the unresolved pc that must still be accounted for. Since it does not account for the tokens in the unresolved segment the second modified context is unable to coalesce at the current deviation-level with any path that does. Thus, it is prevented from contributing to the global parse unless the deviation-level is incremented, and a least-deviant-first explanation is still guaranteed.

In an implementation that permits more than two deviations in an utterance, a discrimination algorithm capturing a more general analysis than the breakdown by cases in Tables 6-1 and 6-2 would be appropriate. Figure 6-22 shows that in CHAMP the case analysis suffices for the error recovery routine, CLOSEOFF. By this time the algorithm should seem straightforward; essentially, the results of error detection are used to select a single or composite recovery function. If ISCOMPLETE returns a list of deviant subcontexts, the **mls** and **tls** computed for each form are augmented by values for the unresolved segments (**urs**), available deviation points (**adp**), additional transpositions (**atls**), and recovery-time constraints (**rtc**). Taken together the six factors determine how many and which of the recovery functions create the least-deviant explanation. If a recovery function does not require a **ur** representing an end subsegment, the **ur** is passed back. When the **adp** is one, only a single function is indexed, although we create a second modified context under the special circumstances in step (4b) to compensate for the anomaly described above. When two deviation points are available more than one composite action may be invoked; each modified context produced for each least-deviant form is returned to EXPAND (step (4c)).

CLOSEOFF returns one of two values to EXPAND: a retry message or a list of modified contexts (OK returns a modified context without modifications). As promised in Section 6.1, Figure 6-23 shows EXPAND's response in each situation. If a retry message is returned, the candidate constituent failed to create a path at the current deviation-level. Under these circumstances, EXPAND caches the retry value and returns without building any higher level nodes (step (2)). If, on the other hand, CLOSEOFF returns a list of modified contexts then EXPAND caches the value "true" for the context and constructs its higher level constituents by incorporating the changes required to explain the user's error with respect to a particular form.

Imagine the set of utterances recognizable by a given grammar as defining a search space. If the user's utterance is not within the space we rely on the concept of a least-deviant-first parse to extend our search to a larger space in a principled way. Each time through the Parse/Recovery Cycle we extend the search space outward to include more deviant utterances until the best explanation for the grammar is produced or the Maximum Deviation-level for the implementation is reached. To traverse the space defined by a given deviation-level efficiently, we must take advan-

```
CLOSEOFF (context)
Let error-info = ISCOMPLETE (context)                                   (1)
IF error-info = retry message                                           (2)
THEN RETURN (RETRY (message))
Compute urs and adp
IF error-info has no mls or tls AND context has no urs                  (3)
THEN RETURN (OK forms)
FOR EACH triple in error-info, DO                                       (4)
   use the values for form, mls and tls in the triple
   IF adp = 1                                                           (4a)
   THEN choose recovery action using chart in Figure 6-1,
              computing atls, rtc and pass back as needed
      add to the modified contexts the value returned by the recovery function
      IF the recovery function is SUBSTITUTE AND the ur is on the end   (4b)
      THEN add modified context: (form (ur) (1 (DELETE ml)))
   ELSE choose composite recovery action(s) using the chart in Figure 6-2,  (4c)
              computing atls, rtc and pass back as needed
         FOR EACH composite action chosen, DO
            add to the modified contexts the value returned by the composite
RETURN list of modified contexts                                        (5)
```

Figure 6-22: CHAMP's CLOSEOFF algorithm for error recovery.

tage of every possible source of constraint, eliminating unprofitable paths as soon as we are certain they cannot explain the utterance. In the model underlying CHAMP, constraint is provided by the violation of expectations. Some types of violations are non-recoverable, including the violation of semantic constraints found in the Concept Hierarchy, the contiguity required of co-constituents, and the need to account for all the words in the sentence. An interpretation that exposes a non-recoverable error is always terminated and its path never re-explored. In contrast, the violation of expectations embodied in the forms that comprise the grammar are considered recoverable. A constituent requiring one or more insertions, deletions, substitutions, or transpositions may be constructed using appropriate recovery functions if the resulting path still lies within the extended search space. In essence, Error Detection & Recovery transforms an explainable path into one that has been explained.

The goal of efficient search is facilitated by creating kernel forms with critical differences. During both phases of the Parse/Recovery Cycle the manifestation of a critical difference by constituents in the utterance eliminates portions of the search space. The presence of a segment in an utterance terminates those paths using forms that do not seek the segment in favor of paths using forms that do. Alternatively, a segment may partition forms in the same formclass according to the amount of

```
EXPAND (context)
Let closeval = CLOSEOFF(context)                                        (1)
IF closeval is a retry message                                          (2)
THEN cache the retry value for the context and RETURN
ELSE cache "true" for the context
FOR EACH modified context, mc=(form (urs) (d-adjust notation)), DO      (3)
  IF the mc has passed back urs
  THEN remove them from the subnodes and move them up the Agenda
         decrease the dlevel of the context by 1 per passed back ur
         cache "true" for the reduced context
   IF the subnodes satisfy all expand-time constraints for the context's class
   THEN create a pnode for the class that spans the subnodes
        IF there is an expand-time ig for the class
        THEN invoke it AND cache the canonical value for the pnode
   FOR EACH active step that seeks the pnode's class, DO
     IF the step has a bind-time constraint AND the pnode satisfies it
     THEN create a pc out of
              the step
              the pnode
              the (possibly modified) subnodes
              the mc's form
              the dlevel of the context + the mc's d-adjust
              the notation
          AND place it on the appropriate level of the Agenda
```

Figure 6-23: CHAMP's EXPAND Algorithm reexamined with attention to the results of Error Detection & Recovery (Extension of Figure 6-10).

deviation required to explain the segment as an instance of the class. Under these circumstances, only the least-deviant paths are preserved.

CHAMP's cache also facilitates efficient search. As the deviation-level increases, the cache prevents the more deviant interpretations of an explained segment from being explored. In addition, CHAMP's cache prevents useless work during each new Coalesce/Expand Cycle by directing search only along paths that previously failed but for which there is evidence of potential success at the current deviation-level.

Whether the result of the Parse/Recovery Cycle is a single explanation of the user's utterance or a set of competing hypotheses concerning the user's intent, the understanding process is not yet complete. In the next chapter we examine Resolution—the phase in which a final effective meaning is assigned to the utterance. Resolving the effective meaning may require any or all of: dividing a set of APTs into equivalence classes based on effect, checking for the consistency of an interpretation against events in the databases, and finding default values for missing information using the Concept Hierarchy, simple inferences, or the user's help.

Chapter 7
Resolution: Choosing Among Explanations

When an utterance is understandable using the current grammar, the result of the Parse/Recovery Cycle is one or more meaning representations of the sentence (APTs) at a particular deviation-level. Although each APT represents an action to be performed in the domain, there is no guarantee that all APTs represent the same action or that any represented action is meaningful in the context established by the contents of the calendar and airline schedule. The Resolution phase of processing is responsible for enforcing database constraints, establishing a single meaning for the utterance, and performing the database action represented by that meaning (to review the position of the Resolution phase in the complete understanding process see Figure 4-1). There are three essential issues in resolution. First, do any of the represented actions correspond to the user's intent? This question must be asked when more than one effect is present or when there is a single effect at a non-zero deviation-level. Second, can the intended action be performed? This question is always pertinent. Third, what form should interaction with the user take? This question relates to the first one—determining the user's intent often requires user interaction.

In many ways the third question is the most difficult. How do we enlist the user's aid intelligently—without inundating her with choices or requiring her to act as linguist or programmer? Consider that a sentence as simple as

"Cancel the mtg June 5 at 3"

produces *twelve* APTs when CHAMP uses the kernel grammar for the calendar domain.[30] Figure 7-1 displays the explanations divided into four sets; explanations within a set differ only by the type of **groupgathering** they identify. In keeping with the notation introduced in Section 2.2, the first group of four corresponds to the hypothesis that **mtg** is an insertion and the head noun has been omitted. In the second set, **mtg** is treated as a substitution for the head noun and the marked form of

[30]Eighteen explanations are produced when both domain kernels are used; in each group in Figure 7-1 there would be an extra explanation for each kind of trip (air and nonair).

the date contains a deletion. In the final group, the head noun is omitted and **mtg** substitutes for the missing date marker. No interpretation is shown corresponding to a substitution of **mtg** for the head noun plus a transposition of the unmarked prenominal date because the transposition is prevented by a **no-trans** recovery-time constraint (we suspended that constraint for demonstrative purposes only in Chapter 5).

1. Cancel the >mtg< June 5 **[meetingwd]** at 3
2. Cancel the >mtg< June 5 **[seminarwd]** at 3
3. Cancel the >mtg< June 5 **[classwd]** at 3
4. Cancel the >mtg< June 5 **[mealwd]** at 3

5. Cancel the *mtg*/**meetingwd** [on] June 5 at 3
6. Cancel the *mtg*/**seminarwd** [on] June 5 at 3
7. Cancel the *mtg*/**classwd** [on] June 5 at 3
8. Cancel the *mtg*/**mealwd** [on] June 5 at 3

9. Cancel the **[meetingwd]** *mtg*/**datemkr** June 5 at 3
10. Cancel the **[seminarwd]** *mtg*/**datemkr** June 5 at 3
11. Cancel the **[classwd]** *mtg*/**datemkr** June 5 at 3
12. Cancel the **[mealwd]** *mtg*/**datemkr** June 5 at 3

Figure 7-1: The twelve explanations produced by the Parse/Recovery Cycle for "Cancel the mtg June 5 at 3" using the calendar kernel.

What is an appropriate method for presenting such a set of alternatives to the user? Certainly the list in Figure 7-1 is inappropriate—it requires that the user be familiar with the internal representation of the grammar as well as a number of notational conventions. An interaction such as the one in Figure 7-2 is somewhat better; the list is shorter and contains neither notation nor obscure references to internal grammatical categories. The format in Figure 7-2 uses a partial error analysis to distinguish alternatives. In this case, we have created the choices solely from hypothesized substitutions. The result is reasonably "friendly" although incomplete. Had we tried to capture the other information in the choices in Figure 7-1 we would have been forced to ask questions such as "Do you want to omit the marker for the date case?" and "Do you want to omit the head noun?" Of course, utterances with errors that are not substitutions would occasion questions like these as well. It seems inappropriate to assume that the user could, in general, answer such questions accurately. If we wish to assume any expertise on the part of the user it should be task expertise, not linguistic expertise.

Do you want:
(1) "mtg" to be a synonym for "meeting"?
(2) "mtg" to be a synonym for "seminar"?
(3) "mtg" to be a synonym for "class"?
(4) "mtg" to be a synonym for "breakfast"?
(5) "mtg" to be a synonym for "lunch"?
(6) "mtg" to be a synonym for "dinner"?
(7) "mtg" to be a synonym for "on"?
(8) none of the above
[number between 0 and 8]:

Figure 7-2: Using error analysis to create an alternative format for user interaction when resolving the meaning of "Cancel the mtg June 5 at 3."

What is wrong with interaction formats like those in Figures 7-1 and 7-2 is that they are designed to help the system, not the user. In contrast, CHAMP's approach to resolution incorporates the belief that for an interaction to make sense to the user it must be conducted within her frame of reference. In short, the user is concerned with accomplishing her task—scheduling calendar events—not with teaching grammar. The question in her mind is not "Will the system learn the substitution?" but "Will the system do the right thing?" Thus, from the user's point of view the goal of resolution is not establishing a unique explanation for the utterance but establishing her intended effect.

The difference this focus makes in the nature of an interaction can be seen in Figure 7-3. The interaction shown in each of the three examples results from mapping the set of explanations produced by the Parse/Recovery Cycle into subsets that have the same effect in the domain. It is the potential effects that are then presented to the user. The user's choice, in turn, determines the subset of root nodes that are passed from the Resolution phase to the adaptation functions. The differences between the interactions result from the differences in the assumed contents of the database.

Let us look at the three scenarios in Figure 7-3 more closely. In EXAMPLE 1 we assume that the database contains the entries shown at the top of the figure: an AI seminar scheduled from 10 a.m. to noon in room 5409, lunch from noon to 1 p.m. in an unspecified location, and a meeting with Ed in the professor's office from 3 to 4 p.m. Under these circumstances CHAMP finds only one effect both present in the list of twelve explanations and possible within the constraints enforced by the database. Note that pinpointing the intended effect reduces the hypothesis set from twelve to

EXAMPLE 1 assumes the following calendar entries for June 5:
(date (6 5 *) starthr 1000 endhr 1200 ggtype seminar location (* 5409) topic ai)
(date (6 5 *) starthr 1200 endhr 1300 ggtype lunch location (* *))
(date (6 5 *) starthr 1500 endhr 1600 ggtype meeting location (* office) parts ed)

Do you want:
to delete: JUNE 5 3:00pm - 4:00pm MEETING in/at OFFICE with ED ?
[y or n]: y
Ok, done.
(returning roots: 204 208 200)

EXAMPLE 2 assumes the following calendar entries for June 5:
(date (6 5 *) starthr 1000 endhr 1200 ggtype seminar location (* 5409) topic ai)
(date (6 5 *) starthr 1200 endhr 1300 ggtype lunch location (* *))
(date (6 5 *) starthr 1600 endhr 1700 ggtype meeting location (* office) parts ed)

Do you want:
(0) to delete: JUNE 5 12:00pm - 1:00pm LUNCH ?
(1) to delete: JUNE 5 10:00am - 12:00pm AI SEMINAR in/at 5409 ?
(2) to delete: JUNE 5 4:00pm - 5:00pm MEETING in/at OFFICE with ED ?
(3) none of the above
[number between 0 and 3]: 2
Ok, done.
(returning roots: 204 208 200)

EXAMPLE 3 assumes no calendar entries for June 5.

There are no events scheduled on June 5.
Please try again.
(returning roots: nil)

Figure 7-3: Resolution in CHAMP: the confirmation of a subset of explanations for "Cancel the mtg June 5 at 3" based on the user's selection of her intended effect.

three: the returned root nodes (pc204, pc208, and pc200) correspond to choices 1, 5, and 9 in Figure 7-1—one of each of the three hypothesized error combinations applied to the **meeting** object.

In EXAMPLE 2 of Figure 7-3, the database is changed slightly so that the meeting with Ed now takes place from 4 to 5 p.m. As a result, no calendar entry is a perfect match to the information contained in any of the explanations. On the other hand, each of the entries matches in part—although the times are wrong, there are explanations that expect to find a meeting, a seminar, and lunch. The partial matches create the choice list shown; when the the user chooses the cancellation of the meeting, the hypothesis set is reduced to the same subset of explanations as in EXAMPLE 1. Note that although the choices offered to the user are different in EXAMPLE 1 and EXAMPLE 2, the returned root lists are the same because the chosen effects are the same.

The final example in the figure shows one variant of CHAMP's behavior when none of the explanations correspond to an effect that is possible. Since the action of deleting an entry is meaningless if no entries are present, the system detects the error condition and returns the most informative message it can. In contrast to the displayed behavior, if there had been entries present, but no perfect or partial matches, the message would have been "No calendar entry fits that description on June 5."

There are two advantages to this approach to resolution, which we call *confirmation by effect*. First, the interaction demands no more of the user than the knowledge of what she intended by the utterance. Second, the system has access to an additional knowledge source to focus the user's choices: the state of the "real world" as represented by the databases. In other words, in the process of trying to answer the question "Do any of the represented actions correspond to the user's intent?" we will automatically answer the question "Can the intended action be performed?" The main disadvantage to the approach is that it does not guarantee a unique explanation in terms of the grammar (although it does guarantee a unique meaning in terms of the database).

Figure 7-4 displays the resolution algorithm in CHAMP. The process is composed of five steps: the transformation of explanations into database action records, the application of default reasoning and inference to incomplete action records, the transformation of complete records into virtual effects, the selection of the intended effect by the user (if necessary), and the performance of the database action. In the remainder of this chapter we examine each of these steps in turn.

7.1. Converting meaning to action

An explanation of an utterance is created by the Parse/Recovery Cycle in the form of an annotated parse tree (APT). The first step in resolution requires that we convert each APT into a *database action record.* Doing so allows the system to place root nodes producing identical database action records into the same preliminary equivalence class.

A database action record contains three pieces of information: the name of the action, a source *database record*, and a target database record (see Figure 7-5). The

RESOLVE (rootlist)
FOR EACH root node, DO (1)
  Transform the root node into a database action record
  Group root nodes with identical records
FOR EACH record, DO
  APPLY-DEFAULT-LOGIC to the record (2)
  IF the record contains all the information required by its database action
  THEN convert the record to a virtual effect (3)
  Group the roots with identical effects
IF there is a single non-error effect AND the deviation-level is 0 (4)
THEN perform the action AND RETURN the roots corresponding to the effect
ELSE IF the effect is an error (5)
    THEN display the appropriate error message
    ELSE pass the effects to USERQUERY (6)
        IF the user confirmed an effect
        THEN RETURN the corresponding roots

Figure 7-4: CHAMP's RESOLVE algorithm which controls Resolution.

list of possible actions is the same in both of CHAMP's domains: **insert, remove, alter,** and **retrieve,** corresponding to the action concepts **add, delete, change,** and **show** in the Concept Hierarchy. A detailed discussion of the database functions can be found in Section 7.3.

Each database action record requires a source database record, but **alter** requires a target record as well (for the other actions the target record is empty). Figure 7-5 shows that the fields in a source or target database record depend upon the domain. EXAMPLE1 and EXAMPLE 2 in Figure 7-3 show instances of database records from the calendar domain in which fields containing nil values have been suppressed.

Database Action Record	Calendar Domain Database Record	Travel Domain Database Record
action	date	date
source database record	ggtype	triptype
target database record	starthr	departure
	endhr	arrival
	location	origin
	participants	destination
	subject	flightnumber
	topic	

Figure 7-5: The record structures used in database interactions.

The creation of a database action record from an APT occurs with the help of *bindvars* and instance generators (*igs*), both of which were introduced in Section 4.2. Each record field has one or more identifying labels associated with it, labels that are placed in the *bindvar* lists of the steps that may fill the fields. In this way a tree-walk over the APT allows us to retrieve the values to associate with the *action*, *source*, and *target* fields regardless of where or how they occur in the utterance. The actual value placed in a field is either the canonical value for the pc satisfying the step, or the tokens associated with the pc if a canonical value is not available. A canonical value may be computable at resolution-time by an ig or may have been previously computed by an expand-time generator. Figure 7-6 demonstrates how the APT for the fifth explanation in Figure 7-1 becomes a database action record (the actual record is shown in Figure 7-7).

Utterance: Cancel the mtg June 5 at 3
Explanation 5: Cancel the *mtg*/**meetingwd** [on] June 5 at 3

APT:
204: *ROOT* (0 6 deleteforms) (ACT2) 2
    daction *in *ROOT*'s bindvar sets action to* **remove** *via* **ig-act**
  1: 705 (0 0 deletewd)
  125: 709 (1 6 m-d-ggforms) (DGG1) 2
    2: 401 (1 1 defmkr)
    56: 403 (2 6 meetingforms) (GG1) (2 (SUBST 0 309))
      dggtype *in 403's bindvar sets source ggtype to* **meeting** *via* **ig-mrgg**
      0: 0 (2 2 unknown) nil 1
      34: 316 (3 4 m-dateforms) (DATE0) (1 (DELETE 201))
        22: 203 (3 4 u-dateforms) (DATE1)
          ddate *in 203's bindvar sets source date to (6 5 *) via* **ig-date**
          3: 101 (3 3 monthwd)
          6: 102 (4 4 number)
      24: 315 (5 6 m-hourforms) (HR0)
        7: 111 (5 5 hrmkr)
        16: 113 (6 6 u-hourforms) (HR1)
          dshour *in 113's bindvar sets source starthr to (3 0 ?) via* **ig-hour**
          9: 4 (6 6 number)

Figure 7-6: Converting an APT to a database action record using *bindvars* to indicate record fields & instance generators to produce canonical values.

The figure shows that the value of the *action* field is computed by the resolution-time instance generator, **ig-act**, when the token **daction** is found on the *ROOT* step's *bindvar* list. **Ig-act** chooses the database action **remove** for pc204 predicated upon the class of the root node (**deleteforms**). Steps 705, 709, and 401 do not contribute to the record but step 403's *bindvar* list contains **dggtype.** Since no *bindvar* list containing the label **target** has been encountered in our recursive descent, we know that we should fill the *ggtype* field of the *source* database record. Again, a resolution-time ig is invoked (**ig-mrgg**) to return a canonical value—in this case the token **meeting.** Just as the value produced for the *action* field relied on the class of the root node rather than the token acting as verb, producing the value **meeting** for the *ggtype* field relies on the class of pc56 (**meetingforms**) rather than the token bound to the step seeking the head noun (step 309). By building database records with canonical values we preserve the important information in the meaning structure even when the referring phrase is unknown, as in the substitution in our example, or when the referring phrase is missing, as in a deletion of the head noun. In other words, every APT refers to some kind of action and object in the domain—the APT rooted at pc204 hypothesizes the existence of a meeting regardless of the actual referring phrase. The canonical value makes comparison against records in the calendar database both easier and more constraining. Consider that if we had filled the *ggtype* field with the previously unencountered token **mtg** instead of **meeting,** comparison against actual database records could result in a partial match at best.

Both the *date* and *starthr* fields in the source record are filled by canonical values computed (and cached) by expand-time instance generators. Step 303 provides the *source date* through **ddate** and **ig-date.** Similarly, step 113 provides the *source starthr* through **dshour** and **ig-hour.** Interpreting the single hour ("at 3") as the *starthr* rather than the *endhr* is an inference that is forced by placing the label **dshour** in step 113's *bindvar* list. The inference stems from the observation that people often do not indicate a definite ending time for an appointment when they schedule it [42].

When the twelve APTs produced by the Parse/Recovery Cycle for our sample sentence have been converted to database action records, four equivalence classes are formed. Figure 7-7 shows that, in terms of effect, the discriminating factor among the explanations is the kind of **groupgathering** object each expects to find in the database. Thus, explanations 1, 5, and 9 (from Figure 7-1) correspond to the removal of a meeting entry from the database, explanations 2, 6, and 10 correspond to the removal of a seminar, 3, 7, and 11 correspond to the removal of a class, and 4, 8, and 12 to the removal of a meal. These equivalence classes stand in contrast with the original grouping in Figure 7-1 which organized the explanations according to similarities in the error recovery combinations.

Action Record for 1, 5 & 9	Action Record for 2, 6 & 10	Action Record for 3, 7 & 11	Action Record for 4, 8 & 12
action remove	action remove	action remove	action remove
source	source	source	source
date (6 5 *)	date (6 5 *)	date (6 5 *)	date (6 5 *)
ggtype meeting	ggtype seminar	ggtype class	ggtype meal
starthr (3 0 ?)	starthr (3 0 ?)	starthr (3 0 ?)	starthr (3 0 ?)
endhr nil	endhr nil	endhr nil	endhr nil
target nil	target nil	target nil	target nil

Figure 7-7: The initial database action records defining four equivalence classes for the explanations in Figure 7-1 (some nil fields suppressed).

As a final observation concerning the database action records produced by the first step in resolution, note that the value left by **ig-hour** remains unresolved in terms of the twenty-four hour clock representation that CHAMP uses internally, and that the *ggtype* **meal** remains unresolved in terms of the choices defined for the domain (breakfast, lunch, and dinner). The problem of transforming unresolved values into values that can be compared against the database brings us to the topic of default knowledge and inference.

7.2. Using default knowledge and inference

One of the early arguments against natural language interfaces to database systems was that user utterances would fail to express legal database commands (see, for example, [56, 72, 54]). Critics observed that in ordinary language use people tend to leave some necessary information implicit, relying on the listener to make use of common knowledge and commonsense reasoning.[31] Interface designers have reacted to the criticism by providing rudimentary forms of the same abilities in their systems. In CHAMP we allow for the user's imprecision by detecting missing information and unresolved values during resolution and using default information and inference to compensate.

Exactly what constitutes necessary but missing information depends upon how the database functions are implemented. In CHAMP the database record fields that require values are determined by the database function in the *action* field and the domain represented by the type field (*ggtype* indicates the calendar domain, *triptype*

[31]Critics also argue that natural language encourages users to form requests outside the system's capabilities—an issue we will not address.

indicates the travel domain). Figure 7-8 displays the relationships. In most cases, only a date must be present in the utterance. When adding an entry to the calendar, however, the *starthr* and *location* fields must also be filled if the object is a **groupgathering**, while the *departure* and *destination* fields must also be filled if the object is a type of trip. **Alter** inherits its requirements from **remove** and **insert** because an **alter** action is implemented as a **remove** of the source followed by an **insert** of the target.

	calendar	travel
retrieve:	date	none
remove:	date	date
insert	date starthr location	date departure destination
alter:	source same as remove target same as insert	source same as remove target same as insert

Figure 7-8: The database record fields that require values, as determined by the database action and the type of database object.

Since the entry for "remove" and "calendar" in Figure 7-8 contains only **date**, we conclude that the database action records in Figure 7-7 have no missing information. The records do, however, have unresolved values. What constitutes an unresolved value also depends upon what the database functions expect. CHAMP's database functions expect dates to be represented as a list containing integers for the day, month, and year, although the year may be represented by a wildcard (*) which indicates "any value." Hours are expected to be represented as wildcards or single integers between zero and 2400 that encode the hour and minutes in the obvious way. Values filling the *location* field must be a list with two elements in the calendar domain, either element may be a wildcard. The grammar and instance generators enforce the convention that the first element in the list corresponds to a major location (a building, school, or business) while the second element is reserved for a room name or room number (5409 or office, for example). In the travel domain, a location must be a major location or the name of a city.

The database functions also expect that one of a fixed set of values fills the *action*, *ggtype*, and *triptype* fields. As we have mentioned, the *action* field must contain one of **remove, insert, alter,** or **retrieve**. The *ggtype* must be one of **meeting, seminar, class, breakfast, lunch,** or **dinner**. The *triptype* field must hold one of **air** or **nonair**.

Given these expectations we see that there are three unresolved values among the database action records in Figure 7-7: neither the *starthr* nor *endhr* have the appropriate form, and the token **meal** is an invalid *ggtype*.

Missing or unresolved values may be corrected by copying default values from the Concept Hierarchy (Section 4.3) or by inference. Consider, for example, the sentence

"Schedule a Prodigy meeting on June 12."

Figure 7-8 shows that the database action record for this utterance must have a *starthr* and *location* in addition to the date that is present. The **meeting** concept provides the default location (*** office**) but no time information to fill the *starthr* or resolve the **nil** *endhr*. We change a **nil** *endhr* to a wildcard based upon the the domain-dependent inference (justified in [42]) that a missing *endhr* reflects an intent by the user to leave the ending time open. To set the *starthr*, CHAMP uses a domain-independent inference and tries substituting the last *starthr* mentioned.

In total, CHAMP has seven strategies to compensate for missing or unresolved values:

- APPLY-DEFAULTS retrieves default values from the Concept Hierarchy based upon the concepts represented in the record fields (another reason that canonical values are important).
- ADJUST-GIVEN-TIMES converts a **groupgathering** time in the form (hour min ?) to a 24-hour value using the inference that an hour between one and seven should be post-meridian. The function also converts unresolved times for non-air trips by user interaction (unresolved times for flights are inferred by ADJUST-FLIGHTINFO).
- ADJUST-EMPTY-TIMES converts to wildcards all unspecified times that are not required by the domain and action.
- ADJUST-FLIGHTINFO is used when the *triptype* is **air** to fill in the complete airline database record from the information in the utterance. If, for example, a flight number is given by the user, then the destination and departure time can be retrieved by looking up the flight in the airline schedule. Similarly, if a destination and departure are given, a unique flight number may be available.
- ADJUST-MEAL is invoked only when the *ggtype* is the unresolved value **meal**. This strategy checks the *starthr* to ascertain the most likely meal. If no *starthr* is given then it replaces the database action record containing *ggtype* **meal** with three new database action records: one each for **breakfast**, **lunch**, and **dinner**.
- LAST-VALUE tries to retrieve a missing, required value from the database action record for the last utterance CHAMP successfully understood. Clearly, LAST-VALUE is not guaranteed to succeed. If the previous interaction was of the wrong type, for example, the desired value will not be available (as when the current utterance is missing a flight destination but the previous utterance concerned a seminar).

- TRANSFER-VALUE is used only for the **alter** action which requires a full target database record; the strategy is responsible for preserving the appropriate values from the source in the target.

The first five strategies in the list are domain-dependent, the last two are domain-independent. Taken together, LAST-VALUE and TRANSFER-VALUE are a weak mechanism for handling some types of ellipsis.

The order in which the seven inference strategies are applied will, in general, affect the contents of the database record produced. If, for example, we apply ADJUST-MEAL before APPLY-DEFAULTS we will have access to the default *starthr* available in the Concept Hierarchy for each of breakfast, lunch, and dinner. If, on the other hand, we do not apply ADJUST-GIVEN-TIMES before ADJUST-MEAL we may not be able to use the *starthr* to determine which meal is most likely. The application order used by CHAMP is shown in the algorithm APPLY-DEFAULT-LOGIC (Figure 7-9). It is not the only possible ordering, nor does it always produce correct results, but it does something useful most of the time.[32] The strategy TRANSFER-VALUE does not appear in the algorithm; it is used only by the database function ALTER (described in Section 7.3).

```
APPLY-DEFAULT-LOGIC (database action records)
FOR EACH database action record, DO
   ADJUST-GIVEN-TIMES                                              (1)
   IF the type of the record is air THEN ADJUST-FLIGHTINFO         (2)
   IF the type of the record is meal THEN ADJUST-MEAL              (3)
   IF there are missing required values THEN APPLY-DEFAULTS        (4)
   ADJUST-EMPTY-TIMES                                              (5)
UNLESS there are records that are complete
   try to fill missing fields in each record using LAST-VALUE      (6)
RETURN only records without missing information                    (7)
```

Figure 7-9: CHAMP's algorithm for using default knowledge & inference.

Notice that the algorithm returns only completed database records (step (7)). This guarantees that the database functions have available the information they need to perform their actions. It also means that APPLY-DEFAULT-LOGIC may change the number of equivalence classes formed by the conversion process in the previous section. To see how this might happen, consider the sentence

"Forget meeting June 12."

[32]We evaluate the degree to which CHAMP's accuracy suffers because of its inferences in Chapter 9.

in which "forget" is unknown. Using the kernel grammar, the Parse/Recovery Cycle produces two roots for this sentence: an **addform** and a **deleteform.** During the first step of resolution, each root, in turn, becomes a distinct database action record (one with the action set to **insert**, the other with the action set to **remove**), creating two equivalence classes of roots with one member in each class. The **remove** action requires only the date that is present. The **insert** action, however, requires each of a date, location, and start time. Thus, after applying default logic only one equivalence class remains—the existence of the complete **remove** record blocks the call to LAST-VALUE (step (6)) that might have compensated for the missing values in the **insert** record. Since the explanation hypothesizing a **remove** requires fewer inferences than the explanation hypothesizing an **insert**, **remove** is preferred.

The effect of the inference process on the database action records in Figure 7-7 is shown in Figure 7-10. ADJUST-GIVEN-TIMES infers that the value **(3 0 ?)** should be 3 p.m., and replaces the old value with **1500.** Subsequently, ADJUST-MEAL notices that 3 p.m. is more likely to be lunch than dinner or breakfast and replaces **meal** with **lunch.** Since the *endhr* field is not required by the combination of **remove** and the calendar domain, ADJUST-EMPTY-TIMES sets the *endhr* to a wildcard.

Final Record for 1, 5 & 9	Final Record for 2, 6 & 10	Final Record for 3, 7 & 11	Final Record for 4, 8 & 12
action remove	action remove	action remove	action remove
source	source	source	source
date (6 5 *)	date (6 5 *)	date (6 5 *)	date (6 5 *)
ggtype meeting	ggtype seminar	ggtype class	ggtype lunch
starthr 1500	starthr 1500	starthr 1500	starthr 1500
endhr *	endhr *	endhr *	endhr *
target nil	target nil	target nil	target nil

Figure 7-10: The database action records defining the four equivalence classes for the explanations in Figure 7-1 after default logic has been applied (compare to Figure 7-7).

With the conversion and inference steps complete a set of database action records are available that are "syntactically correct" from the point of view of the database functions. We are ready, therefore, to tackle the question, "Can the intended action be performed?"

7.3. Interacting with the databases

At the beginning of a session CHAMP must be told which domain to work with: calendar, travel or both. If the choice is "calendar," the system has access to a collection of database records, organized by their *date* fields, which we have been calling the calendar. If the response is "travel" or "both," CHAMP has access to the calendar as well as an auxiliary collection of database records representing an airline schedule. Acting on these databases are the four database functions that serve CHAMP's two domains: REMOVE, INSERT, ALTER, and RETRIEVE. All four functions are defined as operations on the calendar. RETRIEVE is defined as an operation on the airline schedule as well.

In the process of performing the user's intended database action it may be necessary to call any of the database functions in either of two ways: for virtual effect or for actual effect. A synopsis of each function's response under each condition is shown in Figure 7-11. Although the action ultimately taken by each database function is fairly straightforward, the "virtual" effect may not be. In essence, when we call a database function for virtual effect we are looking for the result of a comparison between the information in the source database record and the entries in the calendar on the source date (or in the airline schedule, regardless of date). The purpose of the comparison depends upon the function and is reflected by the kind of error that may occur. If we ultimately wish to INSERT a new calendar entry then we must make sure that the new entry times do not overlap with previously scheduled appointments. If we are trying to REMOVE a calendar entry then such an entry must exist, and the match between the entry we wish to remove and the entry that is present must be close, although not necessarily exact. ALTERing an entry is essentially the same as removing one record and inserting another; thus, any of the errors that might occur during a REMOVE or INSERT might occur during an ALTER as well. In contrast to REMOVE and ALTER, an empty entry for a particular calendar day is not considered an error by RETRIEVE; a response of "There are no appointments for that day." may well have been what the user wanted.

Comparisons against the calendar for REMOVE and ALTER are permitted to be only partially successful. This allows CHAMP to compensate for erroneous knowledge on the part of the user (as in EXAMPLE 2 of Figure 7-3) and to overcome the need for canonical values in all record fields. By permitting a partial match, an appointment "about finances" may still be cancelled by an utterance referring to "the financial meeting." EXAMPLE 1 of Figure 7-3 demonstrates that when a perfect match occurs, those alternatives are offered to the user first.

INSERT (database action record)
    virtual effect: returns database record to be added or *overlap* error
    actual effect: inserts record in calendar on date

REMOVE (database action record)
    virtual effect: returns database record(s) matched, *nomatch* or *noevents* error
    actual effect: removes intended record from calendar

ALTER (database action record)
    virtual effect: returns one or more pairs of database records in which the first record matched and the second record is to be added, or *overlap*, *nomatch*, or *noevents* error
    actual effect: removes intended record and inserts corresponding new record

RETRIEVE (database action record)
    virtual effect: returns record(s) to be displayed from appropriate database
    actual effect: displays record(s) or *emptyday* message

Figure 7-11: The four database functions and the effects they may produce.

To see how the match process works, we switch our attention from the sentence in Figure 7-3 to the sentence

"Change the June 5 mtg from 3-4 pm to 1-2 pm."

In this case the Parse/Recovery Cycle produces only four explanations, interpreting "mtg" as each of a possible **seminarwd**, **meetingwd**, **classwd**, and **mealwd**. The four database action records produced by conversion and inference are shown in Figure 7-12. Notice that at this point the target database records contain only the *starthr* and *endhr*—the values that are explicitly given in the utterance.

Record1 (pc381)	Record2 (pc382)	Record3 (pc383)	Record4 (pc384)
action alter	action alter	action alter	action alter
source	source	source	source
date (6 5 *)	date (6 5 *)	date (6 5 *)	date (6 5 *)
ggtype meeting	ggtype seminar	ggtype class	ggtype lunch
starthr 1500	starthr 1500	starthr 1500	starthr 1500
endhr 1600	endhr 1600	endhr 1600	endhr 1600
target	target	target	target
starthr 1300	starthr 1300	starthr 1300	starthr 1300
endhr 1400	endhr 1400	endhr 1400	endhr 1400

Figure 7-12: The database action records defining 4 equivalence classes for explanations of "Change the June 5 mtg from 3-4 pm to 1-2 pm."

The virtual effect of a call to ALTER for each of these four database action records is shown in Figure 7-13 for one set of June fifth calendar entries. For CALENDAR1, Record1 of Figure 7-12 is a perfect match to entry r3. ALTER records the fact that the match was perfect and that r3 is the record to be removed from the calendar if the effect being constructed is eventually chosen. Record2, Record3, and Record4 of Figure 7-12 produce only partial matches to CALENDAR1; the matches for Record2 and Record4 come from their *ggtypes*, while Record3's match stems from its *starthr* and *endhr* values.

CALENDAR1 for (6 5 *)
    r1 starthr 1000 endhr 1200 ggtype seminar location (* 5409) topic ai
    r2 starthr 1200 endhr 1300 ggtype lunch location (* *)
    r3 starthr 1500 endhr 1600 ggtype meeting location (* office) participants ed

ALTER (Record1):
(perfect r3 (date (6 5 *) starthr 1300 endhr 1400 ggtype meeting
        location (* office) participants ed))

ALTER (Record2):
(partial r1 (date (6 5 *) starthr 1300 endhr 1400 ggtype seminar
        location (* 5409) topic ai))

ALTER (Record3):
(partial r3 (date (6 5 *) starthr 1300 endhr 1400 ggtype class location (* 5409))

ALTER (Record4):
(partial r2 (date (6 5 *) starthr 1300 endhr 1400 ggtype lunch location (* *)))

Figure 7-13: The values returned by calls to ALTER for virtual effect for database action records in Figure 7-12 under CALENDAR1.

Along with the degree of match and a pointer to the record to be removed, ALTER's virtual effect includes a record to be added to the calendar. To create the new record, ALTER calls TRANSFER-VALUE (see Figure 7-14) which uses the source record and the matched record to fill in fields in the target. In general, the algorithm works well if the source type and matched type are the same (Record1, Record2, and Record4 in Figure 7-12, for example), or if the target type differs from the matched type but is given explicitly in the utterance (as in "Change the meeting at 4 to a seminar at 5"). The algorithm tends to give less reliable results when the target type is copied from the source and differs from the matched type (as for Record3 in Figure 7-13 where TRANSFER-VALUE changes the partially matched meeting from 3 p.m. to 4 p.m. in the office with Ed to a class from 1 p.m. to 2 p.m. in room 5409).

TRANSFER-VALUE (source record, target record, match record)
IF the type field of the target is unspecified (1)
THEN copy the source type
FOR EACH empty target field, DO (2)
  IF the target type and match type are the same (3)
  THEN IF the source is empty OR a default AND the match field is not empty
      THEN copy the match value to the target
      ELSE copy the source value to the target
  ELSE IF the field is required (4)
    THEN IF the source field is specified
      THEN copy the source value to the target
      ELSE copy the match value to the target

Figure 7-14: The TRANSFER-VALUE algorithm for preserving information when ALTERing a value in a database record.

The virtual effects produced by ALTER for the same database action records but a different set of calendar entries are shown in Figure 7-15. CALENDAR2 contains the same seminar entry as CALENDAR1 in Figure 7-13 but does not contain CALENDAR1's lunch entry and has different times for the meeting entry. In fact, since r5's *starthr* and *endhr* no longer correspond to those expected by any of the database action records, Record1 is now only partially matched by r5, while Record3 and Record4 have no match at all.

CALENDAR2 for (6 5 *)
  r4 starthr 1000 endhr 1200 ggtype seminar location (* 5409) topic ai
  r5 starthr 1600 endhr 1700 ggtype meeting location (* office) participants ed

ALTER (Record1):
(partial r5 (date (6 5 *) starthr 1300 endhr 1400 ggtype meeting
    location (* office) participants ed))

ALTER (Record2):
(partial r4 (date (6 5 *) starthr 1300 endhr 1400 ggtype seminar
    location (* 5409) general-topic ai))

ALTER (Record3): (error nomatch 5)

ALTER (Record4): (error nomatch 5)

Figure 7-15: The values returned by calls to ALTER for virtual effect for database action records in Figure 7-12 under CALENDAR2.

If we look back at Figure 7-4, the RESOLVE algorithm, we see that the equivalence classes that were originally created by distinctions in the database action records must ultimately be organized by virtual effect (step (3)). The results returned by ALTER did not change the root's equivalence classes under CALENDAR1—each database action record (representing a unique root) produced a distinct effect. Under CALENDAR2, however, Record3 and Record4 produce the same effect, a "nomatch" error. Figure 7-12 showed the correspondence between roots and database action records. Figure 7-16 shows the pairings of roots to effects under each set of calendar entries.

Roots	Effect under CALENDAR1
(381)	(perfect r3 (date (6 5 *) starthr 1300 endhr 1400 ggtype meeting...)
(382)	(partial r1 (date (6 5 *) starthr 1300 endhr 1400 ggtype seminar...)
(383)	(partial r3 (date (6 5 *) starthr 1300 endhr 1400 ggtype meeting...)
(384)	(partial r2 (date (6 5 *) starthr 1300 endhr 1400 ggtype lunch...)

Roots	Effect under CALENDAR2
(381)	(partial r4 (date (6 5 *) starthr 1300 endhr 1400 ggtype meeting...)
(382)	(partial r5 (date (6 5 *) starthr 1300 endhr 1400 ggtype seminar...)
(383 384)	(error nomatch 5)

Figure 7-16: The equivalence classes of roots for "Change the mtg from 3-4 p.m. to 1-2 p.m." as determined by effect under two calendars.

The first three steps in the resolution process are responsible for creating database action records, applying inferences and default reasoning, and mapping completed records into sets of equivalent virtual effects. If these steps result in a single set for all roots then all the explanations produced by the Parse/Recovery Cycle were effectively equivalent. If the roots were at Deviation-level 0 and the effect is not an error, then confidence in the explanation is high enough to simply take the proposed action (step (4) of the RESOLVE algorithm). Under the circumstances where all the roots lead to errors, an error message is chosen and no action is taken (step (5)). The roots for "Change the mtg from 3-4 p.m. to 1-2 p.m.," correspond to neither of these conditions; the roots succeed at Deviation-level 1 and create multiple possible effects (not all of which are errors) under both CALENDAR1 and CALENDAR2. With no more knowledge available to help the system determine the correct action, CHAMP must turn to the user in the final step of the resolution process.

7.4. Confirmation by effect

By the time it reaches the last stage of resolution, the system knows which roots correspond to possible database actions and which do not. It also knows which of the possible effects resulted from perfect matches against the contents of the calendar (or airline schedule) and which from only partial matches. These two pieces of information make the USERQUERY algorithm (called in step (6) of Figure 7-4) extremely simple: first ask the user to choose from among the effects caused by perfect matches, then, if no choice was acceptable (or no matches perfect), offer the effects caused by partial matches. In this way the system receives confirmation of a subset of explanations by displaying the subset's corresponding effect. Once a single, legal database action has been determined, the appropriate database function is reinvoked for "actual effect."

Figure 7-3 showed the choices offered by USERQUERY for the sentence, "Cancel the mtg June 5 at 3" under three sets of calendar contents. The choices offered by USERQUERY for "Change the June 5 mtg from 3-4 p.m. to 1-2 p.m." under CALENDAR1 and CALENDAR2 are shown in Figure 7-17. In EXAMPLE 4, the user chooses the single effect that has survived the resolution process to this point. Effects corresponding to the partial matches in ALTER for CALENDAR1 would be offered to the user only if she finds the perfect match unacceptable. By confirming the effect, the user causes the change to be made to the calendar. She also unknowingly reduces the number of explanations for the utterance from four to one; only the tree rooted at pc381 is passed along to the adaptation and generalization mechanism.

In EXAMPLE 5, none of the alternatives offered to the user were what she intended by the utterance. Since the choices correspond to partial matches, the system has no options left but to continue to search for new explanations at higher deviation-levels. The continuation message is given when the deviation-level of the roots is less than the maximum deviation-level deviation-level permitted by the system (two in CHAMP). If the maximum deviation-level has already been reached the user is told instead to "Please try again" (see EXAMPLE 3 in Figure 7-3). When no effect is confirmed by the user, no database action takes place and no root nodes are passed to the adaptation and generalization mechanism.

We pointed out in Chapter 4 that although the user has a single task (making changes to the calendar), CHAMP has two tasks: performing the database actions requested by the user and learning the user's language. The purpose of resolution from the user's point of view (indeed, the purpose of the system) is to produce her

EXAMPLE 4 assumes CALENDAR1 from Figure 7-13:

Do you want:
  to change: JUNE 5 3:00pm - 4:00pm MEETING in/at OFFICE with ED
          to JUNE 5 1:00pm - 2:00pm MEETING in/at OFFICE with ED?
[y or n]: y

Ok, done.
(returning roots: 381)

EXAMPLE 5 assumes CALENDAR2 from Figure 7-15:

Do you want:
(0) to change: JUNE 5 4:00pm - 5:00pm MEETING in/at OFFICE with ED
          to JUNE 5 1:00pm - 2:00pm MEETING in/at OFFICE with ED?
(1) to change: JUNE 5 10:00am - 12:00pm AI SEMINAR in/at 5409
          to JUNE 5 1:00pm - 2:00pm AI SEMINAR in/at 5409?
(2) none of the above
[number between 0 and 2]: 2

Ok, continuing...
(returning roots: nil)

Figure 7-17: Examples of user interaction for "Change the June 5 mtg from 3-4 p.m. to 1-2 p.m."

intended effect. The purpose of resolution from CHAMP's point of view, however, is both to produce the intended effect and to find the single correct explanation of the utterance. What role should the system's added task play in user interaction? The answer in CHAMP is: none. The interaction is designed to offer the user the most intelligent choices possible by using inference and the constraints imposed by the contents of the calendar and airline databases. By considering the nature of the interaction from the user's point of view we gain ease of interaction for the user at the cost of being able to guarantee a unique explanation for the utterance. Still, the examples in this chapter demonstrate how the process of arriving at the user's intended effect can also significantly reduce the number of explanations that must be considered meaningful. As a result, we know that the APTs preserved by resolution correspond to the minimum set of explanations generated by the current grammar that capture the effective meaning of the utterance. It is from this minimum set that user derived forms are constructed through adaptation and generalization.

Chapter 8

Adaptation and Generalization

In Chapter 6 we transformed CHAMP from a bottom-up parser to a least-deviant-first parser by adding error recovery to the system. While error recovery allows CHAMP to accept a larger language than the kernel grammar alone, the average cost of acceptance (and rejection) increases; although we apply constraints at every opportunity, the fact is that search expanded to a non-zero deviation-level is always larger than a grammatical search would be for the same utterance. If we can modify the grammar to recognize a deviant form directly, subsequent encounters with that deviation will not require error recovery at all. Thus, future sentences containing the deviation will succeed at lower deviation-levels, requiring less search. Giving CHAMP the ability to learn new grammatical components transforms the system from a simple least-deviant-first parser to a least-deviant-first *adaptive* parser.

Modifications to the grammar come about after error recovery has formed one or more hypotheses explaining a deviation (see Figure 4-1 at the beginning of Chapter 4). The process of transforming one or more hypothetical explanations (APTs) into an appropriate set of new grammar components is what we mean by *adaptation.* Out of the potential set of component types—lexemes, lexical definitions, wordclasses, steps, forms, form annotation nodes, and formclasses—we must choose the subset that best responds to each type of recovery notation.

To understand the issues involved in adaptation, consider Figure 8-1, the APT produced at Deviation-level 2 for User 1's third sentence in her first experimental session (U1S13). The APT rooted at pc81 contains the four pieces of information that define the *adaptation context* for U1S13:

1. The particular grammatical constituents needed to understand the utterance.
2. The order in which the constituents appeared in the sentence.
3. The particular forms used to recognize the constituents.
4. The recovery actions needed to modify one or more of the forms.

An extremely conservative approach to adaptation would capture as much of the adaptation context as possible. The result would be a set of highly specialized new components derived, for example, from the steps in boldface in Figure 8-1. Following the structure of the APT, first we would create a new **deleteform** with two ordered steps, 705 and 709', where 709' seeks a new subclass of **m-d-ggforms** with a form whose steps list contains only 403'. In turn, 403' would seek a new subclass of **meetingforms** with a form whose steps list contains, in order, step 305, a new step created to look for the tokens **%apostrophe s**, and steps 307, 309, and 316.

U1S13: "Cancel [the] John>'s< speech research meeting on June 9."
Tokens: (cancel john %apostrophe s speech research meeting on june 9 %period)

81: *ROOT* (0 9 deleteforms) (ACT2) 2
  1: **705** (0 0 deletewd)
  70: **709** (1 9 m-d-ggforms) (DGG1) (2 (DELETE 401))
    46: **403** (1 9 meetingforms) (GG1) (1 (INSERT 0))
      17: **305** (1 1 u-personforms) (IFPERSON1)
        2: 118 (1 1 studentname)
      0: **0** (2 3 unknown) nil 1
      19: **307** (4 5 u-subjectforms) (IFSUBJ)
        3: 129 (4 5 subjname)
      4: **309** (6 6 meetingwd)
      23: **316** (7 9 m-dateforms) (DATE0)
        5: 201 (7 7 dtmkr)
        20: 203 (8 9 u-dateforms) (DATE1)
          6: 101 (8 8 monthwd)
          9: 102 (9 9 number)
  10: 799 (10 10 eosmkr)

Figure 8-1: User 1's first sentence and its explanation (steps in boldface are sources of adaptation in an extremely conservative approach).

This sort of interpretation, corresponding to little more than rote memorization of the utterance, is clearly too extreme. Yet, how much of the information in the adaptation context should we pay attention to? Expressed differently, which of the available pieces of information correspond to the appropriate conditions on usage? Will User 1 always drop the article when the action is **delete** and the object is a **groupgathering**? Will she drop the article *only* under these circumstances? Can the tokens **%apostrophe s** appear anywhere among the prenominal segments of a **meetingform**, or are those tokens always a reliable indication of a preceding unmarked participant? Must the participant always be a student? Must the object always be a **meetingform**? Do we gain anything in terms of reduced search or increased accuracy of interpretation if we can make that discrimination?

What we want to extract from an explained deviation is a set of new grammatical components with two properties: first, the components must be accessible during future parses to understand this sentence *and others like it* directly. Second, and just as important, the new components must not add unduly to the cost of understanding sentences in which they ultimately play no role. Thus, the main issue in adaptive parsing, as in most kinds of learning, is the issue of generalization.

What we mean by generalization in CHAMP is the transformation of the adaptation context into new grammatical components that capture the correct conditions on usage of the deviation. Our goal is to construct the new components for the grammar without either undergeneralizing or overgeneralizing the recovery. Undergeneralization occurs when a component that can explain a segment of the utterance is inaccessible to the parser. For example, when User 1 types, "Move Anderson seminar on June 10 to room 7220" (U1S19), we might tie the previously unknown token **move** to a form that expects a change in the *location* field. Such an adaptation undergeneralizes the actual conditions on usage, as demonstrated by U1S39: "Move PRODIGY meeting on June 11 to 3-4." By tying **move** to the expectation of a change in location, we made it impossible to understand without further adaptation that **move** may also indicate a change in time.

Overgeneralization occurs when a component that plays no role in the APT for an utterance nevertheless creates search paths during the parse. Suppose we had separate kernel forms for the **change** action for each field in a calendar database record. In other words, CHANGE1 would alter the *location* field, CHANGE2 would alter the *participants* field, and so on. Suppose further that all the CHANGE forms shared a step seeking a **changewd**. If we add **move** to the wordclass **changewd** we will prevent the undergeneralization described previously—the parser will treat **move** as a valid verb for either a change in time or a change in location. The new lexical definition overgeneralizes, however; each time **move** is encountered in the future, the parser will have to consider the token as a potential reference to each **changeform**, despite the fact that the word is used in only two ways.

While some type of generalization is needed, the **move** example shows that any mechanism we choose is likely to include or omit appropriate conditions some of the time. When generalizing from a single example this is to be expected. Since there is likely to be a discrepancy between the user's true idiosyncratic conditions on usage and those we can represent, our goal in choosing an adaptation method cannot be absolute accuracy. Instead, we strive for a principled trade-off between increasing linguistic coverage and controlling the increase in search that can result from extending the grammar. We achieve our goal by way of three assumptions:

1. The only portion of the adaptation context that is relevant to learning is the constituent in which the recovery notation occurs (the *local context*).
2. The shared hierarchical structure of the grammar enforces the appropriate degree of generalization.
3. When more than one method of adaptation can bring the deviation into the grammar in a reasonable way, the method that minimizes the actual or potential increase in the size and ambiguity of the grammar is preferable.

The first assumption offers some protection from undergeneralization by reducing the set of potentially relevant conditions on usage to those found locally in the deviant constituent. The second assumption offers some protection from overgeneralization by tying the conditions on usage into the relationships already present in the Formclass Hierarchy. The third assumption offers a guideline for choosing among adaptation methods that conform to the first two assumptions. The third assumption can be paraphrased as: keep the size of the search space at Deviation-level 0 under control. To do this we may have to consider not just the immediate effect of an adaptation on search, but also long-term effects that stem from the introduction of learning biases. When we consider the effects of adaptation on search, we often find that CHAMP's bottom-up parsing style is better suited to compensate for overgeneralization than for undergeneralization in its learning methods.

The remainder of this chapter explores the co-processes of adaptation and generalization in CHAMP. In the next four sections we examine in detail the specific grammatical augmentations associated with each of the recovery actions. In Section 8.5 we tie the individual types of adaptation together under the control of the ADAPT algorithm. Section 8.6 discusses the potential explosion in the size of the grammar that can occur when the Parse/Recovery Cycle produces multiple, effectively equivalent hypotheses; the explosion is controlled by adding a competition mechanism to the basic process of adaptation. In the last section in this chapter we present a detailed example of the effects of adaptation on both system and user performance.

8.1. Adapting to substitution deviations

A substitution is identified by error recovery when there is an unknown word or phrase available to fill an unsatisfied, required step. At first glance the appropriate adaptation for this situation seems simple: create a new lexical definition for the unknown word or phrase as a member of the class sought by the required step. We call this a *liberal* approach to adaptation for substitutions because it ignores the adaptation context completely and relies solely on the Formclass Hierarchy to enforce conditions on usage. Although this is exactly the solution implemented in CHAMP, there are other possible methods for adapting to substitution deviations that are less extreme. It is important to understand what we gain and what we lose by a liberal choice.

To illustrate the trade-offs, let us suppose that we have an explanation requiring a substitution in step *k* of form S1 in Figure 8-2. If we add the new word or phrase to the lexicon as an instance of **class4**, every form containing a step that seeks that wordclass will now recognize the new phrase. This generalization across the grammar is a natural effect of the grammar's shared structure.

```
S1                      S2
  isa class1              isa class1
  steps                   steps
    i class class2          j class class3
    k class class4          k class class4
  rnode (i k)             rnode (j k)
```

Figure 8-2: An example of potential overgeneralization under the liberal approach. Adding a phrase to **class4** as a response to a substitution in S1 generalizes to S2 despite the critical differences between the forms.

In particular, the new phrase will be accepted by S2. Observe, however, that S1 requires step *i* and S2 requires step *j*—a critical difference between the two forms. Since the hypothetical utterance is explainable by a substitution in S1 (and not by a substitution in S2) we can conclude that step *i* was satisfied and step *j* was not. Thus, the liberal approach ignores part of the adaptation context inherent in the presence of *i* and the absence of *j*. Yet it is precisely the retention of this type of local context that we assumed was important in the previous section.

Ignoring local context eliminates the possibility of capturing a reliable co-occurrence of co-constituents. To the extent that the co-occurrence is a real condition on usage, ignoring it overgeneralizes the conditions under which paths relying on the new component are considered during search. User 1, for example, substitutes the word "move" for a kernel member of **changewd** at the end of her first experimental session. The substitution occurs in the context of ACT3, a **changeform** whose steps seek a **changewd**, a marked **groupgathering**, and a source-target pair. The fifteen subsequent occurrences of **move** in User 1's log file also take place in the context of ACT3. Because CHAMP uses the liberal approach, however, the system simply learns "move" as a member of the class **changewd**; the reliable co-occurrence of "move" with a marked **groupgathering** and a source-target pair is lost. Since **changewd** is sought by a step shared among six kernel forms (three for each kernel domain), each time "move" is encountered after adaptation the list of forms it indexes may include all six, instead of just ACT3.

The liberal approach also prevents capturing the interdependence of a substitution deviation and another deviation in the constituent. Consider User 3's tenth sentence during session two (U3S210, Figure 8-3). The APT in the figure is only one of three explanations offered for the utterance at that point in the development of her grammar, but it is the only explanation relevant here (for the other explanations, see Figure 8-17 in Section 8.6). The sentence is explained by a substitution and transposition in ACT3 which expects an imperative form of the **change** command. In this utterance there is a clear relationship between the change in the verb's position and the change in its voice and tense. Unfortunately it is a relationship that is not captured by CHAMP. Learning the phrase "has been changed" as a member of **changewd** divorces the two deviations and overgeneralizes both the substitution and the transposition. Instead of suggesting only a highly specific set of predictions when the phrase is seen in subsequent interactions, the new lexical definition simply invokes the same predictions in the presence of "has been changed" as those invoked for any **changewd**. After adaptation those predictions include, but are not restricted to, the combined substitution and transposition.

A final limitation of the liberal approach to substitution adaptations is that it is insensitive to the value of the referring phrase. In other words, we cannot make discriminations based on the tokens themselves. We can only inherit from the shared structure of the grammar those discriminations already associated with the substituted wordclass.

Is it possible to capture critical differences between forms as conditions on usage, incorporate dependent adaptations into the same derived component, make discriminations based on the tokens themselves rather than their wordclass, and still rely on the shared structure of the grammar for generalization? The answer is "yes" if we adapt by the following procedure (the *conservative* approach):

1. Create a new wordclass, $\mathbf{subst}_i$.
2. Add the new word or phrase to the lexicon as an instance of $\mathbf{subst}_i$.
3. From the form that succeeded via the substitution (the *parent*), derive a new form to add to the grammar. The derived form is identical to its parent with two exceptions: first, the derived form must incorporate any other deviations in the constituent. Second, the steps list of the derived form contains a step seeking $\mathbf{subst}_i$ in place of the step that required the substitution.

U3210: "Lunch with VC on June 13, 1986 <u>*has been changed*</u> from Station Square
to VC Inc."

Abbreviated APT:
349: *ROOT* (0 17 changeforms) (ACT3) (2 (SUBST 0 706) (TRANS (0 80)))
  80: 709 (0 7 m-d-ggforms) (DGG2)
    66: 404 (0 7 mealforms) (GG4)
      1: 313 (0 0 mealwd)
      55: 319 (1 2 m-participantforms) (PART0) ...
      56: 316 (3 7 m-dateforms) (DATE0) ...
  0: 0 (8 10 unknown) nil 1
  86: 711 (11 16 stpforms) (STP1)
    70: 406 (11 13 locsrcforms) (LOCSRC1)
      12: 321 (11 11 sourcemkr)
      21: 304 (12 13 buildingforms) (LOC7)
        13: 133 (12 13 buildingname)
    72: 407 (14 16 loctgtforms) (LOCTGT1)
      15: 322 (14 14 targetmkr)
      49: 326 (15 16 u-locationforms) (IFLOC2)
        17: 114 (15 16 businessname)
  18: 799 (17 17 eosmkr)

Figure 8-3: An example of the interdependence of multiple deviations.

How does the conservative method compensate for the inadequacies of the liberal approach? By creating a new wordclass with only the new phrase as its member, the tokens themselves index the specific set of expectations represented by the derived form. Those expectations capture the local context in the deviant constituent by inheriting all the relationships present in the parent form (class, *unodes*, and so on) except the ones that gave rise to the substitution and any other deviation. By inheriting the parent's class, generalization occurs naturally through the Formclass Hierarchy; every location in the grammar that seeks a member of the new form's class now accepts the new form as a valid way of recognizing a member of that class.

The conservative approach solves some problems, but introduces others. Specifically, it undergeneralizes in a particularly harmful manner. To see how, consider Figure 8-4. The substitution of **mtg** for a recognizable **meetingwd** in the first sentence creates five APTs during the Parse/Recovery Cycle: one for each type of object left active after segmentation (the **flight** object is eliminated because AISys is not a legitimate flight destination). Interaction with the user during Resolution reduces the set to the single APT containing the substitution for a **meetingwd.** Conservative adaptation, in turn, adds GG1' to the grammar. GG1' looks for the token **mtg** specifically—a critical difference with respect to GG1. Note that the liberal approach would simply add **mtg** to **meetingwd**.

Si: "schedule AISys *mtg* on june 3 at 4 pm"
P/R: mtg/meetingwd, mtg/seminarwd, mtg/classwd, mtg/mealwd, mtg/tripwd
Resolution: mtg/meetingwd
Adaptation: mtg/$subst_1$, GG1' seeking $subst_1$

Sj: "schedule AISys *appt* on june 8 at 7 pm"
P/R: appt/meetingwd, appt/seminarwd, appt/classwd, appt/mealwd, appt/tripwd, appt/$subst_1$
Resolution: appt/meetingwd and appt/$subst_1$
Adaptation: appt/$subst_2$, GG1'' seeking $subst_2$

Sk: "schedule AISys [meeting] on june 11 at 11 am"
P/R: delete meetingwd, delete seminarwd, delete classwd, delete mealwd, delete tripwd, delete $subst_1$, delete $subst_2$
Resolution: delete meetingwd, delete $subst_1$, delete $subst_2$
Adaptation: GG1''' deleting meetingwd

Sl: "schedule *taxi* on june 15 at 3 pm"
P/R: taxi/meetingwd, taxi/seminarwd, taxi/classwd, taxi/mealwd, taxi/tripwd, taxi/$subst_1$, taxi/$subst_2$, insert taxi/GG1'''
Resolution: taxi/tripwd
Adaptation: taxi/$subst_3$, TRIP1' seeking $subst_3$

Figure 8-4: An example of the explosive growth in the search space caused by the conservative approach.

At some future point in time, the user types sentence *Sj*. Now *six* interpretations are produced by Parse/Recovery, the extra one stemming from a substitution in GG1' because the critical difference between GG1 and GG1' is not manifested in the utterance. Resolution can narrow the field only as far as an equivalence class containing GG1 and GG1'. In turn, conservative adaptation creates a derived form for each parent form. We assume that the system is smart enough to detect that the two derived forms are identical (because they posit the same substitution for the step that distinguishes their parents), and add only one of them (GG1'') to the adapted grammar. It is possible, however, to create a slight variation on GG1' through a transposition in a non-required case. Such a change would appear to be an additional critical difference between GG1 and GG1' to any straightforward test procedure, but would not be manifested by the utterances shown. Under those circumstances, derived forms for both GG1 and GG1' would be added to the grammar. In other words, had we chosen to make the example in the figure more complex, we could have created an exponential increase at each stage rather than a simple linear increase.[33] Note that under the liberal method, the amount of processing required to explain the second sentence would have been unaffected by the adaptation from the first sentence: the same four paths would have succeeded during Parse/Recovery, one explanation would have survived Resolution, and **appt** would have been added to the lexicon as a **meetingwd**.

If we move forward in time to sentence S*k* we find that the steady increase in processing time caused by the conservative approach may continue via other deviations as well. The figure shows that when the user drops the head noun altogether (a common occurrence), interpretations must be followed for each of *seven* paths despite the fact that three of the paths now correspond to the same effective meaning. Again, a smart algorithm would notice that the same derived component suffices for all three paths in this example and would create only GG1''' in response. Under a liberal approach, however, we would still have had only four paths succeed in Parse/Recovery and only one APT survive Resolution.

In the last sentence of the example, another substitution appears, but in a new object. To find the correct explanation we must now generate *eight* hypotheses at Deviation-level 1: seven substitutions and one insertion into the form that no longer requires the head noun. Under the liberal method we generate only five (the original four plus the insertion). Observe that the last incident of adaptation in the figure looks just like the first. Sentence S*l* starts the propagation of effectively equivalent forms in a new portion of the grammar.

In general we characterize the trade-off between the liberal and conservative approaches as one of overgeneralization versus undergeneralization (of course, less liberal or less conservative methods than those discussed would contain some combination of the problems of each the extremes). In CHAMP, the balance tips in favor of overgeneralization when we consider the relative increase in search under each approach. Figure 8-4 demonstrates that CHAMP is poorly suited to compensate for the effects of undergeneralization. When a substitution is tied to a critical difference between a parent and its derived form and that critical difference does not reflect a true condition on usage, future adaptations create multiple paths during Parse/Recovery. The equivalence of the interpretations along the paths cannot be established until the Resolution phase, *after* a lengthy search.

---

[33]Conservative adaptation algorithms for substitution and insertion were implemented in an early version of CHAMP. They produced the same kind of harmful expansion in the grammar (including instances of exponential growth) that is shown in this simplified example.

On the other hand, CHAMP is well-suited to compensate for overgeneralization. The system begins with a kernel grammar in which each form contains a critical difference with respect to every other form. The liberal method of adapting to substitutions does not change that situation; adding a new phrase to a wordclass leaves the relationships between the forms unaffected. If the user employs the new phrase in the full range of structures that seek the phrase's class, then liberal adaptation has generalized correctly. Even if the user employs the new phrase in only a subset of the structures indexed by its class, those structures are still critically different from the others in the set; the critical differences guarantee that the unsuccessful forms are weeded out early in the Parse/Recovery Cycle by COALESCABLE. In short, the shared structure of the grammar permits full generalization by the simple addition of a lexical definition, while the parsing algorithm takes advantage of the actual conditions on usage during search.

8.2. Adapting to insertion deviations

An insertion notation is added to an APT by error recovery whenever there is an unknown word or phrase in the utterance and at least one path through the search space with no unsatisfied, required steps. Since the inserted phrase is not tied to a step in the grammar, it has no associated *bindvar* and cannot contribute to the effective meaning constructed for the utterance during Resolution. A liberal response to an insertion deviation would simply add the phrase to the lexicon as a member of the wordclass **insert**, then throw away segments in that class in subsequent parses. In this way, the "insertion" generalizes to all locations in the grammar. The approach has two advantages: first, it is extremely efficient in both its implementation and performance. Second, it is intuitively appealing if the majority of insertions are truly content free.

In what sense might an inserted node carry information if it has no associated *bindvar* to map its tokens into a database field? If the deviation is employed consistently by the user, and only in certain contexts, then its presence could be taken as an indicator of those contexts. By acting as a predictor of a context, the existence of that segment in a future utterance would influence the space of explanations to be explored.

Unfortunately, an insertion deviation usually represents a family of contexts. Recall that the Parse/Recovery Cycle is designed to bubble the inserted node up to the highest constituent that captures it (see Section 6.5). The resulting APT is just a shorthand for a set of hypotheses that are recoverable by a procedure akin to a tree-walk (see Figure 8-5). We cannot know *a priori* which constituent, if any, will be consistently indexed by the inserted phrase. Consequently, to use the presence of the phrase as a reliable indicator of a context, we would have to create critically different new forms for all the interpretations and let future utterances determine the correct one (Section 8.6 demonstrates how this could be done).

```
U5S23: "Cancel class 15-731 on June 16>th< from 1:30-3:00."
Tokens: (cancel class 15 %hyphen 731 on june 16 th from 1 %colon 30 %hyphen 3
        %colon 0 %period)

Abbreviated APT:
                127: *ROOT* (0 17 deleteforms) (ACT2) 1
                  1: 705 (0 0 deletewd)
                  111: 709 (1 16 m-d-ggforms) (DGG1') 1
                    109: 403 (1 16 classforms) (GG3) (1 (INSERT 0))
                      2: 311 (1 1 classwd)
                      37: 312 (2 4 classnumforms) (CLNUM1) ...
                      55: 316 (5 7 m-dateforms) (DATE0) ...
                        9: 201 (5 5 dtmkr)
                        49: 203 (6 7 u-dateforms) (DATE1)
                          10: 101 (6 6 monthwd)
                          13: 102 (7 7 number)
                      0: 0 (8 8 unknown) nil 1
                      57: 314 (9 16 m-intervalforms) (INT0)
                        14: 204 (9 9 ivlmkr)
                        51: 206 (10 16 u-intervalforms) (INT1) ...
                  28: 799 (17 17 eosmkr)

Hypotheses based on members of the insertion family:
    th indicates GG3: classforms m-dateforms th m-intervalforms
    th indicates DATE0: dtmkr u-dateforms th
    th indicates DATE1: monthwd number th
    th indicates INT0: th ivlmkr u-intervalforms
```

Figure 8-5: The family of insertions represented by the APT for U5S23. The members can be retrieved by a modified infix tree-walk for the subtree rooted at pc109 by using leftmost paths in right subtrees and rightmost paths in left subtrees.

It should come as no surprise that a conservative approach to insertion adaptations—one that tries to tie the inserted phrase to critical differences among forms—carries with it the same type of harmful undergeneralization we saw with conservative substitutions. Moreover, the types of insertions found in the data from our user experiments served as very poor indicators of context, both with respect to forms in the kernel grammar and with respect to forms in each user's adapted grammar. Consequently, CHAMP uses the liberal approach and "throws away" inserted segments during the parse by allowing them to JOIN with any pc (in Section 8.6 it will become clear why we cannot actually remove the phrase from future utterances during segmentation).

8.3. Adapting to deletion deviations

A deletion is detected when a required step cannot be satisfied by a segment in the utterance. We label a step "required" in the kernel grammar for one of two reasons: either we believe that satisfying the step makes a strong prediction for the presence of the complete form, or we believe that the value to be bound to the step is critical to understanding. Steps seeking markers are required for the first reason while a step that binds to the object of a verb is required for the second reason. As in the cases of substitution and insertion adaptations, we can contrast liberal and conservative methods for responding to a deletion recovery notation. Unlike the previous cases, however, this time we take the conservative path; the change in attitude stems from a desire to maintain the unique properties of required steps in the grammar.

Recall from Section 4.2.2 that a step is required by a form if it appears in the form's *rnode* list. Let us assume that the grammar contains a form, S1, with a required step, *k*, unsatisfied by the utterance (Figure 8-6(a)). A liberal adaptation would modify S1 directly by deleting *k* from the form's *rnode* list (producing $S1_{new}$ in the figure). Such an action does create a form in which *k* is no longer required. At the same time, however, it removes a source of context from the adapted grammar that was considered important when the kernel grammar was designed.

S1	$S1_{new}$	S2	S3
isa class1	isa class1	isa class1	isa class1
steps	steps	steps	steps
j class class2	j class class2	j class class2	j class class2
k class class3	k class class3	k class class3	rnode (j)
rnode (j k)	rnode (j)	rnode (j)	
(a)	(b)	(c)	(d)

Figure 8-6: Adapting to a deletion deviation in S1 by removing an *rnode* annotation directly (b) or in a new form (c), or by deleting the step (d).

Removing that source of context has two effects: first, it introduces a bias toward overgeneralization in future explanations. To see how, assume we simply remove the step from the *rnode* as in $S1_{new}$. Now suppose that an utterance appears requiring an adaptation of $S1_{new}$. That adaptation occurs either in the presence or the absence of a member of *k*'s class. By having removed the *rnode*, $S1_{new}$ now succeeds at the same deviation-level under either set of circumstances—any further adaptation of $S1_{new}$ generalizes to both conditions. Since *k* was considered to be strongly predictive in the kernel, we want to be careful about how we remove its predictive capabilities: saying that a member of **class1** can be present without *k* should be different from saying that the presence of *k* is no longer a good indicator of **class1**.

The second effect of removing the *rnode* annotation for *k* also biases learning. If *k* is no longer required, then **class3** can no longer be the target of substitutions. Recall from Section 6.5 that we decided to treat substitution as an appropriate recovery action only for required steps because considering substitutions into all the steps in a form would have created an unreasonable number of deviation hypotheses. Thus, once S1 is replaced by a form in which *k* is no longer required, all new phrases that legitimately play the same role as members of **class3** will be learned as insertions. The presence of a segment in the class **insert** produces no constraint on search during the parse. The presence of a segment in any other wordclass produces whatever constraint is inherent in the grammar for that class at the time of use. Thus, removing the possibility of learning the substitution also removes the constraint that substitution might have on search.

A less liberal approach is shown in Figure 8-6(c): we create a new form from S1 without the *rnode* annotation for *k*. Thus, S2 is identical to $S1_{new}$ except that it exists in the grammar in addition to S1 rather than in place of S1. With *k* removed from its *rnode*, S2 succeeds whenever S1 fails because step *k* is unsatisfied; the grammar as a whole has been extended to include constituents of S1's class that do not require *k*. In addition, the extension to the grammar maintains a form in which *k* is a required step so that substitutions into **class3** are still possible. Unfortunately, this solution preserves the context in S1 at the cost of introducing a form without a critical difference. Whenever S1 succeeds, so will S2 because S2 can (but need not) recognize the sub-constituent in step *k*. In essence, S2 introduces the same bias toward overgeneralization in future explanations as did $S1_{new}$.

Figure 8-6(d) presents the conservative approach to deletion adaptations implemented in CHAMP. The adaptation leaves the *rnode* annotation for *k* intact in S1 and creates a new form from S1 that omits step *k* altogether. This approach uses critically different forms to preserve the separate contexts corresponding to the presence or absence of the deleted step. Generalization occurs through the Formclass Hierarchy because the parent (S1) and its derived form (S3) share the same class; any constituent seeking a subsegment recognizable by the parent now accept candidates recognized by the derived form as well.

Figure 8-7 shows a ubiquitous example of deletion deviation and subsequent adaptation. Although the sentence is taken from User 7's protocol (U7S19), every user studied eventually dropped the articles from some of her utterances. Two APTs are initially constructed for the utterance by the Parse/Recovery Cycle because **AISys** is defined in the lexicon as a **businessname** (a business may refer to either a location or a set of participants). Resolution finds that only the interpretation of **AISys** as a set of participants matches a calendar entry. Since the APT contains a deviation it is only a hypothetical explanation of the utterance; consequently the user is asked to confirm the system's interpretation despite the fact that there is a perfect match. When confirmation is given, adaptation creates USTRAT0 from DGG1 by deleting the step in DGG1 that seeks the definite article. Note that USTRAT0 inherits from DGG1 all those field values that are not directly affected by the deletion.

```
next> cancel AISys meeting on June 14
P/R: (39 38)

Do you want:
   to delete: JUNE 14   10:00am - 12:00pm MEETING with AISYS ?
  [y or n] y

Creating USTRAT0 from DGG1 via (DELETE)
Ok, done.

                 Parent Form                Derived Form
                 DGG1                       USTRAT0
                   isa m-d-ggforms            isa m-d-ggforms
                   steps (401 403)            steps (403)
                   rnode (401 403)            rnode (403)
                   snode (all)                snode (all)
```

Figure 8-7: A common type of deletion detection and adaptation.

8.4. Adapting to transposition deviations

When the order relation on two steps is violated in an utterance we say that a transposition error has occurred. Since there is direct evidence for the new order and either direct or *a priori* evidence (in kernel forms) for the old order, we could adapt by joining the steps with a *unode* annotation in the deviant form. Alternatively, we could create a new form that reflects the transposed order directly. The latter method is implemented in CHAMP.

To see why, let us assume that the user's grammar contains form S1 in Figure 8-8(a). We further assume that the user's utterance does not contain the optional constituent in step *j* but does contain constituents *i* and *k*, in the wrong order. Figure 8-8(b) and (c) demonstrate how each solution introduces a different bias into the hypothesis space.

S1	$S1_{new}$	S2
isa class1	isa class1	isa class1
steps	steps	steps
i class class2	i class class2	j class class3
j class class3	j class class3	k class class4
k class class4	k class class4	i class class2
rnode (k)	rnode (k)	rnode (k)
	unodes (i k)	
(a)	(b)	(c)

Figure 8-8: Adapting to a transposition deviation in S by introducing a *unode* annotation (b) or by creating a new form with the transposed order (c).

In Figure 8-8(b) we reflect the transposition by adding a *unode* annotation between *i* and *k* directly in S1. In Figure 8-8(c) we record the transposition explicitly in a new form, S2. Now consider the sets of utterances accepted by (b) and (c). Each solution results in an adapted grammar in which both the order *i*, *k* and the order *k*, *i* are accepted when step *j* is unsatisfied. Only S2 accepts the new order when a constituent for *j* is present, however. For $S1_{new}$ to accept both orderings on *i* and *k* when *j* is present, we would have to add *j* to the *unode* as well, but the utterance gives no evidence for that interpretation. The solution in (c) permits both orderings for which there has been evidence and establishes a critical difference between the parent and derived form when *i* and *k* are present in the utterance. Unfortunately, when *i* is not present both forms succeed.

When constructing a derived form for a transposition, other ordering relations in the parent form must be considered. Figure 8-9 shows the transposition learned for U2S91. At Deviation-level 0, CHAMP finds an explanation for the sentence by attaching the marked date to the target seminar description and using the default date provided at the start of each session (June 5) to infer the source seminar date. Since no calendar entry corresponds to this interpretation during Resolution, CHAMP continues its search into Deviation-level 1. With one deviation point available, the system produces an APT in which the introductory adverbial date has been transposed to the end of the sentence. Because of the *bindvar* in the transposed step, this

```
next> change Natural Language Interfaces Seminar to AI Seminar on June 19
P/R roots: (58)
No calendar entry fits that description on June 5.

P/R roots: (73)

Do you want:
  to change: JUNE 19   10:30am - 11:30am
             (NATURAL LANGUAGE INTERFACES) SEMINAR in/at 5409
         to: JUNE 19   10:30am - 11:30am
             AI SEMINAR in/at 5409
 [y or n] y

Creating USTRAT17 from ACT5 via (TRANS)
Ok, done.

Abbreviated APT:
        73: *ROOT* (0 10 changeforms) (ACT5) (1 (TRANS (22 0)))
          0: 706 (0 0 changewd)
          35: 709 (1 4 m-d-ggforms) (USTRAT1)
            27: 403 (1 4 seminarforms) (GG2) ...
          5: 723 (5 5 targetmkr)
          41: 724 (6 7 m-i-ggforms) (USTRAT0)
            32: 403 (6 7 seminarforms) (GG2) ...
          22: 703 (8 10 m-dateforms) (DATE0)
            8: 201 (8 8 dtmkr)
            17: 203 (9 10 u-dateforms) (DATE1) ...

Parent Form                        Derived Form
ACT5                               USTRAT17
  isa changeforms                    isa changeforms
  steps (701 702 703 706             steps (701 702 706 709
          709 723 724 799)                  723 724 703 799)
  rnode (706 709 723 724)            rnode (706 709 723 724)
  mnodes ((701 702))                 mnodes ((701 702))
  unodes ((701 702 703))             unodes ((701 702))
```

Figure 8-9: An example of deviation detection and adaptation for transpositions.

interpretation maps the date to both source and target during Resolution, allowing the desired calendar entry to be found. Since the APT contains a deviation, the user is asked for confirmation of the effect. When confirmation is given, the calendar is updated and USTRAT17 is created by adaptation, reflecting the new ordering in its steps list. Observe that USTRAT17 contains another difference with respect to its parent: 703 has been removed from the *unode* inherited from ACT5. In general, the transposed step loses its old ordering relations and takes its new ordering relations from its new position. If the new position is contiguous to ordered steps, the transposition is ordered with respect to those steps. If the new step is inserted between unordered steps, it shares the *unode* annotation of those steps in the new form.

8.5. A summary of adaptation in CHAMP

The purpose of adaptation is to bring a deviation into the grammar by deriving new grammatical components from the adaptation context that parse the deviation directly in future utterances. The particular set of new components that are added to the grammar depends upon which deviations are present in the utterance. The choices implemented in CHAMP are shown in Figures 8-10 through 8-13. In addition to describing the type of component added, each figure also reviews the method of generalization and summarizes the implications of the adaptation for learning and future search.

Substitution

- Adaptation: a new lexical definition is added to the grammar for the unknown phrase as a member of the wordclass sought by the step requiring the substitution.
- Generalization: occurs through the Formclass Hierarchy. Everywhere the wordclass was previously sought, the new lexeme is recognized.
- Implications for learning: extends the set of indices for discriminations already present in the grammar—those attached to the substituted wordclass. Loses potential discriminations based upon the tokens themselves, or the co-occurrence of the tokens or substituted class with other classes or deviations present in the adaptation context.
- Effect on search: reduces the deviation-level required to understand future occurrences of the lexeme. If the lexeme was already defined in the lexicon, the new definition increases the amount of lexical ambiguity in the system. This may create additional search paths for utterances that contain the lexeme, but has no affect on the search space for utterances that do not contain it.

Figure 8-10: Summary of adaptation to substitutions.

With respect to generalization, the four figures show that a derived component that recognizes a new way of referring to a particular class of constituents is "inherited upward" through the Formclass Hierarchy to all locations that seek constituents of that class. The main advantage to relying on the Hierarchy for generalization is that it provides a simple, uniform mechanism. The main disadvantage is that making

Insertion

- Adaptation: a new lexical definition is added to the grammar for the unknown phrase as member of the special wordclass **insert**.
- Generalization: occurs throughout the grammar. The new lexeme is allowed to occur without deviation anywhere in subsequent utterances.
- Implications for learning: loses potential discriminations based upon the co-occurrence of the tokens with other classes or deviations present in the adaptation context. Assumes the lexeme carries no meaning.
- Effect on search: reduces the deviation-level required to understand future utterances containing the inserted phrase. If the lexeme was already defined in the lexicon, the new definition increases the amount of lexical ambiguity in the system. This may create additional search paths for utterances that contain the lexeme, but has no affect on the search space for utterances that do not contain it.

Figure 8-11: Summary of adaptation to insertions.

Deletion

- Adaptation: a new form is added to the grammar. The new form is derived from the form in which the deviation was explained. The new form inherits all the information present in its parent that does not relate to the deleted step.
- Generalization: occurs through the Formclass Hierarchy. The derived form may be used anywhere the parent form is used to recognize a constituent. If two deletions or a deletion and a transposition occur in the same constituent, they are tied together in the same derived form.
- Implications for learning: permits future discriminations based on the presence or absence of a class. Permits discrimination based upon some co-occurrences of deviations.
- Effect on search: reduces the deviation-level required to understand future utterances containing the deletion. May introduce structural ambiguity into the grammar if the deleted step represents a critical difference between formclasses.

Figure 8-12: Summary of adaptation to deletions.

generalizations across established boundaries in the grammar requires discrete episodes of learning. Consider, as an example, that the kernel grammar distinguishes **groupgatherings** marked by definite articles from those marked by indefinite articles by assigning the former to the class **m-d-ggforms** and the latter to the class **m-i-ggforms**. The first time a user drops the article from her utterance, she does so

Transposition

- Adaptation: a new form is added to the grammar that explicitly captures the new ordering of steps. The new form inherits all the information present in the parent that does not relate to the ordering of the transposed step. The ordering relations on the transposed step depend on the steps surrounding it after transposition. If the surrounding steps are unordered, the transposed step is added to their *unode* annotation.
- Generalization: occurs through the Formclass Hierarchy. The derived form may be used anywhere the parent form is used to recognize a constituent. If two transpositions or a transposition and a deletion occur in the same constituent they are tied together in the same derived form.
- Implications for learning: permits discriminations based on ordering. Permits discrimination based upon some co-occurrences of deviations.
- Effect on search: reduces the deviation-level required to understand future utterances that reflect the new ordering. If the transposed step is not required, the adaptation may introduce ambiguity into the search space at non-zero deviation-levels whenever the transposed step is not needed to understand the utterance.

Figure 8-13: Summary of adaptation to transpositions.

in one context or the other; CHAMP learns either a new **m-d-ggform** or a new **m-i-ggform**, but not both. The deletion in the other class must be learned separately because the discrimination provided by the separate classes cannot be ignored by the same mechanism that is relying on that discrimination for generalization.

Figures 8-10 through 8-13 make it clear that CHAMP learns discriminations based on the presence, absence, or position of categories in its kernel grammar. The adapted grammar that evolves for a particular user depends, of course, on the history of interactions with that user. Since none of the adaptations introduces new constituents into a derived form, however, some portions of the user's natural language may be out of reach. As an example, consider the following sentences taken from User 10's first session:

U10S120: Change June 11 NY to Pittsburgh from flight 82 to flight 265
U10S121: Change from flight 82 to flight 265 on June 11 NY to Pittsburgh
U10S122: Change flight 82 to flight 265 on June 11

User 10's first two attempts to perform the subtask require learning that is beyond the scope of CHAMP's adaptation mechanism. The problematic segment is "from flight 82" which the parser tries to explain as a source in a source-target pair because of the marker "from." No kernel form permits a full flight object in the source (only a flight attribute), and the system provides no way to introduce the possibility into the language. Thus, in U10S120 the system can compensate for the missing head noun ("Change June 11 NY to Pittsburgh [flight]"), and in U10S121 the system can compensate for the transposed date and origin-destination pair, but in neither instance can the system construct an explanation of the sentence. U10S122 does not contain the misleading marker and is parsed by a kernel form. Giving CHAMP the ability to construct new sets of previously uncombined constituents would be a non-trivial but valuable extension to the system. One mechanism providing that ability is *constructive inference* which is discussed further in Chapter 11.

With respect to search, the summary figures reveal that each type of adaptation may introduce ambiguity into the adapted grammar. Substitution and insertion adaptations may introduce lexical ambiguity if the new definitions act as alternatives to definitions already in the lexicon.[34] The cost of the ambiguity during search depends initially upon the number of additional forms indexed by the new definition. The degree to which the ambiguity propagates through the search space depends upon what other constraining information is available in the utterance.

Deletion adaptations may introduce structural ambiguity into the grammar. Let us reconsider the case of **m-d-ggforms** and **m-i-ggforms**. In the kernel there is only one **m-d-ggform**, DGG1, and only one **m-i-ggform**, IGG1. The forms share the step that seeks the object; the critical difference between the forms is the step in each that seeks the marker. If the user drops both definite and indefinite articles, then the system derives forms omitting each kind of marker: DGG1' seeks only an object and IGG1' seeks only an object. In other words, any unmarked object succeeds at Deviation-level 0 in the adapted grammar as both a member of **m-d-ggforms** and **m-i-ggforms**. Again, the cost of the ambiguity during search depends initially upon the number of additional forms indexed by the incorrect class assignment. The degree to which the cost propagates depends upon the other constituents in the sentence.

Transpositions may introduce ambiguity at non-zero deviation-levels if the critical difference between the parent and the derived form is in an ordering relation that is not manifested by the utterance. In Figure 8-9, for example, USTRAT17 differs from ACT5 by a transposition of the marked date. A sentence containing the unmarked

---

[34]In CHAMP, it is impossible to introduce a new lexical definition for a word or phrase that is already defined without employing extra-linguistic conventions. The method of compensating for the *lexical extension problem* is discussed in Chapter 9. Other aspects of the problem are discussed in Chapter 10.

form of the date, for example, "change the June 20 seminar to a meeting," does not manifest this difference—it would succeed via both forms. At Deviation-level 0 the success of both forms has no effect on processing—EXPAND simply creates a pc with both forms in the *forms* field. On the other hand, if there is a deviation in the constituent, ISCOMPLETE builds a separate modified context for each form (see Section 6.3). Since the separate contexts then EXPAND to distinct sets of higher level constituents, this type of ambiguity always propagate through the search space.

It is important to note that even though each type of adaptation may increase the amount of ambiguity in the current grammar, the future search space for utterances containing the deviation is always significantly smaller than it would have been had we not adapted. The reason is simple: any ambiguous paths at Deviation-level 0 are also part of the much larger search space at higher deviation-levels. Of course the cost of parsing some utterances that were in the grammar prior to the adaptation will have increased, but three factors make the trade-off worthwhile. First, since adaptations tend to reflect preferred forms of expression, utterances relying on the adaptations are likely to reappear—the more often an adaptation is reused the more favorable the trade-off becomes. Second, adaptation brings more of the user's language into the grammar, resulting in fewer rejected parses over time. Since rejecting a sentence requires a search through Deviation-level 2 *plus* the search associated with understanding any subsequent rephrasings, any action that prevents rejections must reduce search overall. Finally, since the frequent user's language is self-bounded, whatever increase in ambiguity results from adaptation must be bounded as well.

Figure 8-14 displays the simple algorithm implementing adaptation in CHAMP: each hypothetical explanation for the user's utterance has its annotated nodes transformed into the grammatical components appropriate for that recovery notation.

When there are multiple hypotheses explaining an utterance, each root APT will correspond to a different set of new grammatical components after adaptation. At least one set of components must be added to the grammar to bring the current sentence into Deviation-level 0, but which set of components should we add? If we choose arbitrarily we may choose the least useful set, adding to the grammar adaptations that may increase ambiguity without significantly increasing the system's explanatory power. If we simply add all the components to the grammar then every sentence that is structurally similar to the current one will always succeed in multiple ways. Since each successful path corresponds to the same meaning, this approach is even more likely to increase ambiguity without increasing explanatory power. What

<u>ADAPT (roots)</u>
FOR EACH root passed on by Resolution, DO
  Descend through the tree for this root (1)
  FOR EACH subnode that contains one or more recovery notations, DO
    Perform the adaptation required by the recovery notation(s) (2)
    Associate the new components with the root
FOR EACH derived component used to explain the sentence, DO (3)
  IF the component required no adaptation
  THEN try to resolve old competitions associated with the component
IF more than one root node created new components (4)
THEN set the components from different roots in competition

Figure 8-14: CHAMP's ADAPT algorithm.

we need is some method of delaying our decision until we have more evidence about which set of changes to the grammar is the most useful. In CHAMP, that method is called *competition*. When the current utterance lends equal support to more than one set of changes, we add all the changes to the grammar as competitors (step (4)). We use subsequent utterances that rely on the derived components to resolve the competition (step (3)).

8.6. Controlling growth in the grammar through competition

Competition helps attain the goal of maximal coverage with minimal ambiguity by delaying commitment to a single set of changes until information is available to make an intelligent choice. The competition mechanism is based on a simple idea: just as one sentence is enough to cause a set of competitors to be added to the grammar, so one sentence is enough to cause a subset to be removed. To preserve the relationships established by multiple APTs, we create a competition relation between grammar components from different APTs and a support relation between grammar components from the same APT. Figure 8-15 illustrates the process.

With respect to the kernel grammar, the first sentence in the figure (U7S118) contains one unknown segment ("what is my"), and two deletions (a verb and a definite article). Due to its position in the utterance, the unknown segment may fill either deleted step; thus, U7S118 creates two APTs during the Parse/Recovery Cycle. Since the APTs correspond to the same effective meaning, both are preserved by Resolution. The first explanation produces two new grammar components during adaptation: the lexical definition for the segment "what is my" as a **defmkr** compensates for the unknown segment and the deletion of the article, while USTRAT5 compensates for the deletion of the verb. The second explanation for U7S118 uses the unknown segment as a substitute for the missing verb and captures the deleted article in USTRAT6. Since only one set of components is required to parse the sentence, but we do not know which set will prove more useful, the last step in adaptation is to place the two sets of components in competition.

In contrast to the competitive relationship between the sets of components created for different APTs, the individual components within a competitor are said to *support* each other. In Figure 8-15, for example, the **defmkr** definition and USTRAT5 support one another. The support relationship reflects the fact that both components are required to explain the current sentence. If a component wins a permanent place in the grammar through competition, it also wins a place for any components it supports. In this way we guarantee that reducing the grammar through competition resolution does not cost us the ability to understand a previous utterance.

```
U7S118: "what is my schedule between 9:00 and 12:00 on JUne 12"

Parse/Recovery and Resolution:
  APT substituting "what is my" for article and detecting showwd deletion
  APT substituting "what is my" for showwd and detecting article deletion

Adaptation:
  (what is my)/defmkr
  USTRAT5 from ACT6 via deletion of showwd

  (what is my)/showwd
  USTRAT6 from MCALSEG1 via deletion of defmkr

  Competitors: ((what is my)/defmkr & USTRAT5) vs.
               ((what is my)/showwd & USTRAT6)

U7S41: "please list schedule for june 12"

Parse/Recovery and Resolution:
  APT using USTRAT6 and treating "please" as an insertion

Adaptation:
  (please)/insert
  remove USTRAT5 and (what is my)/defmkr
```

Figure 8-15: A simple example of the introduction & resolution of a competition.

The four new components remain in the grammar until User 7's fourth session. When she types U7S41, User 7 creates the situation that decides the competition. As the figure shows, Parse/Recovery produces an explanation of U7S41 at Deviation-level 1 by using USTRAT6 as a non-deviant explanation of the missing article and an insertion deviation to explain the unknown segment "please." When the APT is processed by ADAPT, step (3) of the algorithm notices that USTRAT6 is a derived form that succeeded without recovery notations. Since USTRAT6 has an associated competition relation, the APT is examined for evidence of each competitor. In the single APT for U7S41, only USTRAT6 is present. We now have available additional information to decide which explanation to prefer for U7S118: the combination of USTRAT6 and "what is my" as **showwd** helps to understand both utterances, whereas the combination of USTRAT5 and "what is my" as **defmkr** has a more limited use. Since the former combination subsumes the explanatory power of the latter (given the evidence to this point) we preserve only USTRAT6 and the component it supports; its competitor is removed from the grammar. Notice that the system preserves the definition of "what is my" as **showwd** despite the fact that it does not occur in U7S41 because it is supported by USTRAT6.

Competitions are sometimes resolved despite the fact that no new information is available. This learning bias stems from an interaction between the competition mechanism and the Maximal Subsequence Heuristic (Section 5.2). Figure 8-16 illustrates the problem. As shown, U4S15 causes adaptations analogous to those produced in response to U7S118 in Figure 8-15 (two explanations corresponding to alternative substitutions and deletions). The competition set up by U4S15 should not be resolved by U4S31: the two sentences are structurally identical with respect to the portions in competition.[35] Therefore APTs incorporating both competitors should succeed. Only one APT is constructed, however, because the constituent that picks up "commuting time" as a **tripwd** is formed on a lower Agenda-level than the constituent that would use the segment as a **defmkr**. Specifically, at Agenda-level 3 USTRAT3 creates a **tripform** from the prepositional phrases without using the segment "commuting time" (because the head noun is not required in USTRAT3's subcontext). A continuation of this path would pick up the unused segment as a **defmkr**. At the same Agenda-level, however, TRIP1 coalesces the prepositional phrases with "commuting time" as a **tripwd**. Since only the maximal segment is EXPANDed, no path is created that requires the segment as a **defmkr**. At Agenda-level 4, USTRAT2 EXPANDs the maximal subsegment as a marked trip without

[35]CHAMP offers the spelling correction of "commuting time" to "comuting time" for U4S31 during segmentation. When the correction is accepted, the system asks if it should remember the corrected version as well. An affirmative response equates the correct spelling with the original misspelling learned for U4S15.

noticing the absent marker. During adaptation, the success of USTRAT2 and "commuting time" as **tripwd** without the simultaneous success of either USTRAT3 or "commuting time" as **defmkr** in another APT eliminates USTRAT2's competitors from the grammar.

U4S15:
"change comuting time from CMU to Aisys on june 12 from 12p.m. to 2p.m."

Parse/Recovery and Resolution:
APT substituting "comuting time" for tripwd and detecting article deletion
APT substituting "comuting time" for article and detecting tripwd deletion

Adaptation:
(comuting time)/tripwd
USTRAT2 from DTRIP1 via deletion of defmkr

(comuting time)/defmkr
USTRAT3 from TRIP1 via deletion of tripwd

Competitors: ((comuting time)/tripwd & USTRAT2) vs.
((comuting time)/defmkr & USTRAT3)

U4S31:"cancel commuting time from CMU to Aisys on June 12 at 2 p.m."

Parse/Recovery and Resolution:
APT using USTRAT2 and (comuting time)/tripwd succeeds at Deviation-level 0

Adaptation:
remove USTRAT3 and (comuting time)/defmkr from grammar

Figure 8-16: An example of a competition resolved by maximal subsequences.

It would be wrong to infer from the examples in Figures 8-15 and 8-16 that CHAMP's competition mechanism always preserves the components that correspond to linguistically correct analyses of the sentences. Figure 8-17 shows a complex sequence of adaptations and competition resolutions that provides a counterexample. We include the first sentence in the example (U3S110), despite the fact that it creates no competition, because USTRAT1 (a form that does not require an **addwd** for the **schedule** action) contributes to the outcome of a competition further on.

The second sentence in the figure (U3S210) is highly ambiguous at Deviation-level 2. The first competitor incorporates USTRAT4 and corresponds to the explanation that "has been changed" is a substituted and transposed **changewd**. The second competitor explains U3S210 with the same substitution for the verb but considers the

U3S110: "Dinner with Dad June 14, 1986 at 6:00."

Adaptation:
USTRAT1 from ACT1 via deletion of addwd
USTRAT2 from DATE0 via deletion of datemkr

U3S210: "Lunch with VC on June 13, 1986 has been changed from Station Square to VC Inc."

Adaptation:
(has been changed)/changewd
USTRAT4 from ACT3 via transposition of changewd
USTRAT5 from ACT3 via transposition of m-d-ggform
(has been changed)/insert
USTRAT6 from ACT3 via deletion of changewd
USTRAT7 from ACT4 via deletion of changewd
(has been changed)/locationslotwd

Competitors: ((has been changed)/changewd & USTRAT4) vs.
((has been changed)/changewd & USTRAT5) vs.
((has been changed)/insert & USTRAT6) vs.
((has been changed)/locationslotwd & USTRAT7)

U3S311: "Reschedule Craigs meeting on June 11, 1986 to be from 3:00 to 4:00."

Adaptation:
(to be from)/targetmkr
reschedule/defmkr
reschedule/changewd
reschedule/insert

remove USTRAT4, USTRAT5, USTRAT7, (has been changed)/changewd and (has been changed)/locationslotwd

Competitors: (reschedule/defmkr & (to be from)/targetmkr) vs.
(reschedule/changewd & (to be from)/targetmkr) vs.
(reschedule/insert & (to be from)/targetmkr)

U3S345: "reschedule a meeting with Jaime at 2:00 on June 12th."

Adaptation:
remove reschedule/changewd and reschedule/defmkr

Figure 8-17: Using competition to control the growth in the grammar caused by multiple hypothetical explanations.

groupgathering to be the transposed element. The third competitor pairs a deletion of the verb with an insertion of the unknown segment. The final competitor deletes the verb in a kernel form that seeks a **slotform** rather than a **groupgathering** (ACT4) and substitutes "has been changed" for a valid **locationslotwd.**

U3S311 resolves the competition set up for U3S210. Thirteen APTs are produced by the Parse/Recovery Cycle for the sentence, but only three of the APTs survive Resolution. One uses USTRAT6 (which requires no verb), a substitution of "reschedule" for the **defmkr** required by the kernel form DGG1, and a substitution of "to be from" for the **targetmkr**. A second explanation uses a substitution of "reschedule" for the **changewd** still required by ACT3, a form derived from DGG1 that does not require the article, and the **targetmkr** substitution. The final explanation uses USTRAT6 and the form derived from DGG1 to treat "reschedule" as an insertion, and the **targetmkr** substitution to explain "to be from." Since USTRAT6 was used without further adaptation to help explain U3S311, and none of its competitors contributed to an alternative explanation, the competitors are removed from the grammar. This means that the only explanation left in the grammar for U3S210 is the one in which the verb was considered deleted and "has been changed" was considered a meaningless insertion. Although this explanation is inaccurate from a linguistic point of view, it does preserve the most useful subset of adaptations for the two examples.

In addition to resolving an old competition, U3S311 sets up a new competition among its explanations. The new competition is resolved by U3S345, which uses the word "reschedule" as an **addwd** (U3S311 used it as a **changewd**). However, the existence of USTRAT1 (deleted **addwd**) and the definition of "reschedule" as an insertion (along with other prior adaptations) allow the sentence to be understood correctly at Deviation-level 0. Even though no deviations occurred, the APT for the utterance is passed to adaptation to see if old competitions can be resolved. As a result, the prior definitions of "reschedule" as a possible **changewd** or **defmkr** are removed from the grammar. The only definition consistent with both U3S311 and U3S45 at Deviation-level 0 in the adapted grammar is "reschedule" as an insertion.

The example in Figure 8-17 also serves to illustrate why we cannot simply remove segments in the class **insert** from the utterance during segmentation. By removing the segment, we circumvent any competition relations attached to the insertion; the insertion interpretation and any supported components effectively win without having to compete. Since the insertion's competitors are probably not insertions themselves, they are adaptations that index expectations in the grammar, expectations that act as search constraint. Thus, leaving the segment in future utterances

Competition in CHAMP is actually just a type of generalization from multiple examples. While a competition may be fully resolved by a single sentence, it is also possible that more than one sentence is required to eliminate all but one competitor. It is even possible that a subset of competitors will never be removed from the grammar; they may, for example, all share a support relation with a common component that co-occurs any time any of the other components is present. At the other extreme, it is possible (although very rare in our experiments) to learn a component, remove it through competition, and then have to learn it again.

In essence, both the advantages and disadvantages of using competition as a method of controlling grammar growth stem from the mechanism's decisiveness: a single piece of evidence favoring one competitor is considered enough to remove its rivals from the grammar. A quick decision is an advantage if the competitors contribute a great deal of ambiguity to the search—but the same decision can be a disadvantage if it removes a set of components that would have eliminated search in the future. There is no simple, generally correct way to prevent this problem within the mechanism described. In the next chapter we examine the degree to which competition is an effective means of controlling growth in six idiosyncratic grammars. We postpone a discussion of alternative mechanisms to Chapter 11.

8.7. The effects of adaptation on performance

With a clear understanding of how learning is accomplished in CHAMP, we can now examine how adaptation improves the system's performance in the task of understanding the user, as well as the user's performance in the task of keeping an on-line calendar. To begin, let us consider Figure 8-18 which contains a small subset of User 3's sentences, none of which can be understood at Deviation-level 0 using the kernel grammar. Two of the ten sentences can be parsed at Deviation-level 2 (S14 and S210), but the remainder contain three or more deviations with respect to the kernel. If we consider these utterances as delineating a portion of User 3's language space, then CHAMP's calendar kernel covers none of that portion.[36] Even with error detection and recovery for two deviations, the system's coverage increases to only twenty percent.

In terms of the kernel system's performance during processing for these ten sentences, observe that each sentence requires a complete search through Deviation-

[36] Figure 8-18 is only a slight exaggeration of the real situation; actually the kernel is able to parse seven percent of User 3's utterances at Deviation-level 0 (see Section 9.1.4).

S14 "Cancel John's Speech Research Meeting at 9:00 on June 9, 1986."
S210 "Lunch with VC on June 13,1986 has been changed from Station Square to VC Inc."
S33 "Lisp Tutorial class will be held in Room 8220 on June 11, 1986."
S311 "Reschedule Craigs meeting on June 11, 1986 to be from 3:00 to 4:00."
S314 "Schedule time for Jill in the User Studies Lab from 3:00 to 4:30 on June 12th."
S49 "Change Andy's lunch on June 12th to begin at 12:30."
S71 "Speech Project on June 17th will be held in room 7220 instead of 8220."
S716 "Class 15-731 will be held in Room 7220 on June 23rd."
S91 "reschedule AI Seminar to begin at 9:00 instead of 9:30 on June 19th."
S93 "Class 15-731 will be held in Room 5409 instead of 7220 on June 23rd."

Figure 8-18: A subset of User 3's utterances delineating a portion of her language space. None can be parsed directly with the kernel grammar.

level 2 before it can be accepted or rejected. The situation is more serious from the user's point of view—her performance is affected not only by the system's response time (relatively slow for all the utterances), but also by the total number of interactions required to perform the task. For the sample in Figure 8-18, she must generate at least one alternative phrasing eighty percent of the time.

The next two figures demonstrate how adaptation improves the situation. Figure 8-19 shows some of the components added to the grammar as each utterance is encountered in turn (only the winning set of components is shown for sentences that produce competitions). The column labelled "Relies On" lists the sentences from our sample that earlier produced new components used to understand the current utterance. The frequent appearance of previously derived components in the explanations of subsequent utterances clearly demonstrates adaptation's bootstrapping effect. Although eight utterances were originally unparsable, Figure 8-19 shows that with adaptation each sentence is within two deviations of the extant grammar when it is encountered.

Figure 8-20 shows the bootstrapping effect more clearly. In the first column the ten sentences are partitioned according to their degree of deviation with respect to the kernel (K). The remaining columns show the continual repartitioning of User 3's language space as each sentence is understood in turn. The second column, for example, shows that after adaptation and generalization for S14, three utterances that would have been unparsable are now within the reach of error recovery: understanding S33 and S311 at Deviation-level 2 requires the form DGG1' that was produced by S14, while understanding S49 at Deviation-level 2 requires S14's lex-

Sentence	Relies On	Produces
S14		DGG1' derived from DGG1 by deleting **defmkr** (%apostrophe s)/insert added to lexicon
S210		ACT3' derived from ACT3 by deleting **changewd** (has been changed)/insert added to lexicon
S33	S14, S210	ACT3'' derived from ACT3' transposing marked date (will be held in)/targetmkr added to lexicon
S311	S14, S210	reschedule/insert added to lexicon (to be from)/targetmkr added to lexicon
S314		th/insert added to lexicon
S49	S14, S314	(to begin at)/targetmkr added to lexicon
S71	S14, S210, S33, S314	LOC6' derived from LOC6 by deleting **roomwd** (instead of)/sourcemkr added to lexicon
S716	S14, S210, S33	rd/insert added to lexicon
S91	S14, S210, S311, S314, S71	
S93	S14, S210, S33, S71, S716	

Figure 8-19: An example of bootstrapping in User 3's grammar. (The second column mentions only sentences from our sample. The third column shows only the winning set of competitors.)

ical definition of **%apostrophe s** as a member of the class **insert**. After the first eight sentences in the sample have been understood, all of the original utterances are directly parsable by the grammar. More importantly, a great many variations of those sentences, in the same "style" as the originals, are also at Deviation-level 0 due to generalization.

Without adaptation, CHAMP's performance for the sample sentences would have been quite poor, requiring search through Deviation-level 2 for all ten sentences and additional search after rejection for eight. With adaptation, we see an enormous improvement, both in the amount of search required to process the utterances (only half the sentences require search at Deviation-level 2) and the number of utterances accepted (all ten). It is possible to argue, however, that the performance of a non-adaptive interface with a large grammar would be as good or better than CHAMP's adaptive performance. The validity of this argument depends upon two factors: first,

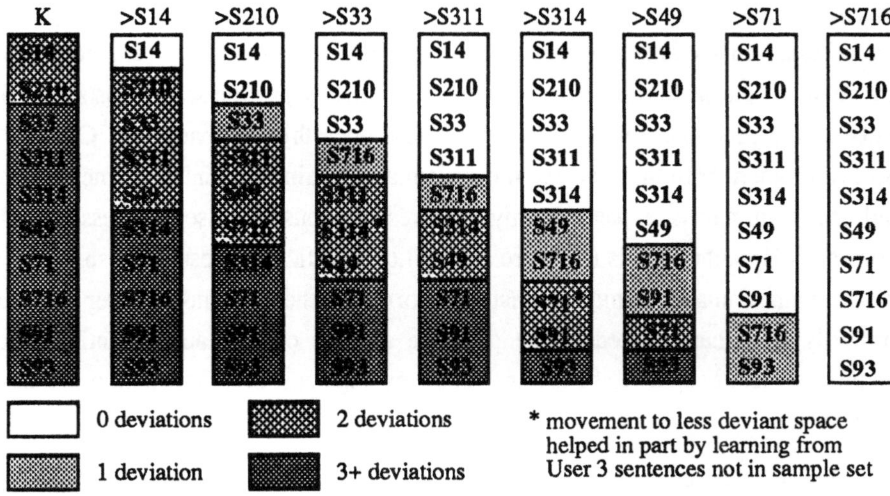

Figure 8-20: Effect of adaptation on the shape of the search space for a portion of User 3's language: as each deviant sentence is brought into the grammar, its derived components reduce the search needed to understand future utterances.

whether or not the larger grammar corresponds to the user's forms of expression, and second, the user's ability to adapt to the subset of language provided.

Given the variety of expression in Figure 8-18 we must question how good the initial correspondence between the user's language and the static system's language is likely to be. With poor correspondence, performance values are dominated by the number of parse failures and required rephrasings. Although it is impossible to predict in the abstract how many rephrasings will be required by a given interface, observe that for the subset of User 3's expressions we have examined CHAMP required none.[37] Of course, to minimize rephrasings, static interfaces rely on both their large grammars and the *user's* ability to adapt—to continue our comparison we assume that the user can adjust to the interface's demands (despite evidence to the contrary presented in Chapter 3).

The Regularity Hypothesis tells us that in the course of adjusting to the non-adaptive system's language, the frequent user comes to rely on those utterances that she remembers as having worked in the past. Regularity on the part of the user

---

[37]The actual number of User 3's sentences that CHAMP could not parse at the time of use was 32/138 (23%). Of these, 20/32 were sentences that would have been accepted by a perfect implementation of the adaptation model described in Chapter 2. Thus, with ideal adaptation, only 12/138 (9%) of User 3's utterances would have required rephrasing.

causes a dilemma for the static interface: if the grammar is large enough to permit a reasonable subset of "natural language" for every user, then the Regularity Hypothesis implies that each particular user is likely to employ only a fraction of that grammar. At the same time, each user must continually pay the search costs over the parts of the grammar she does not use. How does this compare with CHAMP's behavior, where both the user *and* the system adapt? Since the initial kernel is small and the grammar is expanded only in direct response to user expressions, the Regularity Hypothesis tells us that relatively little inefficiency results. In short, when the grammar contains primarily what has worked in the past and the user relies on primarily what has worked in the past, the average cost of an interaction in an adaptive system is likely to be lower than the average cost of an interaction in a large static system.

We began this chapter by claiming that we could improve the interface's performance if we turned the simple least-deviant-first parser from Chapter 6 into a least-deviant-first adaptive parser. Believing that deviations reliably indicate idiosyncratic preference, we have chosen to augment the grammar with new components in response to the explanations of a deviation produced by error recovery. By bringing the deviation into the grammar, future instances of the deviation no longer require extended search. In addition, by tying the new component into the Formclass Hierarchy, the explanation of the deviation generalizes to contexts other than the one which gave rise to the adaptation. The limited performance analysis in this section demonstrates that our method of adaptation and generalization can greatly improve the interaction between the user and system in two ways. First, by reducing the number of interactions required by the user to accomplish her task, and second, by reducing the average amount of search required by the system for each interaction.

This evaluation nevertheless leaves a great many questions unanswered. How does CHAMP perform on User 3's full data set? How does CHAMP's performance compare to the performance of the ideal adaptive system specified by the model in Chapter 2? Is the sort of improvement in performance shown here characteristic across users? Is our assumption that deviations reliably indicate idiosyncratic preference true (in other words, are the components added by adaptation reused)? Is our prediction that an idiosyncratic grammar requires less search on the average than a large static grammar demonstrable? In the next chapter, we answer these questions and others through a detailed analysis of CHAMP's performance for six idiosyncratic grammars.

Chapter 9

Evaluating the Interface

The hidden-operator experiments described in Chapter 3 tested the underlying behavioral assumptions of our model for language adaptation. The experiments demonstrated that an ideal realization of the model could:

1. Capture the within-user consistency that arises from the frequent user's natural, self-bounded language.
2. Accommodate the across-user variability arising from idiosyncratic preferences with a single, general, recovery and adaptation mechanism.
3. Provide a more responsive environment than that provided by a static interface with its fixed subset of natural language.

Recall, however, that the model itself leaves many aspects of any implementation unspecified; it makes no commitment to a particular generalization method, set of knowledge structures, grammar decomposition, or set of inference procedures. Nor does the model require us to confront the computational complexities that lead to the Single Segment Assumption or the Maximal Subsequence Heuristic.

To implement the model in a working interface the unspecified and underspecified must be made concrete. In the previous five chapters we examined one possible implementation, CHAMP, incorporating one possible set of decisions and trade-offs. It is natural to ask how well CHAMP realizes the ideal, or, equivalently, how the implemented system's performance compares to that of the ideal system simulated in the hidden-operator experiments. This comparison is the subject of Section 9.1.

It is also useful to evaluate the system on its own, asking how well CHAMP performs in real user interactions. Section 9.2 examines the system's performance in on-line experiments with two new users (User 9 and User 10). The new experiments extend our sample size without qualitatively changing the results found for the original data.

Overall, our analysis reveals that CHAMP is a good approximation of the model in terms of capturing within-user consistency and accommodating across-user variability. The system provides a slightly less friendly environment than the model predicts due to its higher rate of rejected sentences, but still provides a more responsive environment than does a fixed, monolithic grammar.

9.1. CHAMP's performance on the hidden-operator data

A full description of the hidden-operator experiments is given in Chapter 3. To summarize briefly: users were asked to perform a calendar scheduling task for a fictitious professor/entrepreneur. Each user participated in multiple sessions (three, five, or nine) responding to ten to twelve pictorial subtasks each session. Users in the Adapt and Adapt/Echo conditions of the experiment interacted with a simulated adaptive interface based on the model in Chapter 2 and a grammar that was functionally equivalent to CHAMP's kernel (with a few exceptions, as noted in the next section). Users in the No-Adapt condition interacted with a simulated interface that permitted two-deviation recovery but no adaptation.

The kernel grammar used in the hidden-operator experiments was constructed by simply writing down an informal, BNF-style grammar with one or two forms for each type of action and object required by the stimuli. CHAMP's calendar kernel consisted of functionally equivalent structures represented via steps, forms, and formclasses. The transformation from the BNF representation into CHAMP's case frame grammar took into consideration the patterns and regularities in the *development set*: eighty-five sentences drawn from the log files for User 1 and User 2, pertaining only to the calendar domain. Once a working version of the system had been constructed, CHAMP's kernel grammar for the travel domain was developed; the design of the kernel travel grammar was based only on the travel grammar in the experiments and the representational scheme already established for the calendar domain.

To evaluate CHAMP's performance on the data from the hidden-operator experiments, the system was tested with the 657 sentences from the log files for users in the adaptive conditions (User 1, User 2, User 3, User 4, User 5, and User 7). The 657 sentences in the *test set* include the eighty-five sentences in the development set.

One major change to the system occurred after evaluation began: replacement of conservative adaptations with liberal adaptations for substitution and insertion deviations. The change was in response to the severe undergeneralization that arises from the conservative approach for those types of deviations (see Sections 8.1 and 8.2). It is interesting to note that the problem did not become apparent from working with the development set alone. All measures reported here reflect the mixed liberal-conservative adaptation and generalization method described in Chapter 8.

In the next section we examine the differences between CHAMP and the system simulated during the experiments, discussing the ways in which we compensated for those differences in evaluating CHAMP's performance on the test set. In the remaining subsections of Section 9.1, we look at a number of performance measures, including a comparison of the learning curves for the simulation versus the implementation, an analysis of the reasons for the increased rejection rate in the implementation over the model, and quantification of within-user consistency and across-user variability.

Although CHAMP was tested on the complete set of 657 sentences, our analysis concentrates on CHAMP's performance for the 549 sentences from the log files of the four users in the Adapt condition (User 1, User 2, User 3, and User 4). Each of these users participated in nine experimental sessions, saw the full stimuli set, and had the same opportunities for idiosyncratic expression. In contrast, User 5 and User 7 (Adapt/Echo condition) participated in three and five sessions, respectively, making their data difficult to contrast with the data from Users 1 through 4. The interested reader can find the data for User 5 and User 7 (along with raw data for all users presented in this chapter) in [46]. For the remainder of this section, when we refer to the "test set" we mean the 549 sentences from the four users in the Adapt condition.

9.1.1. Differences between CHAMP and the simulated system

In the process of developing the system it became apparent that there would be sentences accepted during the experiment that CHAMP would be unable to parse as well as sentences rejected during the experiment that CHAMP could understand. To make a meaningful comparison of CHAMP's performance to the ideal performance possible, some way of compensating for these differences had to be found. To understand why, consider that in an adaptive environment the outcome of every interaction may be felt in future interactions: the user avoids forms that lead to rejection and relies on those that are accepted. If a sentence accepted by the hidden-operator lead to adaptations during the experiment but CHAMP cannot accept the sentence, then CHAMP cannot learn the adaptations. If CHAMP does not learn the adaptations then all future sentences relying on those adaptations are likely to be rejected as well. Thus, when a set of adaptations rely on each other (the "bootstrapping effect" we saw in Section 8.7), a difference in learning early in the protocol may be magnified unrealistically. Had the user received negative reinforcement immediately, she would not have been as likely to reuse the form in the future, and the effects of the missing adaptations would not have propagated.

Differences between the simulated system and the implemented system stem from one of three sources:

1. Differences in functionality:
   - User 1 was given the opportunity to create extremely simple macro definitions based on subsequences of events. For example, after three occurrences of "cancel flight *k*" followed immediately by "schedule flight *n*" where the two flights had the same origin and destination, the user was asked if there was a verb that captured this idea. This allowed her to define a "reschedule" macro. Initial experimentation with User 1 made it clear that even a modest macro definition facility would require either very sophisticated inferences on the part of the system or a great deal of user interaction. Consequently, subsequent users were not afforded the same opportunity and CHAMP did not include the facility.
   - Conjunction was allowed in the experiment and is encouraged by the stimuli. CHAMP, however, expects only one database action per utterance.
   - Relative times (for example, "after 5 p.m.") were allowed in the experiment but are not provided for in the kernel grammar or the Concept Hierarchy.
   - For a few concepts, only a subset of the meanings allowed in the experiments were implemented. For example, a **projectname** in CHAMP always represents a group of people. In the experiments, a **projectname** was also a permissible *subject* for a meeting.
   - During the simulation, changes to the database were made overnight rather than on-line. As a result, a user's utterance was never rejected because it was inconsistent with an entry introduced into the database by a previous sentence in the session. CHAMP performs changes on-line and therefore detects such inconsistencies.

Differences in functionality between the simulation and the implementation are compensated for by Rules 2, 3, and 5 in Figure 9-1, below.

2. Differences in inference capabilities:
   - During the simulation, *constructive inference* was used by the hidden operator to build new forms and to eliminate redundant phrases (see Figure 3-2 for the rules followed by the hidden operator). Constructive inference was considered to be possible if all the parts of a legitimate concept were present such that no more that two deviation points had accrued in the constituents. Constructive inference was intended as a way to overcome the arbitrary two-deviation limit when enough information was present in the utterance to satisfy a sentential-level case frame (and, thus, a database action). In the simulation, forms derived by constructive inference were created by joining the tokens and generalized categories present in the confirmed interpretation. Thus, "The 3 o'clock meeting will be held in 5409" creates a **roomform** with the **roomwd** deleted as well as a **changeform** constructed from **m-d-ggform** + "will be held" + **m-locationform**. Without constructive inference, some portions of the users' grammars are simply not learnable (see Section 8.5). Constructive inference is discussed further in Chapter 11.

- Inferences allowed during the Resolution phase of the simulation were more powerful than those implemented. For example, reasoning about time was more complex during the experiment than the sorts of inferences of which CHAMP is capable. In addition, some instances of inference used during the experiment are explicitly prevented by recovery-time constraints. It is not possible, for example, to infer the type of a deleted object from the other constituents in the sentence because steps with **object** *bindvars* are protected by a **no-del** constraint.

Inference differences are compensated for by Rules 4 and 7 in Figure 9-1.

3. Differences arising from lack of specificity in the model:
   - During the simulation, if there was a segmentation of tokens that made the sentence understandable, that segmentation was used. CHAMP, on the other hand, is constrained in its interpretation by the Single Segment Assumption which enforces the view that contiguous unknowns perform a single functional role within the utterance. Consequently, the Single Segment Assumption may prevent CHAMP from finding the correct segmentation and explanation of the sentence. For further discussion of the problem, see Section 5.1.2.
   - The simulation required only that some decomposition of the utterance into constituents be within two deviations of the grammar. In contrast, the Maximal Subsequence Heuristic forces CHAMP's parser to coalesce and expand only the largest subsequence that corresponds to a constituent. This may prevent sentences that are within two deviations of the current grammar from being recognized. For further discussion of the problem, see Section 5.2.
   - The *lexical extension problem* occurs when a known word or phrase is used in a new way. During the simulation it was assumed that CHAMP would be able to treat the relevant tokens as unknowns under these circumstances. CHAMP's current design is unable to ignore the definitions for a word or phrase in the lexicon, however. The system relies on extra-grammatical markers to enforce the interpretation of recognizable tokens as unknowns. Chapter 10 contains a more detailed discussion of the problem.
   - Since the adaptation model makes no commitment to a particular form of generalization, derived forms were integrated into the grammar in the most useful way possible during the experiments. Achieving the best possible generalization of a new form represents an ideal circumstance. CHAMP's method of generalization, while both uniform and useful, is hardly ideal. Thus, the grammatical components derived by CHAMP during adaptation do not always correspond to the same derived components added to the grammar during the experiments (this is especially true when a set of components was derived through constructive inference). The differences are felt primarily as undergeneralization in CHAMP, requiring more learning episodes to capture the user's conditions on usage.

Differences that stem from the underspecified nature of the model are compensated for, in part, by Rules 1 and 7 in Figure 9-1. Figure 9-1 specifies the methods used to compensate for the differences between the simulated and the implemented systems. The primary method of compensation relies on preprocessing the data in the specific ways outlined in Rules 1 through 4. Preprocessing enables CHAMP to accept some sentences that were accepted during the experiment but that CHAMP could not otherwise understand. Rule 1 compensates for the lexical extension problem by introducing extra-grammatical markers that help force the correct behavior. The only justification offered for the rule is that it compensates for an open problem in this research. Rules 2 through 4 change the actual tokens typed by the user. The justification for these rules is simple: had the relevant forms been rejected by the hidden operator at their first appearance (as they would have been by CHAMP), the user would not have relied on them in future utterances.

The second method of compensation described in Figure 9-1 is forced rejection or acceptance. During evaluation of the test set, CHAMP is forced to reject a sentence that it would otherwise have accepted if the hidden operator mistakenly rejected it (Rule 5). On the other hand, if CHAMP found a resolution-time error in a sentence that was accepted in the experiment, the system was forced to adapt anyway (Rule 6). As a last resort, a difference in behavior is prevented from propagating to future interactions by introducing the necessary derived components by hand (Rule 7).

In parentheses after the statement of each rule, Figure 9-1 shows the number of sentences in the test set affected by each type of interference. Only two values are noteworthy. The fact that 145 sentences were preprocessed to remove redundancy (Rule 4) is actually quite misleading: 127 of those sentences were from User 4. She used the day of the week redundantly when specifying the date in almost every utterance. Had the redundancy not been accepted via the rules for constructive inference the first time it occurred, it is unlikely that she would have included it in the remaining 126 sentences. Indeed, this is exactly what happened in User 10's protocol the first time she included a day of the week along with the full date. CHAMP's interaction with User 10 during segmentation of the sentence let her know that the system considered **saturday** an unknown token. As a result, she never included a day of the week as part of the date again.

It is more difficult to dismiss the sixteen percent of the test set sentences that had to be marked to compensate for the lexical extension problem. As we noted above, a solution for this problem within our adaptation model remains an open aspect of this research. We discuss the difficulties involved in parsing sentences that contain lexical extensions in Chapter 10. Here we note only that the problem is significant and cannot be ignored.

1. If a known word is being used in a new way and the hidden operator interpreted it in the new way, then force it to be treated as an unknown by enclosing it in angle brackets. The modified sentence is then treated in accordance with the Single Segment Assumption.(84/539 (16%))
   Example: "the University of Chicago" has one unknown token, **university**, and three tokens being used in new ways. The segment therefore becomes: <the> university <of> <chicago>. When contiguous unknown tokens are combined, segmentation produces **the university of chicago** as a single unknown phrase.
2. Turn conjunctions into separate sentences, distributing shared information. (31/539 (6%))
   Example: "cancel flight #1 on june 16 and schedule flight #2" becomes "cancel flight #1 on june 16" and "schedule flight #2 on june 16" (this counts as two sentences affected by conjunction).
3. If a failure is caused by unimplemented semantics, change the data by replacing the phrase referring to the unimplemented concept with one that refers to an implemented equivalent. (39/539 (7%))
   Example: the unimplemented relative time, "after 7 p.m." is replaced with the concrete time, "from 7 p.m. to 11:59 p.m."
4. If a sentence contains a redundant phrase that was compensated for using constructive inference, then remove each occurrence of the redundant phrase. (145/539 (27%))
   Example: "Monday, June 12" becomes "June 12."
5. If a sentence was accepted during the experiment but CHAMP detects a resolution-time error for the meaning, ignore or correct the error and accept the sentence. (16/539 (3%))
   Example: if the user failed to complete a subtask that removed an event from the calendar then CHAMP will detect the conflict when the user tries to schedule a new event in the occupied time slot.
6. If CHAMP accepts a sentence not accepted during the simulation, then force rejection and prevent adaptation. (5/539 (1%))
   Example: this occurs when the hidden operator mistakenly rejected a sentence as too deviant.
7. If a sentence was accepted during the experiment which CHAMP cannot parse (even after applying the previous rules), then consider whether the adaptations resulting from acceptance are required in the future. If what was learned from the sentence is never used again or CHAMP can learn it the next time it appears, then do nothing. If, on the other hand, what was learned will be required later and CHAMP will not be able to learn it at the next occurrence either, then add to the grammar by hand the minimal number of grammatical components that capture the necessary adaptations. (8/539 (1%) resulting in a total of 13 components being added by hand for the 4 users).
   Example: this occurs when acceptance was by constructive inference or when the hidden operator erroneously accepted.

Figure 9-1: The rules used to preprocess the data from the hidden-operator experiments (and the number of test set sentences affected by each rule).

The purpose of preprocessing the original experimental data and interfering with the normal understanding process in CHAMP is to recreate the conditions of each protocol as closely as possible given the differences between the simulation and the implementation. Although some sentences required more than one kind of interference, most sentences required none (see [46]). We turn now to an examination of CHAMP's performance on the preprocessed test set.

9.1.2. Comparison of performance

A fundamental purpose of the original experiments was to demonstrate the self-bounded linguistic behavior of frequent users in an adaptive environment. Consequently, our primary measure of performance was a calculation of the number of new constructions per interpretable utterance for each user and session (Figure 3-3 in Chapter 3). We found strong evidence for self-bounded behavior in the decrease over time of both the number of new constructions and the number of uninterpretable sentences. Figures 9-2 through 9-5 show the original graphs constructed for each of the four users in the Adapt condition side-by-side with CHAMP's performance for the same measure.[38] The graphs for User 2 show the most similarity, the graphs for User 1, the least. We explain the causes for the apparent differences between the sets of graphs in the remainder of this section. Despite the differences, the general pattern remains: an overall decrease in the number of new constructions and rejected sentences over time, with a local increase after the introduction of the supplementary instructions to work quickly. In short, the implementation's behavior conforms closely enough to the model to capture the regularities present in the test set utterances.

It should be noted that the y-axis in the lefthand graph of each figure is labelled differently from its counterpart in Figure 3-3 where it read, "new constructions/interpretable sentences." For the hidden-operator graphs, the meaning of the new label ("new constructions/learning opportunity") is the same as the old: the number of interpretable sentences is exactly the number of opportunities for learning and exactly the number of sentences accepted. Under the conditions of this evaluation, however, CHAMP's opportunities for learning may be different from the number of sentences the system can interpret. In accordance with the rules in Figure 9-1, we do not consider as opportunities for learning those sentences from the test set

---

[38]The values shown for CHAMP take competition into account. In other words, if six components were added to the grammar as three sets of competitors, only two components (one competitor) were counted as new constructions. Taking competition into account gives a more realistic picture of the asymptotic behavior of the system: as competitions are resolved only one set of components will remain in the grammar. The numbers of new constructions without considering competition can be found in [46].

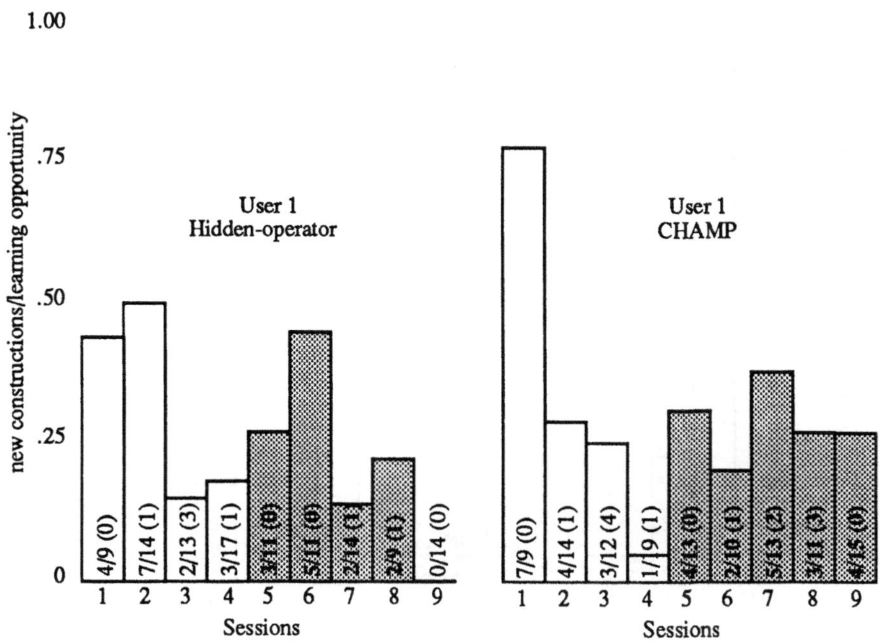

Figure 9-2: Capturing User 1's regularity under the model and in CHAMP (shaded sessions followed the supplementary instructions to work quickly, the number of unparsable utterances for each session is given in parentheses).

that CHAMP understood but was forced to reject (Rule 6), but we do consider as opportunities for learning those sentences CHAMP was forced to accept (Rule 5) as well as those after which we added to the grammar by hand (Rule 7).[39] Note that it is possible to have more than one new construction per opportunity for learning if multiple deviations in the sentence resulted in the addition of multiple derived components to the grammar (see Figure 9-4).

The figures also show the number of unparsable sentences for each session in parentheses after the fraction for new constructions. What it means to be "unparsable" must be defined carefully for CHAMP as well. The number of unparsable sentences in the experiments is exactly the number of utterances rejected. The number of unparsable sentences for CHAMP, on the other hand, includes not only those

[39]None of the graphs includes learning at Deviation-level 0 (new instances of known classes, abbreviations, and stored spelling corrections) because we do not expect the same decrease in these phenomena from self-bounded behavior as we expect for deviations. The number of instances of learning at Deviation-level 0 for each user can be found in [46].

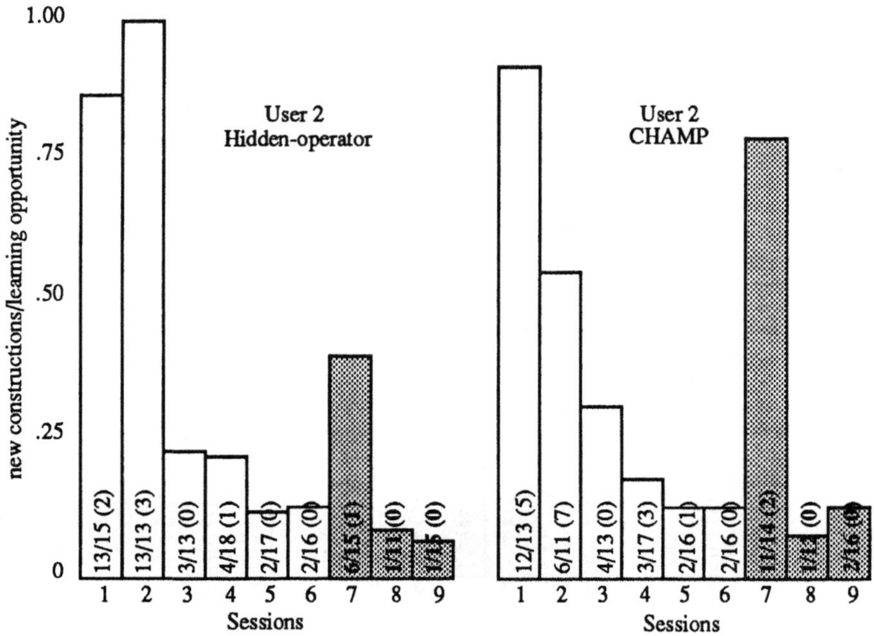

Figure 9-3: Capturing User 2's regularity under the model and in CHAMP (shaded sessions followed the supplementary instructions to work quickly, the number of unparsable utterances for each session is given in parentheses).

sentences actually rejected by the system (some of which lead to adaptations anyway, via Rule 7) but also those rejected by force (Rule 6). Note that under this method of evaluating the implementation it is possible for the same sentence to be both unparsable (showing up in parentheses) and a contributor to the number of opportunities for learning. In the experiment, this was impossible.

Although we attempted to recreate the conditions of the protocol as closely as possible, Figures 9-2 through 9-5 show that CHAMP's performance was not exactly the same as the model's. The differences between the two graphs for each user stem from three sources: the number of rejected sentences, undergeneralization during adaptation, and the redistribution of learning episodes by Rule 7. We analyze the reasons for the increase in rejections in the next section; here we note only that CHAMP does, in general, reject more sentences than does the model. When the number of opportunities for learning decreases, the number of constructions per opportunity, reflected by the height of the bars, increases.

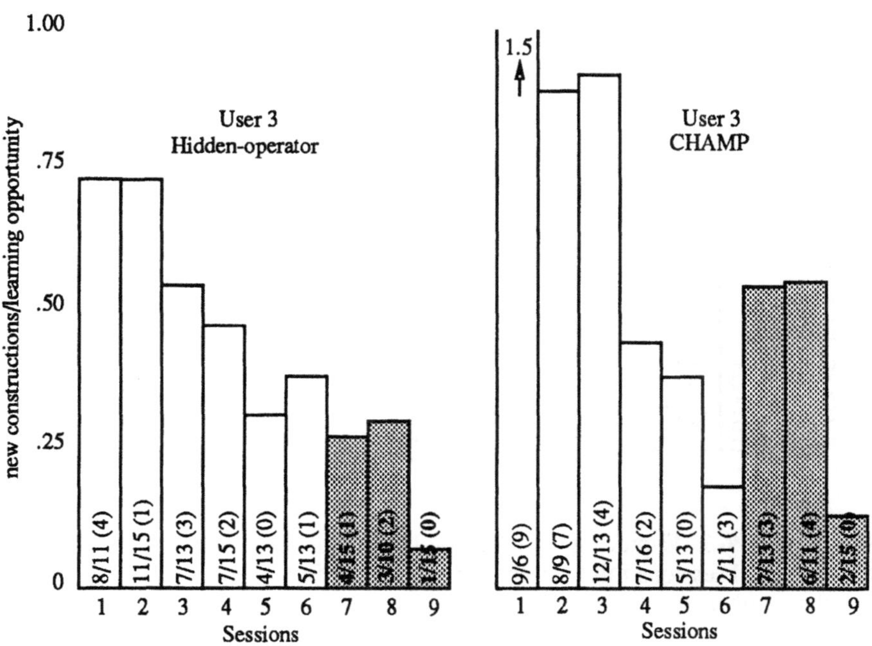

Figure 9-4: Capturing User 3's regularity under the model and in CHAMP (shaded sessions followed the supplementary instructions to work quickly, the number of unparsable utterances for each session is given in parentheses).

CHAMP undergeneralizes in comparison to the hidden operator's behavior primarily because CHAMP lacks constructive inference. In essence, more episodes of learning by straightforward adaptation are required to cover all the cases covered by a single episode of learning via constructive inference and hidden-operator generalization. The lack of constructive inference accounts for many of the differences in the sessions after the supplementary instructions were given; CHAMP had undergeneralized some transpositions and deletions that were crucial as utterances became shorter.

The redistribution of learning episodes occurs because of the uneven compensatory role of Rule 7. Recall that if a component could not be learned by CHAMP but had been relied upon by the user in future utterances, Rule 7 adds the component to the grammar immediately after the sentence that contained the deviation. If the component could be learned at the next occurrence, however, no action is taken. As a result, some components learned during session *i* in the hidden-operator graph may not have been learned until sessions *j* and *k* in CHAMP's graph, depending upon when the next sentence requiring them occurred in the protocol.

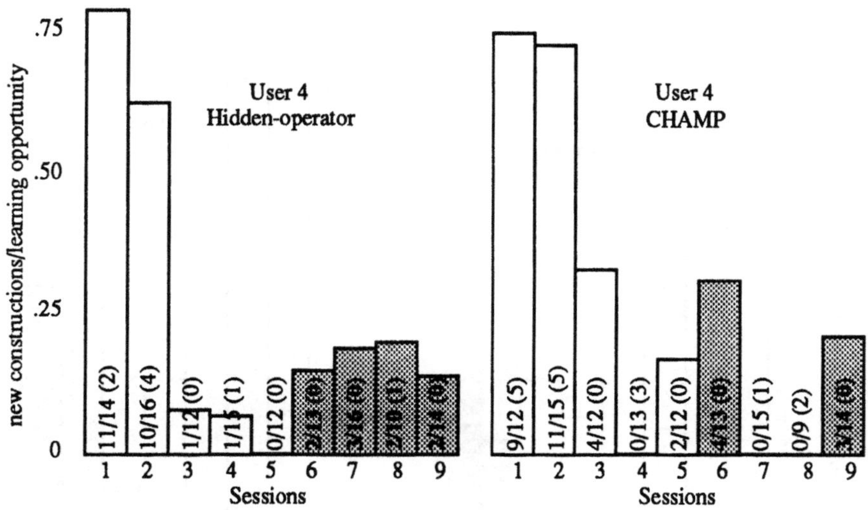

Figure 9-5: Capturing User 4's regularity under the model and in CHAMP (shaded sessions followed the supplementary instructions to work quickly, the number of unparsable utterances for each session is given in parentheses).

Despite these differences, the graphs for performance under CHAMP show the same general pattern as those under the simulation, reflecting the inherently self-bounded nature of each user's utterances and the ability of the implementation to capture her regularity.

9.1.3. Analysis of differences in acceptance/rejection

Having noted that CHAMP accepts fewer sentences from the test set than did the simulation, it is useful to ask what causes the additional rejections. When we factor out hidden-operator errors (five erroneous rejections and seven erroneous acceptances), we find that 38/539 of the test set sentences were truly too deviant with respect to the grammar current at the time of use. Thus, a perfect implementation of the model would have rejected seven percent of the sentences. Factoring out forced rejections, CHAMP fails to accept 73/539 sentences, or about fourteen percent.

Figure 9-6 shows that most of the thirty-five rejections not predicted by the model come from two sources: the lack of constructive inference and the intrusion of the Single Segment Assumption. Note that for the four users in the Adapt condition of the original experiments only one sentence was rejected because of recovery-time constraints and no sentences were rejected because of the Maximal Subsequence Heuristic.

Reason for difference	% of test set
Constructive inference	16/539 (3%)
Single Segment Assumption	18/539 (>3%)
Recovery-time constraint	1/539 (<1%)
Total:	35/539 (7%)

Figure 9-6: A breakdown of the reasons why CHAMP rejects 35 sentences from the test set that were acceptable according to the adaptation model.

Although a three percent increase in rejections from the lack of constructive inference does not seem like a lot, the statistic does not reflect the true value because of Rule 7. Using Rule 7 we added by hand those grammatical components that would be required but still unlearnable later in the user's protocol. Thus the sixteen sentences rejected because of the lack of constructive inference represent only a portion of the sentences truly affected—the portion that contained adaptations that could be learned at the next occurrence. Without constructive inference or Rule 7, CHAMP would have rejected at least eight additional utterances.

Constructive inference figured prominently in the simulation because it is a good mechanism for overcoming bad choices in kernel design. One bad design choice in the kernel, for example, affected every user's ability to accomplish the class of subtasks that added a value to an empty slot in a database record. From a database update point of view these subtasks correspond to a **change** action in which the source value for the slot is not specified (for example, "Change the speaker of the AI seminar [from nil] to John"). Thus, it was expected that the kernel **changeforms** adequately indexed the action. Unfortunately, none of the users thought about those subtasks in that way. Instead, they seemed to think about the subtasks as "amendment" actions, distinct from both **schedule** actions and **change** actions (for example, "Add John as the speaker for the AI seminar."). In the experiment, this conceptual difference posed no serious problem because each user eventually employed a deviant **changeform** acceptable via constructive inference. In CHAMP, this would not have been possible, and users would have had to battle a conceptual mismatch as well as a two-deviation limit on error recovery. We examine the issues involved in extending CHAMP to include constructive inference in Chapter 11.

The Single Segment Assumption was also responsible for rejecting three percent of the sentences that were recognizable by the model. The effect is modest for this user group and task. While the experiments with new users do not result in a higher percentage, it is unclear whether the problem might be more pervasive given a different task or domain. We briefly examine ways in which to extend the system to compensate for single segment violations in Chapter 11.

9.1.4. Analysis of the utility of adaptation and generalization

Although we were able to draw many useful conclusions from the hidden-operator experiments, the underspecification of the model made it impossible to give quantitative answers to a number of questions we would have liked to ask. It is difficult, for example, to derive the utility of adaptation in any sort of precise way from the results of the simulation when generalization by the hidden operator provided some of the power of the learning mechanism. An implementation of the model, on the other hand, allows access to quantitative measures. The purpose of this section, then, is to provide a sense of the overall utility of our method of adaptation and generalization by answering the following questions for CHAMP's performance on the test set:

- What is the effectiveness of learning? How much actual improvement in understanding the user's language comes from adaptation?
- What is the cost of learning? What effect does adaptation and generalization have on the level of ambiguity in the grammar?
- How effective is competition as a method of controlling grammar growth?
- Given a uniform (non-human) method of adaptation and generalization, how truly idiosyncratic are the derived grammars?

To answer the first of these questions, we contrast for each user the number of her sentences accepted by the kernel and the number accepted by her final grammar—any increase is due to learning. Figure 9-7 shows that the increase is significant for each user. On the average, the kernel accepts only 16% of a user's utterances while her own derived grammar accepts 88%.

	User 1	User 2	User 3	User 4
G_{kernel}	18/127 (14%)	34/144 (24%)	9/138 (7%)	25/130 (19%)
G_{final}	115/127 (91%)	127/144 (88%)	112/138 (81%)	118/130 (91%)

Figure 9-7: The effectiveness of learning as measured by the differences in the number of utterances understood by the kernel and by the user's final grammar.

To carry the analysis further, we measure the utility of each learning episode by computing the average number of sentences brought into the grammar each time a deviant utterance is explained. The value is computed by subtracting the number of sentences accepted by the kernel from the number accepted by a user's grammar and dividing by the number of learning episodes. For Users 1, 2, 3, and 4, respectively, the values are: 3.3, 2.7, 2.3, and 3.7 sentences per episode. These values represent a kind of "bootstrapping constant" that reflects the way in which CHAMP's particular implementation of adaptation and generalization captures within-user consistency. An alternative implementation would probably produce very different values. Consider, for example, an implementation using conservative substitution adaptations (as described in Chapter 8). The tendency of the conservative approach to undergeneralize is likely to appear as a decrease in the utility of each learning episode: the user's final grammar might result in the same number of acceptances but at the cost of requiring more instances of adaptation. Thus, the boostrappping values themselves are less important than the fact that our ability to compute them provides a metric for comparing design choices.

The second question posed at the beginning of the section concerns the cost of adaptation. As we bring more of the user's language into the grammar we increase the likelihood that we will understand her future utterances. But is the increase in understanding, as measured by acceptances, negated by a larger increase in the cost of understanding, as measured by search? We know that the user's language is self-bounded, but it may still be quite ambiguous. The question, then, is not whether we can prevent the rise in search stemming from inherent ambiguity in the user's idiolect, but whether the system as a whole suffers disproportionately as ambiguity increases.

We measure the rise in ambiguity in an adapted grammar in two ways. First, holding the test sentences constant, we compare the average number of parse states considered by successive grammars during search at Deviation-level 0. As the level of ambiguity in the grammar increases through the adaptations of each session, so will the average amount of search required to accept at Deviation-level 0. Second, we examine the average number of explanations (roots) produced by the Parse/Recovery Cycle for each sentence accepted at Deviation-level 0. This value reflects a rise in ambiguity that is somewhat independent of the increase in search because of the way annotated parse trees share substructure. A rise in search need not give rise to additional explanations. Conversely, additional root nodes may indicate only a modest increase in search. From the user's point of view increased search corresponds to decreased response time while a rise in the number of explanations corresponds to an increase in the number of interactions required during resolution.

Figures 9-8 through 9-11 display the measurements for the successive grammars for each user. The figures show, session by session, the growth in the average number of states and roots over all the user's sentences that are non-deviant with respect to the state of the grammar at the end of the session. Thus, the first row of Figure 9-8 shows that the kernel grammar, G(0), accepts eighteen sentences from User 1, examining nineteen parse states and producing one explanation per sentence, on the average. The second row of the same figure reflects changes in performance due to learning in User 1's first session. The derived components are responsible for bringing sixty-one sentences from that user's total protocol into Deviation-level 0 with no significant rise in search and only a small increase in the average number of explanations produced.

Grammar after session(*i*)	Number of non-deviant sentences	Average number states to accept	Average number roots produced
G(0)	18	19.3	1.0
$G_1(1)$	79	37.0	1.1
$G_1(2)$	86	37.4	1.3
$G_1(3)$	88	38.3	1.3
$G_1(4)$	90	37.7	1.3
$G_1(5)$	96	36.4	1.2
$G_1(6)$	98	36.2	1.3
$G_1(7)$	104	37.2	1.4
$G_1(8)$	111	36.8	1.5
$G_1(9)$	115	37.6	1.5

Figure 9-8: The change in the cost of parsing User 1's sentences at Deviation-level 0 as a function of grammar growth.

For three of the four users, the increase in the number of parse states examined is proportionally far less than the increase in the number of sentences understood. By the end of the ninth session, the search for User 1 has expanded by a factor of two but the number of her sentences that are now non-deviant has expanded by a factor of six. User 3's trade-off is even more favorable: twelve times as many sentences are accepted by the final grammar as by the kernel, at a cost of only two and a half times the search. User 4 gains almost five times as many sentences at slightly less than twice the search. User 2 has the most balanced case: a factor of 3.5 increase in accepted utterances and a factor of three increase in search.

Grammar after session(*i*)	Number of non-deviant sentences	Average number states to accept	Average number roots produced
G(0)	34	21.9	1.0
$G_2(1)$	78	25.8	1.1
$G_2(2)$	91	26.5	1.1
$G_2(3)$	94	28.7	1.2
$G_2(4)$	103	57.6	1.4
$G_2(5)$	107	61.5	1.6
$G_2(6)$	114	59.4	1.6
$G_2(7)$	121	59.4	1.6
$G_2(8)$	123	59.8	1.6
$G_2(9)$	123	59.8	1.6

Figure 9-9: The change in the cost of parsing User 2's sentences at Deviation-level 0 as a function of grammar growth.

Grammar after session(*i*)	Number of non-deviant sentences	Average number states to accept	Average number roots produced
G(0)	9	18.0	1.0
$G_3(1)$	21	30.3	1.1
$G_3(2)$	28	30.8	1.5
$G_3(3)$	71	34.6	1.4
$G_3(4)$	83	46.7	2.1
$G_3(5)$	92	44.6	2.1
$G_3(6)$	93	44.2	2.1
$G_3(7)$	103	43.2	1.9
$G_3(8)$	109	43.6	1.9
$G_3(9)$	112	43.3	2.0

Figure 9-10: The change in the cost of parsing User 3's sentences at Deviation-level 0 as a function of grammar growth.

If increase in search corresponds to increase in response time, what do these values tell us? In short, response times will get slower over all but will not grow exponentially as a function of the increase in the language accepted. Since the grammar itself is bounded by the user's natural behavior, the increase in response time is bounded as well. Even with kinds of increases seen for these users, response times were usually under ten seconds.

The near-monotonic increase in the size of the search goes hand-in-hand with a near-monotonic increase in the average number of explanations produced for each accepted utterance. Where exactly is the ambiguity coming from? The users do

Grammar after session(i)	Number of non-deviant sentences	Average number states to accept	Average number roots produced
G(0)	25	21.0	1.0
$G_4(1)$	62	28.0	1.1
$G_4(2)$	78	30.9	1.3
$G_4(3)$	95	37.3	1.3
$G_4(4)$	106	36.9	1.3
$G_4(5)$	112	38.8	1.3
$G_4(6)$	116	40.2	1.3
$G_4(7)$	116	40.2	1.3
$G_4(8)$	116	40.2	1.3
$G_4(9)$	118	40.7	1.5

Figure 9-11: The change in the cost of parsing User 4's sentences at Deviation-level 0 as a function of grammar growth.

introduce some lexical ambiguity into their idiosyncratic grammars, but lexical ambiguity contributes primarily to small, local increases in the size of the search space. As paths representing the correct constituents are joined, the Maximal Subsequence Heuristic eliminates useless alternative paths which, in turn, keeps the effects of lexical ambiguity from propagating very far up the Agenda.

Most of the increase in ambiguity comes from adaptation to deletion deviations. As the user's language becomes increasingly terse, the system builds forms in which the content words that correspond to critical differences between forms are deleted. As a result, there is an increase in the number of constituents that are satisfied by each segment; the increase propagates to each level of the Agenda and, eventually, to the root nodes themselves.

Consider as a simple example what happens if the user drops both a marker and a head noun (a common occurrence). From that point on, every sentence indexing the derived components produces multiple roots: "Schedule 7 p.m. on June 4 with John" produces two effectively equivalent roots if neither a **meetingwd** nor an **hourmkr** is required by the grammar. One tree contains "7 p.m." as a normal unmarked prenominal constituent in the **meetingform** with the **meetingwd** deleted. The second tree explains the same time segment as a postnominal constituent using both of the components derived by deletions. If the marker for the date is also optional in the adapted grammar (another common occurrence), and we change the sentence slightly to, "Schedule 7 p.m. June 4 with John," then four roots result from the obvious combinatorics (unmarked prenominal versus marked postnominal for each modifier). If the user has derived forms for more than one type of

groupgathering, each of which has the head noun deleted (a somewhat less common occurrence), the same sentence produces four roots for each **groupgathering** that can be recognized without its head noun. Similar problems arise when the user relies on derived forms without verbs.

The third question we posed at the beginning of the section concerns the effectiveness of competition as a method of controlling grammar growth. Competition allows the system to postpone choosing among alternative sets of adaptations that explain the same deviations. Thus, the issue of grammar growth is related to but not identical to increased ambiguity. Competitions arise from ambiguities already present in the grammar; the purpose of competition is to keep those ambiguities from proliferating exponentially via further adaptations.

What do we mean by the "effectiveness of competition?" In short, we want to know whether competition allows the system to eliminate all but one subset of explanations from a set of effectively equivalent adaptations. The reoccurrence of a competitor is necessary but not sufficient to resolve a competition; it is possible for all competitors to succeed when any one succeeds. If competition is a useful mechanism then it provides the system with a way of choosing among alternatives, favoring components that explain an idiosyncratic constituent in more than one context. We consider competition harmful, however, if most competitors are preserved even with repeated use; under these circumstances, it would have been less costly to have the system choose arbitrarily among the initial set of alternative adaptations.

Figure 9-12 displays the relevant competition values for users in the Adapt condition. With the exception of User 4, most of the competitions that had a chance to be resolved were resolved the next time a competitor was required to understand a sentence. For User 4, subsequent uses of competitors generally occurred in utterances that were structurally identical to those that gave rise to the competition initially. As a result, all explanations succeeded repeatedly and the competition remained unresolved.

Considering Figures 9-8 through 9-12 together, we conclude that although competition is fairly successful at stopping the exponential proliferation of existing ambiguities, some additional mechanism for removing ambiguity would be useful as well (see Chapter 11 for further discussion).

The final question we posed at the beginning of the section concerns across-user variability. Recall from Chapter 3 that a strong argument can be made in favor of adaptation at the interface if users' grammars are truly idiosyncratic. With high

	Number resolved competitions	Number unresolved competitions	Number left unresolved with chance to resolve
User 1	0	1	0
User 2	1	5	1
User 3	7	10	2
User 4	1	4	4

Figure 9-12: Controlling grammar growth by preserving only the most useful explanations for deviations through competition.

variability in preferred expression across users, a single grammar capable of understanding all users actually penalizes each individual user during search for forms she does not use. Although the simulation resulted in little overlap among the users' final grammars, one could argue that the perceived idiosyncracy was an artifact of the hidden operator's freedom when generalizing the derived form. CHAMP's uniform adaptation and generalization mechanism provides the opportunity to examine across-user variability in a more meaningful way.

We attain a quantitative measure for idiosyncracy by examining the acceptance rate for each user's utterances under her own and each of the other users' final grammars (Figure 9-13). If each final grammar accepts approximately the same language, then there should be no significant difference in the acceptance rates. In contrast, Figure 9-13 clearly demonstrates a wide range of variability: User 3's final grammar is able to parse 59% of User 1's sentences, but User 4's final grammar can parse only 14% of the utterances from User 3. Observe that in no instance did the grammar for another user come close to the performance of the user's own final grammar. Taken in conjunction with the high acceptance rates by each user's idiosyncratic grammar, we conclude that the method of adaptation and generalization realized in CHAMP is adequate to accommodate the very real variability in preferred expression that exists across users.

9.1.5. Adaptive versus monolithic performance

To what degree did the size of CHAMP's kernel grammar affect the analyses in the previous section? Did we stack the deck in favor of adaptation by choosing a small kernel? It could be argued that with a larger grammar, learning might not be necessary at all—whatever small mismatches exist between the user's natural language and the system's natural language might be easily overcome by user adaptation. Even across-user variability is unimportant if everyone can be understood. In short, wouldn't a monolithic, non-adaptive grammar have performed just as well?

Final Grammar for	Applied to All Sentences of: User 1	User 2	User 3	User 4
User 4	**115/127 (91%)**	72/144 (50%)	40/138 (29%)	60/130 (46%)
User 3	59/127 (46%)	**127/144 (88%)**	15/138 (11%)	74/130 (57%)
User 2	75/127 (59%)	71/144 (49%)	**112/138 (81%)**	66/130 (51%)
User 1	48/127 (38%)	66/145 (46%)	19/138 (14%)	**118/130 (91%)**

Figure 9-13: Measuring across-user variability by computing the acceptance rate for each's utterances under her own & each of the other users' final grammars.

The answer is no. To see why, let us build the best monolithic grammar possible for the four users we have been studying, best in the sense that it is guaranteed to understand every sentence understood by any of the users' individual grammars. We construct the grammar by adding to the kernel the union of the users' final grammars minus any redundant components. Figure 9-14 demonstrates what happens when we use the monolithic grammar to parse the test set.

User	Average $States_{user}$	Average $States_{mono}$	Average $Roots_{user}$	Average $Roots_{mono}$	Additional sentences
1	37.6	109.6	1.5	7.7	4
2	59.8	155.5	1.6	8.5	4
3	43.3	156.5	2.0	9.3	1
4	40.7	148.3	1.5	7.1	1

Figure 9-14: A comparison of the relative costs of parsing with a monolithic grammar versus parsing with the idiosyncratic grammars provided by adaptation. (The last column shows the number of additional sentences for each user that could be parsed by the monolithic grammar but not the user's final grammar).

In every instance the average number of search states examined by the monolithic grammar is significantly greater than the number required by the user's idiosyncratic grammar. Of course, we do gain the ability to understand ten additional sentences in the test set (this occurs when adaptations learned for User *i* are able to parse a sentence that was rejected for User *j*). The trade-off hardly seems favorable, however. User 1 would find a three percent increase in the number of her sentences understood by the interface (4/127) at a cost of almost three times the search. User 2 also receives about a three percent increase (4/144) at a cost of about two and a half times the search. User 3 and User 4 suffer the most: each receives an increase of less than one percent in accepted sentences but must wait through 3.6 times the amount of search.

The trade-off seems even less favorable when we consider the difference in the number of roots produced under each type of system. The monolithic static grammar produces about five times as many roots on the average as a user's adapted grammar—five times as many incorrect or redundant explanations. Even for a system able to make the kinds of resolution-time inferences that CHAMP can, a significant portion of multi-root sentences cannot be resolved by inference and constraints from the databases alone. Thus, in addition to waiting through longer searches, the users are likely to be subjected to more interactions as well.

In Chapter 1 we argued from a theoretical point of view that a monolithic approach to interface design must engender some degree of mismatch between the language accepted by the system and the language employed by any particular user. The mismatch comes in two forms: language the user prefers but that cannot be understood by the interface and language the interface understands that is never employed by the user. In this section we have controlled for the first kind of mismatch by guaranteeing that the monolithic grammar could parse at least as many sentences in the test set as could CHAMP. Figure 9-14 shows the price paid by each user for the second kind of mismatch during every search over those portions of the system's language she will never use. We know that we cannot control for the second kind of mismatch because of the real variability of expression across the users in our sample. Although it may be possible to achieve the same acceptance rate with less ambiguity in a much more carefully crafted monolithic grammar, the across-user variability is not going to disappear.

In contrast to the monolithic system's performance, adaptation minimizes both kinds of mismatch without requiring inordinate skill as a grammar designer. By learning the user's preferred forms of expression and engendering only those mismatches required by its small kernel, an adaptive interface keeps the cost of understanding each user in proportion to the inherent ambiguity in her idiosyncratic language.

9.2. CHAMP's performance in real user interactions

The performance analysis in Section 9.1 seems to argue strongly in favor of an adaptive interface design for frequent users. Still, one might argue that the sorts of interference we needed to employ to compare the implementation with the simulation, the use of the development set during system design, previous exposure to the entire test set during the experiments, and the small user sample all contributed to an exaggerated evaluation of the system's effectiveness.

To guard against this possibility, CHAMP was tested in on-line experiments with two new users (User 9 and User 10) performing the same task as the original users. The two new users were drawn from the same population as the first eight (female professional secretaries between twenty and sixty-five years of age who keep a calendar as part of their jobs but who have no prior experience with natural language interfaces). The experimental condition was the same as that described in Section 3.2 for the Adapt users, including initial instructions, supplementary instructions, pictorial stimuli, and a limit of three attempts per subtask. The kernel grammar used in the on-line experiments can be found in [46].[40]

The role of the hidden operator in the on-line experiments was reduced to adding extra-grammatical markers to compensate for the lexical extension problem before passing the user's sentence to CHAMP. Of the 385 sentences for the new users, thirty-one (8%) required hidden-operator intervention.

In the next three sections, we evaluate CHAMP's performance in the on-line experiments in terms of the same measures examined for the original users. A variety of other measures (including a response-time synopsis) can be found in [46]. The analysis shows the same patterns for spontaneous inputs as it did for the modified test set from the initial experiments. This validates our previous results and suggests that the modifications themselves played no significant part in the system's performance. Note also that the increase in sample size, albeit modest, did not introduce qualitatively different results.

---

[40]The kernel grammar for the experiments differed from the kernel grammar used to evaluate the original data in two ways. First, a set of kernel **changeforms** were added to compensate for the conceptual problem of amendments discussed in Section 9.1.3. Second, the kernel form recognizing marked calendar segments had its marker changed from required to optional. This made it more likely that user preferred forms for the **show** action would succeed (in the original experiments, user preferred **showforms** were usually learned by constructive inference). Many subtasks required the user to look at the calendar or airline schedule before actually performing the indicated action. Thus, making user **showforms** slightly closer to the kernel made it less likely that users would be prevented from carrying out multiple subtasks because of one unacceptable form.

9.2.1. Synopsis of user and system performance

The self-bounded behavior of the two new users is evident in Figure 9-15. Each user shows the same overall decrease in the number of new constructions per interpretable sentence as the original users, as well as the same local increase and return to stabilization after the supplementary instructions are given.

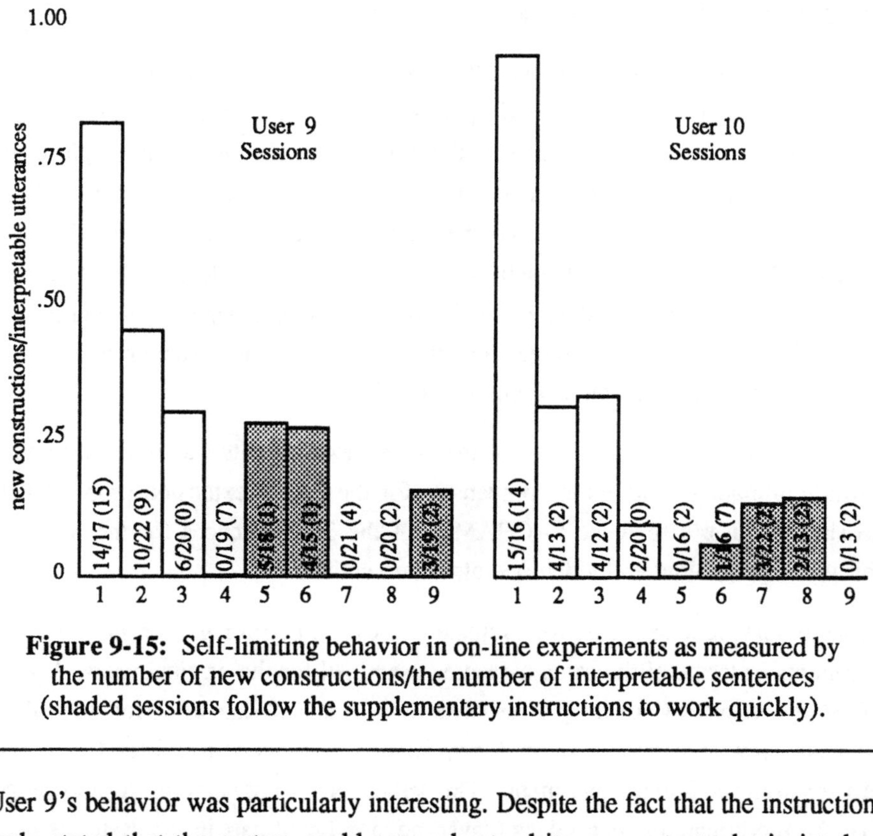

Figure 9-15: Self-limiting behavior in on-line experiments as measured by the number of new constructions/the number of interpretable sentences (shaded sessions follow the supplementary instructions to work quickly).

User 9's behavior was particularly interesting. Despite the fact that the instructions clearly stated that the system could not understand its own output, she insisted on using the system's messages as a template for her own commands (User 7 had shown a less extreme form of the same behavior). Figure 9-16 demonstrates one such episode. By the end of her third session, User 9 had essentially bootstrapped the system to where it could parse a terser form of its own already terse output.

User 10's natural grammar was quite different from the kernel, resulting in both a high rejection rate and high number of new constructions on the first day. Of the ten users studied, however, she was by far the most adaptive and rapidly settled into a comfortable mix of kernel forms and derived forms. In fact, at the end of her third session, User 10 commented that she found it more natural to use a form she

```
next> show schedule for June 10

Tracking...9...13...16...18...20...21...21...21...done.

JUNE 10    10:00am - 12:00pm MEETING in/at OFFICE with AISYS

Ok, done.

next> cancel 10:00am Meeting in/at Office with AISys June 10

Trying to understand IN/AT. Does it refer to a/an:
(0) DATE, (1) TIME-INTERVAL, (2) SINGLE-TIME, (3) PARTICIPANT,
(4) LOCATION, (5) SUBJECT, (6) GENERAL-TOPIC,
(7) none of these? [give number]: 7

Tracking...16...28...37...41...49...50...50...50...done.
Tracking...52...54...61...67...79...82...82...82...done.

Do you want:
  to delete: JUNE 10    10:00am - 12:00pm MEETING in/at OFFICE with AISYS?
[y or n] y

Creating LOCMKR from IN/AT via SUBST
Ok, done.
```

Figure 9-16: An example of User 9's tendency to formulate her utterances based on CHAMP's output ("Tracking" shows the node count at each Agenda-level and deviation-level. It was a device to keep the user's attention focused during search.)

believed the system would understand than to use an alternative form that she preferred but that she believed the system could not understand. Figure 9-15 demonstrates that CHAMP was doing a significant amount of learning despite User 10's belief that only she was adapting.

As was the case with the original users, both of the new users finished most of the subtasks in the experiment. On three occasions a new user was unable to effect the correct change to the calendar due to the system's incorrect inferences (twice for User 9, once for User 10). User 10 was also stopped once by the Maximal Subsequence Heuristic. She was the only user to have sentences rejected for this reason (three sentences corresponding to one subtask). The exact cause of the rejections is explained by Figure 5-14. Except for a slight increase after the supplementary instructions were given, each new user also showed a steady decrease in the number of utterances per task over time as her natural language and her adapted grammar converged.

9.2.2. Analysis of rejections

Extrapolating from the analysis of rejected sentences for users in the original Adapt condition, we expect CHAMP to reject about twice as many sentences as the model considers unparsable. Figure 9-17 confirms the prediction. Eight percent of the new test set was either too deviant with respect to the grammar current at the time of use or corresponded to meanings that conflicted with information in the database at that time. CHAMP rejects an additional eight percent of the test set for implementation-dependent reasons.

Reason for rejection	% of test set
Deviance or resolution-time conflict	31/385 (8%)
Implementation	29/385 (8%)
Operator	4/385(1%)
User	10/385 (3%)
Total:	74/385 (20%)

Figure 9-17: **Reasons for rejected sentences in the on-line experiments.**

In addition, four sentences were rejected because the hidden operator failed to notice occasions of lexical extension. The ten rejections attributed to the user represent cases where CHAMP produced the correct interpretation of the sentence typed, but the user rejected the interpretation during Resolution. Usually this meant that the user had misunderstood the stimuli, but occasionally she had simply changed her mind about what to add to the calendar.

Figure 9-18 breaks down the implementation-dependent rejections by cause. The largest subgroup is formed by sentences in unreachable portions of the user's language space. These deviations cannot be learned because each one tries to introduce a subconstituent into a formclass that does not expect it. We saw an example of an unreachable deviation for User 10 in Section 8.5: "Change June 11 NY to Pittsburgh from flight 82 to flight 265" (U10S120). Since no kernel form expects a full **flight** object in the source case of a source-target pair, CHAMP cannot understand the segment "from flight 82." Further, CHAMP cannot learn to understand the segment because the system adapts only in the presence or absence of expected categories. Were the system extended to include constructive inference, however, each of the fourteen unlearnable deviations would be within reach.

Overall, the pattern of rejections for the new users conforms to the pattern we saw in the original test set. In a perfect implementation of the model, the average accep-

Reason for rejection	% of test set
Unlearnable deviations	14/385 (4%)
Maximal Subsequence Heuristic	3/385 (<1%)
Single Segment Assumption	3/385 (<1%)
Recovery-time constraints	6/385 (2%)
Incorrect inferences	3/385 (<1%)
Total:	29/385 (8%)

Figure 9-18: The causes of implementation-dependent rejections.

tance rate for user utterances is about 92%. Given the constraints on understanding imposed by the design choices in CHAMP, acceptance falls to about 84%. A significant portion of the implementation-dependent rejections could be reversed by the addition of constructive inference to the system.

9.2.3. Analysis of the utility of adaptation and generalization

Measurements other than rate of acceptance show the same patterns for the new users versus the original users as well. If we compare Figure 9-7 with Figure 9-19, for example, we find that the learning effects for Users 9 and 10 are comparable to the learning effects for Users 1, 2, 3 and 4: an average increase via adaptation of 78% for the new users and an average increase of 72% for the original users. Notice that CHAMP did quite a bit of learning for User 10 despite her belief that she was doing all the adapting.

	User 9	User 10
G_{kernel}	20/212 (9%)	19/173 (11%)
G_{final}	192/212 (91%)	148/173 (86%)

Figure 9-19: The effectiveness of learning as measured by the increase in the number of utterances understood for each new user via adaptations.

In Section 9.1.4 we defined a measure called the "bootstrapping constant" to reflect the utility of each learning episode. To compute the constant we divide the number of utterances brought into the grammar by adaptation by the number of learning episodes. The values for Users 1, 2, 3, and 4 were 3.3, 2.7, 2.3, and 3.7, respectively. The constants were somewhat higher for both Users 9 and 10: 5.7 and 5.6, respectively.

Another measure we examined for the original users was the rise in ambiguity in the grammar over time due to adaptation. Figures 9-20 and 9-21, like Figures 9-8 through 9-11, show that as more of the user's language is brought into the grammar, more work is required to understand each utterance at Deviation-level 0. The trade-off is extremely favorable for User 10 (Figure 9-21): she gains almost eight times as many accepted sentences with virtually no increase in search. The trade-off is less favorable for User 9 (almost a factor of ten increase in the number of her sentences accepted at a cost of about six times the search) but is still within the general trade-off ratios seen among Users 1,2, 3, and 4.

Grammar after session(*i*)	Number of non-deviant sentences	Average number states to accept	Average number roots produced
G(0)	20	13.0	1.1
$G_9(1)$	99	29.6	1.1
$G_9(2)$	155	54.9	1.9
$G_9(3)$	171	65.9	2.3
$G_9(4)$	171	65.9	2.3
$G_9(5)$	183	68.8	2.3
$G_9(6)$	188	76.7	2.5
$G_9(7)$	189	77.2	2.5
$G_9(8)$	189	77.2	2.5
$G_9(9)$	192	80.9	2.6

Figure 9-20: The change in the cost of parsing User 9's sentences at Deviation-level 0 as a function of grammar growth.

Of all the users, User 9 shows the largest increases in both the average amount of search required to accept and the average number of explanations produced for each accepted sentence. The reason is simple: her idiosyncratic grammar included derived forms omitting almost every content word in the kernel. Specifically, by the end of session three she had successfully dropped most markers for postnominal cases, three of the four verbs, and two of the four **groupgathering** head nouns (not to mention a few other, less easily characterizable deletions). As a result, almost every sentence she typed in the last seven sessions that was not a request to see the calendar or airline schedule created at least two effectively equivalent meanings. Whatever markers she had not dropped by session three were eliminated after the supplementary instructions were given at the start of session five. On the last day the simple sentence, "Dinner June 24 with Allen," created twelve roots at Deviation-level 0. A different decomposition of the kernel grammar into formclasses and forms would have had an enormous effect on the rise in ambiguity for this user without reducing the number of sentences accepted. The relationship between kernel design, adaptation, and ambiguity is discussed further in Chapter 10.

Grammar after session(*i*)	Number of non-deviant sentences	Average number states to accept	Average number roots produced
G(0)	19	40.4	1.1
$G_{10}(1)$	121	37.7	1.6
$G_{10}(2)$	131	38.2	1.7
$G_{10}(3)$	135	40.3	1.7
$G_{10}(4)$	142	42.3	1.7
$G_{10}(5)$	142	42.3	1.7
$G_{10}(6)$	144	40.7	1.7
$G_{10}(7)$	147	42.8	1.7
$G_{10}(8)$	148	45.8	1.7
$G_{10}(9)$	148	45.8	1.7

Figure 9-21: The change in the cost of parsing User 10's sentences at Deviation-level 0 as a function of grammar growth.

Evaluation of the protocols for the new users reveals nothing unexpected with respect to CHAMP's competition mechanism. Figure 9-22 shows that most of the competitions that had a chance to be resolved were resolved the next time a competitor was required to understand a sentence.

	Number resolved competitions	Number unresolved competitions	Number left unresolved with chance to resolve
User 9	3	5	2
User 10	1	2	1

Figure 9-22: Competition results for Users 9 and 10.

The final measure described for Users 1, 2, 3, and 4 was across-user variability. We found a significant variation among the final grammars of the original users by examining the rate of acceptance for each user's sentences under her own final grammar and the final grammars of the others. Figure 9-23 shows the results for the same computation for Users 9 and 10.[41] The two grammars overlap by about half; as

[41]We do not measure the new sentences with the original users' grammars or the original sentences with the new users' grammars because of differences in the kernels under which each set of sentences was accepted. The differences in the kernel would show up as increased variability, biasing the results in adaptation's favor.

in Figure 9-13 the explanatory power of a user's individual grammar far outweighs that of another user.

Final Grammar for	Applied to All Sentences of User 9	Applied to All Sentences of User 10
User 10	192/212 (91 %)	87/173 (50%)
User 9	120/212 (57%)	148/173 (86%)

Figure 9-23: Measuring across-user variability for Users 9 and 10 by computing acceptance rates for each's utterances under her & the other user's final grammar.

9.2.4. Adaptive versus monolithic performance

Given the results for across-user variability, it is not surprising that a comparison of monolithic versus adapted performance for the test set from Users 9 and 10 reaffirms our previous conclusions. Figure 9-24 displays the increase in both search and the number of explanations produced under a monolithic grammar built from the union of the kernel and the final grammars of Users 9 and 10 with redundant components removed.

User	Average $States_{user}$	Average $States_{mono}$	Average $Roots_{user}$	Average $Roots_{mono}$	Additional sentences
9	80.6	96.7	2.6	2.6	0
10	45.8	68.2	1.7	3.4	0

Figure 9-24: A comparison of the relative costs of parsing with a monolithic grammar versus parsing with the adapted grammars for Users 9 and 10. (The last column shows the number of additional sentences for each user that could be parsed by the monolithic grammar but not the user's final grammar).

User 9 would notice little difference between interactions with this monolithic grammar and those with CHAMP. User 10, on other hand, would notice some difference, primarily in the number of interactions required to resolve the extra explanations produced by the monolithic interface. Most of the extra work required to accept User 10's sentences is contributed by User 9's grammar. In other words, in a monolithic design, User 10 must pay for User 9's idiosyncracy.

9.3. Summary of results

In total, CHAMP has been tested on 1042 utterances most of which represent unmodified spontaneous input by frequent users whose profession includes calendar scheduling as part of its duties. The full test set of 1042 sentences is given in [46] (with modifications indicated). We found no qualitative differences between CHAMP's performance for utterances in the original test set (gathered by simulation of the model) and the system's performance for spontaneous utterances from on-line interactions. The results of evaluating the interface can be summarized as follows:

1. CHAMP is able to understand about 84% of each user's utterances using error recovery, adaptation, and generalization to learn their idiosyncratic forms of expression. This rate of acceptance was adequate for users to be able to accomplish the task.
2. CHAMP's acceptance rate is about eight percent lower than that predicted by the model for the same set of utterances. The difference is caused primarily by deviations that require the system to introduce a new subconstituent into a context that does not expect it. CHAMP's current understanding process can adapt only in the presence or absence of expected categories. Extending the system to include constructive inference would solve the problem.
3. Design choices such as the Single Segment Assumption, the Maximal Subsequence Heuristic, and the use of recovery-time constraints had only a small effect on CHAMP's acceptance rate. Given their power to constrain search, we consider these mechanisms to have been good solutions to some of the problems that arose in trying to realize the model computationally. The lexical extension problem, on the other hand, remains an open issue that cannot be ignored.
4. CHAMP's mixed liberal-conservative adaptation mechanism combines with generalization through the Formclass Hierarchy to learn the user's language effectively. The cost of learning is an increase in ambiguity in the current grammar. The increase seen in CHAMP reflects, in part, the inherent ambiguity in the user's idiolect. The remainder of the added ambiguity, however, comes from the decomposition of the initial experimental grammar into the particular set of formclasses and forms chosen for the kernel. Although competition keeps the effects of ambiguity from proliferating, and response times for most utterances were in a reasonable range, a better understanding of the relationship between kernel design, adaptation technique, and the rise in ambiguity would be worthwhile.
5. Given the chance to use their own natural language, users manifest significant variability in their preferred forms of expression for the same task. An adaptive interface like CHAMP accommodates this variability more efficiently than a monolithic, static design.

By the end of Chapter 3, we had proven all but one of our theoretical hypotheses:

H3: The Fixed Kernel Hypothesis: The kernel grammar for an adaptive parser need contain only a small set of system forms—in general only one form of reference for each meaningful domain action and object. Any user can be understood by then extending the grammar as a direct result of experience with the individual, using the paradigm of deviation detection and recovery in a least-deviant-first search.

Since we have shown that one adaptive interface design, CHAMP, is adequate to capture within-user consistency and accommodate across-user variability, we now conclude that the Fixed Kernel Hypothesis is proven as well.

Chapter 10
Critical Issues

Despite the evaluation's clear demonstration of the usefulness of adaptation at the interface, both theoretical and practical problems remain. The discussion in this chapter is offered as a kind of friendly warning to others interested in adaptive language acquisition for spontaneously generated input. The issues raised here are probably inherent in learning from real user interactions; regardless of the model you choose or the implementation you design, these problems are not likely to disappear. The best one can do under such circumstances is to try to understand the tradeoffs involved in each issue and find the appropriate balance within one's particular framework.

10.1. The effect of kernel design on learning

The tenor of the discussion in Chapter 8 suggests that the choice of adaptation mechanism is the only variable affecting generalization. In reality, the structure of the kernel grammar is crucial as well.

The structural bias in CHAMP's kernel is toward undergeneralization. Consider the case of transposition over the kernel **changeforms**. Each of ACT3, ACT4, and ACT5 is a **changeform** which may contain an introductory adverbial phrase specifying the time or date of the **change** action (see Figure 10-1). Despite sharing steps 701, 702, and 703, the three forms nevertheless use different steps to seek the source and target objects of the change. Because the three forms contain critical differences, an utterance that succeeds via one form cannot succeed via the others. Thus to learn to transpose one of the introductory adverbial phrases under every **change** context requires a separate deviant utterance—a separate learning episode—for each form. Many of the learning episodes in later sessions of the users' protocols reflect this particular source of undergeneralization.

Critical differences exist across formclasses too. Members of **addforms** and of **deleteforms** contain critical differences with respect to each other and with respect to the members of **changeforms** as well. Still, each **addform** and each **deleteform** may be introduced by the same adverbial phrases as ACT3, ACT4, and ACT5.

ACT3
steps (701 702 703 706 709 711 799)
rnode (706 709 711)
unodes ((701 702 703))
mnodes ((701 702))

ACT4
steps (701 702 703 706 710 799)
rnode (706 710)
unodes ((701 702 703))
mnodes ((701 702))

ACT5
steps (701 702 703 706 709 723 724 799)
rnode (706 709 723 724)
unodes ((701 702 703))
mnodes ((701 702))

701: class m-hourforms
702: class m-intervalfroms
703: class m-dateforms
706: class changewd
709: class m-d-ggforms
710: class m-d-slotforms
711: class stpforms
723: class targetmkr
724: class m-i-ggforms
799: class eosmkr

ACT345
steps (701 702 703 706 709 710 711 723 724 799)
rnode (706 709 710 723 724)
unodes ((701 702 703))
mnodes ((701 702) (709 710) (711 710) (723 710) (724 710) (723 711) (724 711))

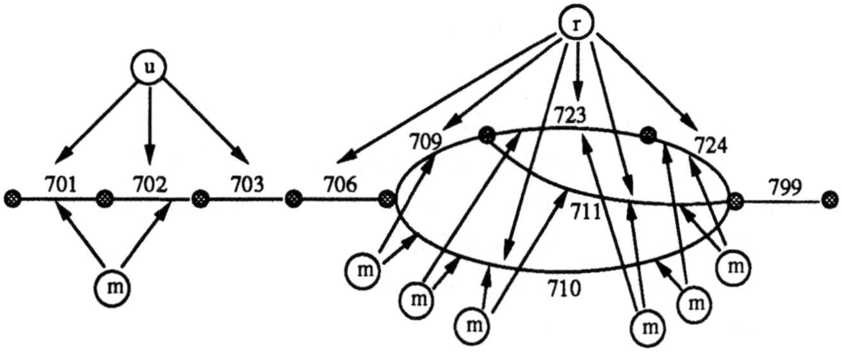

Figure 10-1: Three equivalent representations of the kernel changeforms ACT3, ACT4, and ACT5: as they appear in CHAMP, merged into a single case frame, and as a shared, annotated graph structure. The graph is constructed by joining links representing form steps with unlabelled nodes. Variations on a straight path through the graph are signalled by control nodes ("u"= unordered, "r"= required, "m"= mutually-exclusive).

Again, each critically different form requires its own positive example to learn what could be considered a shared adaptation.

There are at least two ways to eliminate the bias toward undergeneralization in CHAMP's kernel. First, we could add a mechanism to adaptation that explicitly compensates for the bias. Such a mechanism might, for example, look for all forms sharing the deviant step and then try to perform the same adaptation for each form. This approach would leave intact the search control provided by critical differences.

Alternatively, we could redesign the kernel so that all forms in a formclass are merged into a single form using mutual-exclusivity relations.[42] ACT345 in Figure 10-1 demonstrates how this approach would affect ACT3, ACT4, and ACT5 within the case frame representation. ACT345 trades the search control provided by critical differences for the inclusion of more of the grammar in the adaptation context when the form succeeds. The bottom portion of the figure shows the representational shift that is the logical conclusion to the suggested redesign: the Formclass Hierarchy as a set of embeddable, shared, annotated graph structures, reminiscent of ATNs [76]. In this view, graph links correspond to form steps, while the parsing algorithm itself corresponds to following a path through the graph subject to the controls represented by the arrows. Control arrows emanating from a node labelled "r" point to required links on the path just as the *rnode* field captures the required steps in the steps list. Similarly, control arrows emanating from a "u" node point to links that may be unordered and those emanating from an "m" node point to mutually-exclusive links.

By bringing more of the grammar into the adaptation context—either explicitly at adaptation-time or through restructuring the kernel—both solutions clearly run the risk of overgeneralizing. In fact, either mechanism may derive components that increase search but serve no useful function in the grammar. Consider the case of a transposed step shared by ACT3, ACT4, and ACT5. In CHAMP's kernel, the utterance that succeeds via the transposition satisfies only one of these critically different forms (let's say ACT3). The order of the constituents in the utterance determines the new order of the steps in the derived form, ACT3'. If we want to generalize across the formclass during adaptation, however, we must create new orderings for the other forms as well. Without an utterance containing the critically different constituents in ACT4 and ACT5 we have no way to dictate the ordering of the deviant step with respect to the steps seeking those unsatisfied constituents. Our only choice is to rely on some general method of reasoning (analogy, for example) to determine the orderings. Unless the reasoning method is fairly clever, however, the

[42]The idea can be carried further: merging all the forms that share a step, for example, or even all the forms at the same Agenda-level.

derived components it creates for the forms that did not actually succeed (i.e. ACT4' and ACT5') may never correspond to a structure produced by the user. In essence, we will have created exactly the kind of mismatch between the system's grammar and the user's grammar that we were trying to avoid by moving from a monolithic to an adaptive interface design.

The example teaches a simple lesson: any representation of the grammar biases what is learned from a single event. In building CHAMP, we made a conscious choice not to try to compensate for the kind of undergeneralization created by the kernel design. In general, the grammar design in any system that has fixed grammatical categories in fixed relations to each other involves a similar choice.

10.2. The effect of kernel design on search

In an ideal implementation, the rise in ambiguity in an adapted grammar over time would reflect only the ambiguity inherent in the user's idiosyncratic language. In Chapter 9 we saw that CHAMP's performance is not ideal: the decomposition of the kernel grammar into a particular set of forms and formclasses contributed significantly to the rise in ambiguity in most of the users' adapted grammars.

To review the example presented in Chapter 9, we assume that previous interactions with the user have created both a derived form deleting the head noun in a **meetingform** (GG1') and a derived form deleting the hour marker in an **m-hourform** (HR0'). Under these circumstances the sentence "Schedule 7 p.m. on June 4 with John" produces two effectively equivalent roots. One tree contains "7 p.m." as a normal unmarked prenominal constituent in GG1' using the kernel **u-hourform**, HR1. The second tree explains the same time segment as a postnominal constituent in GG1' using the derived **m-hourform**, HR0'. If the marker for the date is also optional in the adapted grammar, and we change the sentence slightly to, "Schedule 7 p.m. June 4 with John," then four roots result: unmarked prenominal versus marked postnominal for each modifier. If the user has derived forms for more than one type of **groupgathering**, each of which has the head noun deleted, the same sentence produces four roots for each **groupgathering** that can be recognized without its head noun. The ambiguity that results from these simple deletions occurs because the combined effect of the adaptations eliminates the critical differences between formclasses. When neither the head noun nor the postnominal marker is required, an unmarked time segment may legitimately serve two roles in the grammar without deviation: as a **u-hourform** and as an **m-hourform**.

The examples demonstrate how an interaction between adaptation and the kernel representational choices for noun phrases and prenominal and postnominal modifiers leads to ambiguity. Note that the combinatoric effect of even a small number of such deletions can be quite expensive at higher deviation-levels. Even if a grammar does not contain the additional deleted date marker, for example, a search that expands to Deviation-level 1 is likely to include a path that follows that interpretation; at each deviation-level we search as if the grammar contains derived components that compensate for the hypothesized deviation.

Although we have shown only one set of examples, there were other kernel choices that led to similar interactions. While it is difficult to assign the blame to any one choice, there is no question that part of the rise in ambiguity seen in the users' grammars stems from these interactions rather than the ambiguity inherent in the users' idiolects.

In CHAMP, combinations of adaptations can interact to eliminate critical differences among forms and formclasses. The lesson is that an aspect of the knowledge representation that significantly controls search under some circumstances can be transformed by the adaptation mechanism into a source of increased search under other circumstances. In general it is important to make certain that the usefulness of the components we derive is proportional to their cost, but it may be that any seemingly efficient grammar organization can be made less efficient by the effects of adaptation.

10.3. The effect of search constraints on system predictability

CHAMP contains features other than critical differences that also help to control search: the Maximal Subsequence Heuristic, the Single Segment Assumption, and the various constraints that are applied at the different stages of processing (segmentation-time, bind-time, and so on). The performance evaluation in Chapter 9 showed that the number of sentences rejected by these features is fairly low. Given this result we might be tempted to conclude that the features are unqualifiedly advantageous. In reality, each feature contributes to rigid boundaries on understanding and learnability that the user may find perplexing.

Let's consider a few examples:

Example 1: In the session during which it is first encountered U7S33 (''change ending time from 4:00 to 4:30 for user studies lab with jill on june 11'') is parsable at Deviation-level 1. Yet the same sentence is outside User 7's final grammar. How can this happen? The discrepancy is caused by an interaction between the Maximal Subsequence Heuristic and an adaptation during session five in which **for** is learned as an insertion. The effect of the interaction when User 7's final grammar is run on U7S33 is to make "4:30 for user studies lab with jill on june 11" maximal during each Parse/Recovery Cycle, with "4:30" interpreted as a prenominal time modifier and "for" ignored as an insertion. The maximal sequence masks the embedded and correct interpretation of "4:30" as the target end time. Had she typed a sentence like U7S33 after session five, User 7 might have thought it odd that a once acceptable structure was now rejected.

Example 2: How can "June 15 3 p.m." be a segment parsable at Deviation-level 0, when "June 7 3 p.m." is both unparsable and unlearnable with respect to every adapted grammar? The answer is: through an interaction between the Maximal Subsequence Heuristic and the bind-time constraint on **hour**. In the unlearnable segment "June 7 3 p.m." **3** has an interpretation as a value for **minutes** and **7** passes **hour**'s bind-time predicate. As a result, "7 3 p.m." becomes the maximal subsegment, masking the embedded subsegment "3 p.m." and ultimately causing the parse to fail. The problem does not arise for the segment "June 15 3 p.m." because **15** does not satisfy **hour**'s bind-time predicate and thus never coalesces with the interpretation of **3** as minutes. Although she was the only user to encounter this apparent inconsistency, User 10 found the difference in the interface's responses for the relevant utterances confusing.

Example 3: When each of "Drew," "McDermott," and "speaking" is an unknown token, the segment "with Drew McDermott speaking about Non-Monotonic Logics" produces an interaction with the user in which she is asked whether or not "Drew McDermott speaking" is a member of one of the system's extendable classes. The segment "with Drew McDermott about Non-Monotonic Logics," on the other hand, produces an interaction referring to "Drew McDermott" alone. The difference between the interactions is caused by the Single Segment Assumption. Although users quickly learn to respond "no" in the first case, and "yes" in the second, they are nonetheless frustrated by the unpredictability of which type of event will occur for a given utterance.

Any solution to the lexical extension problem is likely to exacerbate the effects of the Single Segment Assumption. Consider the phrase "on the topic of Non-Monotonic Logics." To compensate for new uses of known lexemes in CHAMP's kernel, this phrase must be marked by the hidden-operator prior to segmentation as follows: <on> <the> topic <of> Non <-> Monotonic Logics. Since the unbracketed tokens are truly unknown and the bracketed tokens are treated as unknowns, the entire phrase is presented to the user as a candidate new instance of an extendable class.

Example 4: Because of a **no-trans** recovery-time constraint, "cancel class 15-731" is acceptable, but "cancel the 15-731 class" is not. Similarly, the American date form "<month> <day> <year>" is parsable but the common European date form "<day> <month> <year>" is neither parsable nor learnable. In both examples, the recovery-time constraint is necessary to prevent more circumstances under which the Maximal Subsequence Heuristic masks the correct interpretation. To the user, however, there is no easily inferred explanation of why some transpositions are acceptable but others are not.

The lesson from these examples is that a system may have to incorporate a tradeoff in at least two variables that affect the user's ability to accomplish the task efficiently: response time and the ease with which the user can predict the system's behavior. In CHAMP, the additional search control mechanisms probably help more than they hurt, although the user may never realize it.

10.4. The lexical extension problem

When a word or phrase has one or more lexical definitions in the current grammar, none of which reflects the word's meaning in the current sentence, the system is faced with an instance of the *lexical extension problem.* In CHAMP, as in most expectation-driven parsers, when a word has definitions in the lexicon, those definitions are automatically indexed by the presence of the word in the input. Without some mechanism for ignoring existing definitions when they are inapplicable to the current situation, the knowledge the system thinks it has causes the global parse to fail.

Examples of the lexical extension problem occur throughout the user data. During evaluation we found that an average of fourteen percent of the utterances from all users contained instances of lexical extension with respect to the grammar at the time. From a practical point of view, to reject fourteen percent of a user's utterances in addition to the average of sixteen percent already rejected by the implementation seems unreasonable. From a theoretical point of view, note that lexical extension can be thought of as the precursor of lexical ambiguity. Since lexical ambiguity is commonplace in natural language, we conclude that the lexical extension problem is not one we can ignore.

It is technically possible to solve the lexical extension problem within our adaptive model by brute force. When the parse fails globally, we could simply treat each token in turn as an unknown and reparse. If there is no case in which considering a single token as an unknown leads to global success, then we could try pairs, triples, and so on. In other words, we hypothesize single words as instances of lexical extension before we hypothesize increasingly large phrases as unknowns. Of course, the brute force approach is clearly intractable. In addition, it is doomed to produce vacuous results; most sentences are parsable (but meaningless) if we ignore large enough subsegments.

Unfortunately, there does not appear to be a simple solution to the lexical extension problem that is also computationally tractable. One heuristic was suggested by an analysis of the experimental data but ultimately proved untenable. About two-thirds of the instances of lexical extension in the user data corresponded to new uses of tokens from closed linguistic categories (articles, prepositions, punctuation). This suggests replacing the less ambiguous categories in the grammar with more ambiguous ones as a partial solution. For example, we might replace the relatively restricted class **datemkr** with the more general class **preposition**. The change permits any preposition to introduce the date; we no longer have to worry about unanticipated, idiosyncratic use of prepositions being unparsable in those circumstances. This solution is unsatisfactory in CHAMP because it is extremely costly at non-zero deviation-levels. If every preposition can mark every case, then most marked subsegments will succeed as most types of constituents given enough deviation points.

Another heuristic stems from the fact that the grammar consists of a fixed set of categories. This property suggests adding superclass information to the Formclass Hierarchy to detect lexical extensions in cases of substitution. For example, both hour markers and time interval markers might be given the superclass **marker** (or, perhaps, the more specific category **time-related-marker**. Then, when an otherwise recognized time interval was introduced by an unexpected hour marker (as in "at 3 to 4 p.m.") the shared superclass could be used to permit the substitution of **at** into the class **ivlmkr** (note that unlike the previous heuristic, here we insist that there be some other evidence for the constituent). Unfortunately this heuristic provides only a partial solution to the problem—primarily because it does not address the issue of lexical extensions that are insertions. For our user data, the heuristic correctly compensates for only fifty percent of the instances of lexical extension.

It is interesting to note that little is said about the lexical extension problem in the literature. The few interface researchers that recognize that the problem exists offer no solution, instead making the explicit assumption that the lexicon contains either the applicable definition for a word or no definition at all [20, 51]. Most of the remaining researchers seem unaware of the problem and, consequently, implicitly make the same assumption. The spontaneously generated user input collected during our experiments shows how unreasonable such an assumption is. To this point, Zernik's research on learning idioms [82] and Guo's research on interactive vocabulary acquisition [27] appear to be the only other work that tries to address the lexical extension problem.[43] Both Zernik's system, RINA, and Guo's system, XTRA, try to solve the problem by indexing wrong definitions and then reasoning about the semantic inconsistences those definitions produce.

In essence, RINA performs a kind of deviation detection and error recovery over its semantic knowledge. In this respect Zernik's paradigm seems to fit in well with our own. Unfortunately, RINA incorporates the assumption that all deviations stem from semantic errors, never from syntactic ones. CHAMP assumes the opposite: any deviation can be explained syntactically but the semantics of the domain are fixed. Thus, to use Zernik's approach to solve the lexical extension problem within our adaptive model would seem to entail a potential exponential blow-up during search. Each time an expectation is violated we would have to consider both syntactic and semantic causes. In addition, there is the issue for CHAMP of the complexity of determining which semantic concepts are the inconsistent ones. By the time the global parse has failed at Deviation-level 2, there may be more than a thousand nodes on the Agenda. Allowed two deviation points, most subsegments will index more than one concept. How do we decide which concepts are legitimately indexed by deviant forms and which are erroneously indexed by instances of lexical extension? Are there useful heuristics to help make the determination? Zernik's work does not address the inherent complexity of the problem because the examples he studied rarely indexed more than one suspect concept. Thus, despite providing a direction for future work, Zernik's research does not guarantee a tractable solution.

Guo's system explores misspellings and metaphoric uses before assuming that the violation of a semantic preference rule signals the need for lexical extension. With these two exceptions, Guo's assumptions are similar to Zernik's and the problems in

[43] In addition, see Zernik's more recent work on lexical acquisition [83] in which he discusses the inherent (and still unresolved) problem of identifying the *lexical gap*.

adopting the heuristics used by XTRA are essentially identical to those outlined above. Thus, no lesson is offered here, just the observation that the challenge to solve the lexical extension problem in real user data remains.

10.5. Summary

Each of the issues raised in this chapter represents a tradeoff along some dimension of what Watt, in 1968, called the "habitability" of the interface [72] and what we, in modern parlance, call its "user-friendliness." The choice of kernel representation involves balancing possible increases in response time from additional learning episodes against possible increases in response time from additional search. Kernel design also involves balancing response time during search in a tightly-constrained grammar against response time during search as adaptation negates those constraints. The choice of search control mechanisms involves juggling response time, rejection rate, and predictability in the behavior of the interface. In building and using lexical knowledge, there is a tradeoff involved in the power of additional knowledge to increase understanding and the power of that same knowledge to confound a system that always assumes its knowledge is correct.

CHAMP represents a single point in the multidimensional space of tradeoffs just described. The placement and evaluation of other adaptive interfaces in that space should provide valuable (and necessary) insights into how these limitations can be overcome.

Chapter 11
Conclusions and Future Directions

The point of this work has been to demonstrate that adaptive parsing is a desirable and expedient aspect of natural language interface design when users act in a linguistically idiosyncratic and self-bounded manner. In this chapter we review the main results supporting this idea and discuss future directions for research.

11.1. Main results

Through both hidden-operator and on-line experiments, we demonstrated that with frequent interactions a user limits herself to a restricted subset of forms that is significantly smaller than the full subset of natural language appropriate to the task, and quite different from the restricted subsets chosen by others.

- Self-bounded behavior was demonstrated by constructing a performance graph for each user in an adaptive experimental condition. Each graph showed decreases over time in both the number of new grammatical constructions per utterance and the number of rejected utterances per session (Figures 3-3, 3-4, and 9-15).
- Idiosyncracy was demonstrated by measuring overlap in the final, adapted grammars of users whose experimental conditions shared the same kernel. To measure overlap, each user's sentences were parsed under her own final grammar and under the final grammar of each of the other users in her condition. The results showed both significant across-user variability and within-user consistency: acceptance rates by other users' final grammars ranged between eleven percent and fifty-nine percent, while acceptance rates by users' own final grammars ranged between eighty-one percent and ninety-one percent (Figures 9-13 and 9-23).

The hidden-operator experiments also demonstrated that a model of adaptive language acquisition based on deviation detection, error recovery, and grammar augmentation is capable of learning different idiosyncratic grammars with a single, general mechanism.

- Deviation detection and error recovery support a user's idiosyncratic style by increasing the likelihood that the user's natural form of expression will be accepted. Adaptation adds to that support by learning each explained deviation as an extension to the grammar; the ability to continually redefine what is grammatical enables an adaptive interface to bootstrap itself toward a point where the system's grammar and the user's grammar converge. The success of adaptation as a learning method, in theory, was demonstrated by the convergence shown in the users' performance graphs. As simulated by the hidden operator, the model was adequate to learn a number of idiosyncratic grammars, despite significant disparities between the kernel grammar and the preferred expressions of each user.

- The simulation also demonstrated that adaptation provides a more responsive environment than that provided by a static interface if the user's natural grammar differs significantly from the system's and the user herself adapts poorly. Given the same stimuli and a similar degree of initial deviation in her language with respect to the kernel, a user in the non-adaptive condition was unable to show the same improvements in her task performance as did users in the adaptive conditions.
- Adaptation supports the transition of an individual from naive to expert user by allowing her to develop a concise, idiosyncratic command language. This was demonstrated when users were given the supplementary instructions to work as quickly as possible. In response to the instructions, users tended to employ terser, less English-like forms. The same mechanism of deviation detection, error recovery and adaptation that had provided initial convergence was able to incorporate the new forms into the grammar and reestablish convergence with the user's new preferred language.

CHAMP's performance for the utterances from the hidden-operator experiments and in on-line interactions with real users demonstrated the computational viability of the model. Evaluation of the system's performance for a test set of 1042 sentences from eight different users showed each of the following results:

- CHAMP's performance was comparable to that of the model with respect to capturing within-user consistency. The performance graphs for Users 9 and 10 (Figure 9-15) clearly show the expected decrease over time of new constructions per utterance and rejections per session. With respect to Users 1, 2, 3, and 4, differences between the performance graphs under the simulation and the implementation were due largely to CHAMP's higher rejection rates and the methods used to compensate for discrepancies between the two conditions.
- In addition to capturing within-user consistency, CHAMP was able to accommodate significant across-user variability. The idiosyncracy observed informally after the hidden-operator experiments was validated and quantified by the implementation.
- CHAMP rejected about twice as many utterances as were predicted by the model, both in the hidden-operator and on-line experiments. The model accepted about ninety-two percent of each user's utterances while CHAMP's average acceptance rate was eighty-four percent. Although this rate of acceptance is well within the range of seventy-five to ninety percent suggested by Waltz [71] as necessary for natural language interfaces, the discrepancy between the model's rate and the implementation's rate indicates that there is room for improvement. An analysis of the reasons for rejections suggests that a significant increase in acceptance rates is possible by extending the implementation to perform constructive inference.

- Acceptance of user utterances relied significantly on adaptation. This was demonstrated by a comparison of acceptance rates for each user's complete set of sentences under the kernel (from seven percent to twenty-four percent) and under the user's final grammar (from eighty-one percent to ninety-one percent).
- The adaptations themselves resulted in only a modest rise in ambiguity in each adapted grammar with CHAMP's competition mechanism helping to control the increase. Even with the rise in ambiguity, we demonstrated that performance under an idiosyncratic, adapted grammar is better than performance under a monolithic grammar with the same coverage. Adaptation produced significantly less search (thus, better response time) and fewer explanations (requiring less user interaction) than the monolithic approach.
- The system was able to perform effectively in the presence of spontaneous user input. No hidden-operator intervention was required in ninety-two percent of the utterances in the on-line experiments. Eight percent of the utterances did require intervention in the form of extra-grammatical markings to signal instances of lexical extension. Although no solution to the lexical extension problem is offered by this work, some possible research paths were suggested in Chapter 10.
- Adaptation, as we have designed and implemented it, is a robust learning method; CHAMP was able to learn very different grammars, corresponding to very different linguistic styles, with a single general mechanism.

11.2. Future directions

There are no easy solutions to the problems raised in Chapter 10, each demands extensive study. Here we present more immediate and tenable concerns: extensions to CHAMP and a number of future directions for our particular style of adaptive interaction.

Relaxing the Single Segment Assumption: As mentioned in Chapter 10, the Single Segment Assumption may be a source of frustration to the user when an unknown phrase contains an embedded instance of an extendable class. In the current version of CHAMP there is no way for the user to indicate that subsegments within the phrase serve distinct functional roles. It may be possible to eliminate the Single Segment Assumption by relying on user interaction to disambiguate segmentation. A relatively straightforward extension to the system would allow the user to designate the subsegment of an unknown phrase that corresponded to a new instance of a known category. In this way, the user could delineate "Non-monotonic Logics" as the true subject within the unknown phrase "on the topic of Non-monotonic Logics." The issue here is not whether such an extension is possible (it is), but whether users could employ it effectively.

Redefining "deviation:" CHAMP's view that all deviations are created equal may be less useful than a view that considers some deviations more deviant than others. In the current implementation it takes one deviation point to compensate for a violated expectation regardless of which expectation was violated, the cost of detecting the deviation, or the cost of explaining it. In addition, deviation is treated as strictly additive. We are no more confident of an explanation of deviations in separate constituents than we are of an explanation of the same number of deviations within a single constituent. Using simple additivity over equal deviation weights, the size of the search space and the quality of the explanations produced at higher deviation-levels forces CHAMP to restrict processing to its two-deviation limit. To break the two-deviation barrier, the system needs a more complex method for evaluating the effects of a deviation, based on either the cost of processing, the credibility of the resulting explanation, or both. An important question is whether we can increase the amount of deviance the system can tolerate, creating a more robust and flexible interface, without compromising performance.

Implementing constructive inference: The adaptation mechanism implemented in CHAMP responds only to the presence or absence of *expected* constituents. As a result, we found that some portions of a user's idiosyncratic language were unreachable. Specifically, CHAMP cannot learn structures that can be explained only by the introduction of a subconstituent into a strategy not designed to expect it. The problem is clearly in the implementation, not the model; theoretically any set of constituents can be mapped into any other set of constituents using the four general recovery actions. The problem stems from the fact that insertion is not fully implemented in CHAMP—only meaningless tokens may be inserted into a constituent, not meaningful but unanticipated grammatical constituents.

To overcome the problem we have suggested the use of a mechanism called *constructive inference.* As simulated by the hidden operator during the original experiments, constructive inference tries to build a legitimate database operation from the constituents that are present in the utterance. Constructive inference would be an extremely useful though non-trivial extension to CHAMP. To understand the difficulties involved, consider that when Deviation-level 2 is exhausted there may be more than a thousand constituents from which to try to create the intended action. We cannot afford to try all the combinations of constituents, nor can we assume that only the least-deviant ones or those covering the largest portions of the utterance are correct. A fairly complex method of composition is required (perhaps a method similar to CRITIQUE's [35, 36] but taking advantage of both syntactic and semantic constraint). In addition, even if we manage to construct one or more legitimate database actions, how do we then construct the new strategies to which they correspond? Since the inserted constituents carry meaning, they cannot be ignored in the way insertions are currently ignored in CHAMP. As we demonstrated in Section 8.2, however, an insertion usually corresponds to a family of hypothetical explanations any of which may represent the correct or most useful generalization of the structure of the utterance. How do we decide which explanation to include? Could the competition mechanism accommodate the additional burden or would the system simply collapse under the load? These are questions that can and should be explored, although they require significant changes in the implementation.

Relaxing the Fixed Domain Assumption: Trying to integrate Zernik's work into our model of adaptation is important not only as a possible way of solving the lexical extension problem, but also as a way of further relaxing the Fixed Domain Assumption. CHAMP's only exception to the demand of a fully and correctly specified domain is its support of extendable classes. Even with this concession, the assumption seems unrealistic. Is it not likely that users are idiosyncratic in the way they think about a task as well as in the way they express the thought? Is it not also likely that frequent performance of a task leads to the development of stereotypical subtasks which the user may want to reify? In the airline domain, for example, a user might ask the system to

"Center the trip to Boston around 2 p.m."[44]

The actual meaning of the sentence can be paraphrased: schedule a trip arriving in Boston around noon and leaving at about 4 p.m. (allowing the user time to get from the airport to her meeting and back). The required concept, that of **centering** a trip, is not included in CHAMP's kernel and is unlikely to be included *a priori* in any scheduling interface. The constituents from which such an idiosyncratic concept could be constructed are present in the kernel, however. A system combining the ideas in Zernik's research with our model of adaptation might be able to learn semantic idiosyncracy in essentially the same way it learns syntactic idiosyncracy: as deviation detection and recovery in the expectations of semantic forms.

Learning to forget: As demonstrated in the experiments, adaptation offers a partial solution to the problem of supporting the transition of users from naive to expert behavior. Others have shown that as the naive user becomes increasingly expert in her interactions she may want the convenience and speed usually associated only

---

[44]The example was suggested by someone who actually uses this phrase with his travel agent.

with a system-supplied command language. An adaptive interface permits the transition to an idiosyncratic command language as part of its natural function. Thus, despite the general validity of the Regularity Hypothesis, we expect that over sufficiently long periods the user's preferred language will change. In essence, we expect to see regularity for a time followed by mild destabilization as she introduces terser forms, followed by restabilization until, eventually, an idiosyncratic command language develops.

Over the course of nine experimental sessions, we saw this kind of destabilization and reconvergence only when we introduced the supplementary instructions to work quickly. While the artificial impetus did demonstrate that CHAMP could accommodate the transition, we did not address the problem of how to remove obsolete forms once the new adapted grammar has stabilized. This is a crucial issue for long-term adaptation. Since forms may be tied to domain subtasks having irregular periodicity, it seems unlikely that a simple measure of frequency or recency would be adequate to determine when a form has become obsolete. A more practical measure might involve an evaluation of the degree of search constraint versus the degree of ambiguity contributed by a form over time. As an added benefit, the same evaluation function could supplant the competition mechanism CHAMP currently uses, providing a less arbitrary method for learning from multiple examples.

Comparing and evaluating other theories: Our model of adaptive language acquisition based on deviation detection, error recovery, and grammar augmentation is capable of learning different idiosyncratic grammars with a single, general mechanism. CHAMP implements the model using a modified bottom-up parsing algorithm and a decomposition of its kernel grammar into a particular case frame representation. As an initial adaptive interface design CHAMP stands as a challenge to proponents of other parsing paradigms and grammar representations. Could a least-deviant-first search be accomplished as efficiently using an ATN-like representation such as the one suggested in Chapter 10? Is it possible to define processes analogous to deviation detection and recovery in a unification-based parser? In general we must ask how systems based on other paradigms and representations compare to CHAMP both in terms of what is theoretically learnable and in terms of performance for the same set of test sentences along dimensions such as rejection rate and response time.

In Chapter 2 we referred to CHAMP's four general recovery strategies as a linguistic weak method for problem-solving when the understanding process goes awry. We argued that a relatively knowledge-free approach made sense in an initial exploration of adaptive language acquisition. Yet many of the poor explanations CHAMP produces are created because the system's recovery strategies are so linguistically naive. It would be interesting to see what the effect on performance would be if we replaced CHAMP's recovery strategies with more linguistically sophisticated knowledge. Would such a change create a more robust interface with better response, or would it simply create more rigidity and unpredictability from the user's point of view? To take the issue a step further, we might embed a competence model (such as transformational grammar [13]) in the recovery process as a way of pinpointing, and perhaps quantifying, the discrepancies between such models and real performance.

Expanding to other domains and languages: We demonstrated the generality of our method of adaptation both across domains and across users. Still, a full demonstration of the model's generality demands at least two additional tests: across tasks and across natural languages. The creation of a new kernel for a non-scheduling task as well as the creation of a new kernel for a different natural language (especially a non-Romance and non-Germanic language) would undoubtedly provide additional insight into the interactions among the design of the kernel grammar, search, and adaptation.

These are just a few of the possible extensions and modifications that would enable CHAMP to better support its users; undoubtedly there are others. Still, the system described here is a first step toward efficient, habitable interfaces and meeting the goal of providing users with a truly *natural* language environment.

References

1. Anderson, J. R., "Induction of Augmented Transition Networks," *Cognitive Science*, 1977.

2. Anderson, J. R., *The Architecture of Cognition*, Harvard University Press, Cambridge, MA, 1983.

3. Ballard, B. W., Lusth, J. C., Tinkham, N. L., "LDC-1: A Transportable, Knowledge-Based Natural Language Processor for Office Environments," *ACM Transactions on Office Information Systems*, Vol. 2, No. 1, 1984.

4. Berwick, R. C., "Learning Word Meanings from Examples," *Proceedings of the Eighth International Joint Conference on Artificial Intelligence*, August 1983.

5. Berwick, R., *The Acquisition of Syntactic Knowledge*, MIT Press, Cambridge, MA, 1985.

6. Berwick, R.C., and Pilato, S., "Learning Syntax by Automata Induction," *Machine Learning*, Vol. 2, 1987.

7. Brown, J. S., and Burton, R. R., "Multiple Representations of Knowledge for Tutorial Reasoning," in *Representation and Understanding*, D. G. Bobrow and A. Collins, eds., Academic Press, 1975.

8. Burton, R. R., "Semantic grammar: An engineering technique for constructng natural language understanding systems," *BBN Rep. 3453, Bolt, Beranek, and Newman, Boston, Mass.*, 1976.

9. Burton, R. R., and Brown, J. S., "Toward a natural language capability for computer-assisted instruction," in *Procedures for Instructional Systems Development*, O'Neil, H., eds., Academic Press, 1979.

10. Carbonell, J. G., "Towards a Self-Extending Parser," *17th Annual Meeting of the Association for Computational Linguistics*, 1979.

11. Carbonell, J. G., *Subjective Understanding: Computer Models of Belief Systems*, PhD dissertation, Yale University, 1979.

12. Carbonell, J. G. and Hayes, P. J., "Recovery Strategies for Parsing Extragrammatical Language," *American Journal of Computational Linguisitics*, Vol. 9, No. 3-4, 1983.

13. Chomsky, N., *Aspects of the Theory of Syntax*, MIT Press, Cambridge, MA, 1965.

14. Cobourn, T. F., "An Evaluation of Cleopatra, a Natural Language Interface for CAD," Master's thesis, Carnegie Mellon University, December 1986.

15. Davidson, J., and Kaplan S. J., "Parsing in the Absence of a Complete Lexicon," *18th Annual Meeting of the Association for Computational Linguistics*, 1980.

16. Durham, I., Lamb, D. A., and Saxe, J. B., "Spelling Correction in User Interfaces," *Communications of the ACM*, Vol. 26, 1983.

17. Fain, J., Carbonell, J. G., Hayes, P. J., and Minton, S. N., "MULTIPAR: A Robust Entity-Oriented Parser," *Proceedings of the Seventh Annual Conference of The Cognitive Science Society*, 1985.

18. Fillmore, C., "The Case for Case," in *Universals in Linguistic Theory*, Bach and Harms, eds., Holt, Rinehart, and Winston, 1968.

19. Fink, P. K., and Biermann, A. W., "The Correction of Ill-Formed Input using History-Based Expectation with Applications to Speech Understanding," *Computational Linguistics*, Vol. 12, No. 1, 1986.

20. Frederking, R. E., *Natural Language Dialogue in an Integrated Computational Model*, PhD dissertation, Carnegie Mellon University, 1986.

21. Furnas, G. W., "Statistical Semantics: Analysis of the Potential Performance of Key-Word Information Systems," *The Bell System Technical Journal*, Vol. 62, No. 6, 1983.

22. Furnas, G. W., Landauer, T. K., Gomez, L. M., Dumais, S. T., "The Vocabulary Problem in Human-System Communication," *Communications of the ACM*, Vol. 30, No. 11, 1987.

23. Gazdar, G. and Mellish, C., *Natural Language Processing in POP-11, An Introduction to Computational Linguistics*, Addison Wesley, Workingham, England, 1989.

24. Good, M. D., Whiteside, J. A., Wixon, D.R., and Jones, J.J., "Building a User-Derived Interface," *Communications of the ACM*, Vol. 27, No. 10, 1984.

25. Granger, R. H., "FOUL-UP: A Program That Figures Out Meanings of Words from Context," *Proceedings of the Fifth International Joint Conference on Artificial Intelligence*, 1977.

26. Grosz, B., "TEAM: a Transportable Natural Language Interface System," *Conference on Applied Natural Language Processing*, 1983.

27. Guo, C., "Interactive Vocabulary Acquisition in XTRA," *Proceedings of the Tenth International Joint Conference on Artificial Intelligence*, August 1987.

28. Harris, L. R., "A System for Primitive Natural Language Acquisition," *International Journal for Man-Machine Studies*, 1977.

29. Harris, L. R., "Experience with ROBOT in 12 Commercial Natural Language Database Query Applications," *Proceedings of the Sixth International Joint Conference on Artificial Intelligence*, 1979.

30. Harris, L. R., "Experience with INTELLECT," *The AI Magazine*, Vol. V, No. 2, 1984.

31. Hass, N., and Hendrix, G. G., "Learning by Being Told: Acquiring Knowledge for Information Management," in *Machine Learning, An Artificial Intelligence Approach*, Michalski, R. S., Carbonell, J. G., and Mitchell, T. M., eds., Tioga Publishing Company, 1983.

32. Hauptmann, A. G., Young, S. R., and Ward, W. H., "Using Dialog-Level Knowledge Sources to Improve Speech Recognition," *Proceedings of the Seventh National Conference on Artificial Intelligence, American Association for Artificial Intelligence*, 1988.

33. Hendrix, G. G., "Human Engineering for Applied Natural Language Processing," *Proceedings of the Fifth International Joint Conference on Artificial Intelligence*, August 1977.

34. Hendrix, G. G., Sacerdoti, E. D., Sagalowicz, D., and Slocum, J., "Developing a Natural Language Interface to Complex Data," *ACM Transactions on Database Systems*, Vol. 3, No. 2, 1978.

35. Jensen, K., Heidorn, G. E., Miller, L. A., and Ravin, Y., "Parse Fitting and Prose Fixing: Getting a Hold on Ill-formedness," *American Journal of Computational Linguistics*, Vol. 9, 1983.

36. Jensen, K., Heidorn, G. E., Richardson, S. D., and Haas, N., "PLNLP, PEG, and CRITIQUE: Three Contributions to Computing in the Humanities," *IBM Research Report RC 11841*, 1986.

37. Kaplan, S. J., *Cooperative Responses from a Portable Natural Language Data Base Query System*, PhD dissertation, University of Pennsylvania, 1979.

38. Kay, M., "Experiments with a Powerful Parser," *The Rand Corporation, Report Rm-5452-PR*, 1967.

39. Kelley, J. F., *Natural Language and Computers: Six Empirical Steps for Writing an Easy-to-Use Computer Application*, PhD dissertation, Johns Hopkins University, 1983.

40. Kelley, J. F., "An Iterative Design Methodology for User-Friendly Natural Language Office Information Applications," *ACM Transactions on Office Information Systems*, Vol. 2, No. 1, 1984.

41. Kelley, J. F., "CAL—A Natural Language program developed with the OZ Paradigm: Implications for Supercomputing Systems," *Proceedings First International Conference on Supercomputing Systems*, 1985.

42. Kelley, J. F., and Chapanis, A., "How professional persons keep their calendars: Implications for computerization," *Journal of Occupational Psychology*, No. 55, 1982.

43. Keyes, J., "Wall Street Speaks English," *AI Expert*, July 1988.

44. Kwasny, S. C., and Sondheimer, N. K., "Ungrammaticality and Extra-grammaticality in Natural Language Understanding Systems," *17th Annual Meeting of the Association for Computational Linguistics*, 1979.

45. Langley, P., "A Model of Early Syntactic Development," *20th Annual Meeting of the Association for Computational Linguistics*, 1982.

46. Lehman, J. Fain, *Adaptive Parsing: Self-extending Natural Language Interfaces*, PhD dissertation, Carnegie Mellon University, 1989.

47. Lehman, J. F., and Carbonell, J. G., "Learning the User's Language, A Step Towards Automated Creation of User Models," in *User Modelling in Dialog Systems*, Wahlster, W., and Kobsa, A., eds., Springer-Verlag, 1989.

48. Malhotra, A., "Knowledge-Based English Language Systems for Management Support: An Analysis of Requirements," *Proceedings of the Fourth International Joint Conference on Artificial Intelligence*, 1975.

49. Malhotra, A., "Design Criteria for a Knowledge-Based English Language System for Management: An Experimental Analysis," *Technical Report MAC TR-146, Massachusetts Institute of Technology*, 1975.

50. Michaelis, P. R., Chapanis, A., Weeks, G., and Kelly, M. J., "Word Usage in Interactive Dialog with Restricted and Unrestricted Vocabularies," *IEEE Transactions on Professional Communication*, Vol. PC-20, No. 4, 1977.

51. Miller, P. L., "An Adaptive Natural Language System that Listens, Asks and Learns," *Proceedings of the Fourth International Joint Conference on Artificial Intelligence*, 1975.

52. Minton, S. N., Hayes, P. J., Fain, J. E., "Controlling Search in Flexible Parsing," *Proceedings of the Ninth International Joint Conference on Artificial Intelligence*, 1985.

53. Mitchell, T., Keller, R., Kedar-Cabelli, S., "Explanation-Based Generalization: A Unifying View," *Machine Learning*, Vol. 1, No. 1, 1986.

54. Montgomery, C. A., "Is Natural Language an Unnatural Query Language?," *ACM Annual Conference*, 1972.

55. Neal, J.G., and Shapiro, S. C., "Talk About Language !?," *Technical Report, S.U.N.Y. at Stony Brook*, 1985.

56. Petrick, S. R., "On Natural Language Based Computer Systems," *IBM Journal of Research and Development*, Vol. 20, 1976.

57. Pinker, S., *Language Learnability and Language Development*, Harvard University Press, Cambridge, MA, 1984.

58. Rich, E., "Natural Language Interfaces," *Computer*, Vol. 17, No. 9, 1984.

59. Salveter, S. C., "On the Existence of Primitive Meaning Units," *18th Annual Meeting of the Association for Computational Linguistics*, 1980.

60. Schank R. C., *Conceptual Information Processing,* North-Holland, Amsterdam, 1975.

61. Schank, R., and Abelson, R., *Scripts, Plans, Goals, and Understanding,* Lawrence Earlbaum Associates, Inc., Hillsdale, NJ, 1977.

62. Selfridge, M., "A Computer Model of Child Language Acquisition," *Proceedings of the Seventh International Joint Conference on Artificial Intelligence,* 1981.

63. Selfridge, M., "A Computer Model of Child Language Learning," *Artificial Intelligence,* Vol. 29, 1986.

64. Selfridge, M., "Integrated Processing Produces Robust Understanding," *Computational Linguistics,* Vol. 12, No. 2, 86.

65. Sells, P., *Lectures on Contemporary Syntactic Theories,* CSLI/Stanford, Stanford, CA, 1987.

66. Shieber, S. M., *An Introduction to Unification-based Approaches to Grammar,* CSLI/Stanford, Stanford, CA, 1986.

67. Siklossy, L., "Natural Language Learning by Computer," in *Representation and Meaning: Experiments with Information Processing Systems,* Simon, H. A., and Siklossy, L., eds., Prentice-Hall, Inc., 1972.

68. Slator, B. M., Anderson, M. P., and Conley, W., "Pygmalion at the Interface," *Communications of the ACM,* Vol. 29, No. 7, 1986.

69. Tennant, H., *Evaluation of Natural Language Processors,* PhD dissertation, University of Illinois at Urbana-Champaign, 1981.

70. Thompson, B. H., and Thompson, F. B., "Introducing ASK: A Simple Knowledgeable System," *Conference on Applied Natural Language Processing,* 1983.

71. Waltz, D. L., "An English Language Question Answering System for a Large Relational Database," *Communications of the ACM,* Vol. 21, 1978.

72. Watt, W. C., "Habitability," *American Documentation,* July 1968.

73. Weischedel, R. M., and Black, J. E., "Responding Intelligently to Unparsable Inputs," *American Journal of Computational Linguisitics,* Vol. 6, No. 2, 1980.

74. Wilensky, R., "Talking to UNIX in English: An Overview of an On-line Consultant," *The AI Magazine,* Vol. V, No. 1, 1984.

75. Winograd, T., *Language as a Cognitive Process,* Addison-Wesley, Reading, MA, 1983".

76. Woods, W. A., "Transition Network Grammars for Natural Language Analysis," *Communications of the ACM,* Vol. 13, No. 10, 70.

77. Young, S. R., Hauptmann, A. G., Ward, W. H., Smith, E. T., and Werner, P., "High Level Knowledge Sources in Usable Speech Recognition Systems," *Communications of the ACM,* Vol. 32, No. 2, 1989.

78. Young, S. R., and Ward, W. H., "Towards Habitable Systems: Use of World Knowledge to Dynamically Constrain Speech Recognition," *Second Symposium on Advanced Man-Machine Interfaces through Spoken Language*, 1988.

79. Zernik, U. and Dyer, M. G., "Failure-Driven Acquisition of Figurative Phrases by Second Language Speakers," *Proceedings of the Seventh Annual Conference of The Cognitive Science Society*, 1985.

80. Zernik, U., "Learning Idioms -- With and Without Explanation," *Proceedings of the Tenth International Joint Conference on Artificial Intelligence*, 1987.

81. Zernik, U., "Language Acquisition: Learning a Hierarchy of Phrases," *Proceedings of the Tenth International Joint Conference on Artificial Intelligence*, 1987.

82. Zernik, U., *Strategies in Language Acquisition: Learning Phrases from Examples in Context*, PhD dissertation, University of California, Los Angeles, 1987.

83. Zernik, U., "Lexicon Acquisition: Learning from Corpus by Capitalizing on Lexical Categories," *Proceedings of the Eleventh International Joint Conference on Artificial Intelligence*, 1989.

Index

GPSR Compliance

The European Union's (EU) General Product Safety Regulation (GPSR) is a set of rules that requires consumer products to be safe and our obligations to ensure this.

If you have any concerns about our products, you can contact us on ProductSafety@springernature.com

In case Publisher is established outside the EU, the EU authorized representative is:

Springer Nature Customer Service Center GmbH
Europaplatz 3
69115 Heidelberg, Germany

Batch number: 10682323

Printed by Printforce, the Netherlands